Psychoanalytic Theory

For Jean and Keith Elliott

Psychoanalytic Theory
An Introduction

Anthony Elliott

BLACKWELL
Oxford UK & Cambridge USA

Copyright © Anthony Elliott 1994

The right of Anthony Elliott to be identified as author
of this work has been asserted in accordance with the Copyright,
Designs and Patents Act 1988.

First published 1994

Blackwell Publishers
108 Cowley Road
Oxford OX4 1JF
UK

238 Main Street
Cambridge, Massachusetts 02142
USA

British Library Cataloguing in Publication Data
A CIP catalogue record for this book is available from
the British Library.

Library of Congress Cataloging-in-Publication Data
Elliott, Anthony.
    Psychoanalytic theory : an introduction / Anthony Elliott.
        p.   cm.
    Includes bibliographical references and index.
    ISBN 0-631-18846-0 (alk. paper). – ISBN 0-631-18847-9 (pbk. : alk. paper)
    1. Psychoanalysis.   I. Title.
BF173.E63   1994
150.19′5 – dc20   93-29372
                                                                                      CIP

Typset in Sabon on 10.5 pt
by CentraCet Limited, Cambridge
Printed in Great Britain T.J. Press (Padstow) Ltd., Padstow, Cornwall

This book is printed on acid-free paper

Nothing but a wish can set our mental apparatus at work.

Sigmund Freud, *The Interpretation of Dreams*

It is one and the same enterprise to understand Freudianism as a discourse about the subject and to discover that the subject is never the subject one thinks it is. The reflective reinterpretation of Freudianism cannot help but alter our notion of reflection: as the understanding of Freudianism is changed, so is the understanding of oneself.

Paul Ricoeur, *Freud and Philosophy*

The primary processes are present in the mental apparatus from the first, while it is only during the course of life that the secondary processes unfold, and come to inhibit and overlay the primary ones.

Sigmund Freud, *The Interpretation of Dreams*

The time-lag between consciousness and the unconscious is itself the stigma of the contradictory development of society. Everything that has got left behind is sedimented in the unconscious and has to foot the bill for progress and enlightenment.

Theodor Adorno, 'Sociology and psychology'

Contents

Acknowledgements

Many people have contributed to the writing of this book. In particular, I am indebted to Simon Prosser, of Blackwell Publishers, who played an instrumental role in helping to define the conceptual boundaries of the project. I wish to thank him for his valuable advice and editorial support. A number of people read, and commented upon, draft chapters. I would like in particular to thank John Cash, Jane Flax, Stephen Frosh, Tony Giddens, Stan Gold, John B. Thompson, Madelon Sprengnether, Nick Stevenson, and Elizabeth Wright. Albert J. Paolini read the manuscript in a typically painstaking way, and I am grateful to him for many helpful suggestions. I would also like to thank Sheila Dallas for her conscientious copy-editing. A number of institutions should be mentioned for the support they have given. I would like to thank the Australian Research Council for awarding me a Postdoctoral Fellowship. I would also like to thank colleagues and students in the Department of Political Science at the University of Melbourne. Thanks to Kriss McKie, Anthony Moran, Deborah Elliott-Maxwell, Carmel Meiklejohn, Cameron Barnett, Taren McCallan, Aisling O'Conner, Ingrid Scheibler, Rosa Frassoni, Michael Crozier, and Grant Parsons. Finally, extra special thanks to Nicola Geraghty, my deepest source of hope and encouragement, who has regularly and intensively discussed with me the nature of contemporary psychoanalysis.

Anthony Elliott
June 1993

Introduction

In the face of Sigmund Freud's monumental discoveries about psychical life, and its complex interaction with cultural forms, the nature of critical practice in the human sciences has undergone deep alteration. Focusing on individual subjectivity, on the complex, contradictory emotional experiences of people in relation to society and politics, on the quality of human social relationships, on gender relations and our unequal sexual world, and on the fundamental assumptions of Western knowledge and science, psychoanalytic theorists have instigated a powerful restructuring of our social-theoretical traditions. Despite the central place of psychoanalysis within the social sciences, however, the current perspectives and advances of the discipline are generally regarded as a terrain for specialist debate. Indeed there has been a genuine difficulty for students and the general reader searching for a critical introduction to the field.

This book sets out to provide a reasonably comprehensive discussion of developments in psychoanalytic theory. The chapters that follow explore various traditions in psychoanalysis, setting them within the broader context of contemporary debates in the human sciences. Throughout, I have tried to examine psychoanalytic perspectives in a judicious manner, comparing and contrasting Freudian theory, American ego-psychology and self-psychology, British object relations theory, French Lacanian and post-Lacanian psychoanalysis, Kleinian theory, feminist, and postmodern psychoanalysis. However, an introductory discussion such as this will necessarily involve certain simplifications, omissions, and gaps. It would be too simplistic to attempt to represent the key conceptual problems of a discipline as complex as psychoanalysis. For this reason, I have opted for focusing on the work of particular theorists, highlighting certain themes and issues, similarities and differences, linking psychoanalysis throughout with developments in contemporary thought.

This is not a clinical study; but an expository and comparative introduction to the current state of psychoanalytic theory. I am not attempting to provide a history of all psychoanalytic ideas or an account of the institutional divergences between various psychoanalytic schools. Nor do I consider the complex issue of the scientific verification of psychoanalytic theories. A reader searching for such a discussion will have to look elsewhere.[1] Rather, my aim is to provide, through a critical appraisal of the complexity and heterogeneity of conceptual approaches, an informative overview of the contemporary relevance of psychoanalysis to theory and social practice.

Particular attention is devoted throughout the book to analysing the social, political, and cultural dimensions of psychoanalytic theory. On the whole, this emphasis reflects the historical development of psychoanalysis itself. Psychoanalytic criticism today is pursued less by psychoanalysts than by cultural and literary critics, feminists, media and communication analysts, and social and political theorists. This tradition of analysis and critique has led to some of the most important innovations and developments in psychoanalytic theory this century. On a deeper level, however, I contend that the radicalizing possibilities of psychoanalytic theory are unlikely to amount to much unless the discipline turns reflexively upon itself, examining the institutional, social-historical conditions in which it is embedded. I shall argue that the subversive influence of a radical psychoanalytic criticism depends upon connecting theoretical perspectives to a more general cultural analysis.

Central Themes

There are three central themes of this book. The first concerns the analysis of *human subjectivity*. At issue here is our understanding of the personal domain, self, and self-identity. Psychoanalytic theory is of vital importance for understanding the fundamental conditions of selfhood. Whereas the social sciences have tended to see human agents as rational and autonomous, psychoanalysis recasts the relations between selfhood and desire, reason and passion. In psychoanalytic terms, the self is not a stable or unified entity. Rather, the human subject is constituted to its roots through the representational dynamics of desire itself, the self emerging as an outcrop of the unconscious. From this angle, we cannot really speak of the self outside desire, fantasy, sexuality, and gender identification – indeed, issues of gender are fundamental to the psychoanalytic reconceptualization of subjectivity. As we shall see, existing versions of psycho-analytic theory conceptualize the impact of unconscious desire upon self-organization in distinctly different ways. For some theorists, the presupposition of an authentic sense of selfhood is crucial to psycho-analytic critique. For others, the self is seen as an imaginary fiction, a psychic strategy of accommodation aimed at masking the painful realities of desire itself. Many of the following chapters thus trace the consequences of these differing theoretical standpoints for conceptualizing the self, self-identity, and subjectivity.

The second theme of the book is the *relation between self-organization and the contemporary social and political world*. Fol-lowing directly from the first theme, psychoanalytic theorizing about selfhood carries important implications for analysing the wider context of social and political relations. That is, our understanding of the psychic conditions of self-organization can be used as a tool for generalizing about modern social experience – interpersonal relations, the quality of social bonds, political community, and so on. Particular attention is therefore given throughout the book to current debates on modernity and postmodernity. For, in so far as psycho-analytic theory maps the internal world of individual subjectivity, it is therefore well placed to assess the links between human experience and the contemporary cultural and historical period.

The third theme of the book concerns *epistemological issues* – issues about psychoanalytic knowledge and its relation to individual and collective autonomy. As a model of social critique, psychoana-lytic theory is concerned with uncovering asymmetric forms of power. This involves the study of the complex ways in which human beings question, alter, or reinforce their affective relations with others and with the social world. Psychoanalytic critique gives explicit recog-nition to the possibility of disinvesting from certain ideological forms, and to the creative transformation of the self. Thus, many of the following chapters trace the manifold ways in which psychoanalytic critique enhances our understanding of, and therefore contributes to possibilities for, human emancipation.

Overview

The chapters that follow explore these core issues from differing psychoanalytic standpoints. Broadly speaking, they are all concerned with important advances in theoretical thinking about the constitution and structuring of unconscious desire within the social institutions of modern culture. Thus the chapters trace a certain psychoanalytic narrative, the interconnections between self and society. However, I have tried to highlight the distinctive concerns and preoccupations of the theoretical traditions under consideration in each chapter. Therefore, chapters can be read in various orders, and theoretical traditions can be studied according to the reader's interest. To facilitate this, every chapter is prefaced with an introductory overview as well as concise table summaries. In addition, the book concludes with an extended list for further reading in psychoanalytic theory.

The opening chapter provides a broad overview of the various conceptual traditions in psychoanalytic theory today, with the issue of the self to the fore. The concepts examined in this introductory chapter include the unconscious, repression, sexuality, fantasy, gender identity, and power. In chapter 2, I concentrate on how various psychoanalytic concepts have been used to analyse culture, society, and individual subjectivity, with repression as a central theme. This chapter examines developments in psychoanalytic-cultural criticism, from the Freudian-Marxist exploration of the modern world, through critical theory and psychoanalysis, to the contemporary American Left. In chapter 3, I examine the psychoanalytic traditions of object relations, Kleinian theory, and self-psychology. In this chapter, the connections between interpersonal relations and the internal world of the self are explored.

Chapter 4 examines French Lacanian psychoanalysis, post-Lacanian criticism, and the theoretical current known as poststructuralism. Several key issues are assessed in this context: the reinterpretation of Freudian psychoanalysis in the light of structuralist and poststructuralist theories of meaning; the interweaving of language and the unconscious; and the structuring of desire within the socio-symbolic order of modern societies. In chapter 5, I consider developments in psychoanalytic feminism, tracing key conceptual differences between Anglo-American and Continental perspectives. The major themes in this chapter include the unconscious dimensions of patriarchy, sexual difference, and the possibilities for transforming gender relations. Chapter 6 traces current debates about modernity and postmodernism, examining their social and cultural ramifications for identity. This chapter explores contemporary directions in psychoanalytic theorizing, ranging from French anti-psychoanalysis to postmodern theory. Finally, in the conclusion, I sketch out the prospects for a radical psychoanalytic criticism today, reframing the subversive potentials of the discipline within the plurality of perspectives and debates at the current time.

1

The Making of the Self

Divergences in Psychoanalytic Theory

In this opening chapter, I examine certain divergences in contemporary psychoanalytic theory by looking at the nature of the self. As regards selfhood, psychoanalysis raises important issues about the psychic processes in which human experience and emotional development are structured. Indeed, as developed by some theorists, psychoanalysis problematizes the very notion of subjectivity itself. The basic issues to be addressed in this chapter include the following. What is the self? How does a sense of selfhood emerge? What are the precarious, yet profoundly important, psychical mechanisms which link self and desire, reason and emotion? And what are the interconnections between selfhood and culture, and the links between personal meanings and the contemporary social world? In exploring these issues, this chapter ranges widely across core premises of Freudian psychoanalysis, ego-psychology, object relations theory, Kleinian theory, Lacanian, and post-Lacanian theory. In doing so, the chapter traces some of the connections of these standpoints with contemporary cultural and social criticism.

Imagining the Self

What is meant by the notion of selfhood? At first sight, the answer seems obvious. In everyday life, a person's selfhood is usually understood to refer to their defining elements of personality and character. Implicit in this is the belief that there is something stable and durable about the self. I believe myself to be the same 'self' as I was yesterday; and, for purposeful social life to be possible at all, I must also believe that others have a fairly coherent sense of their own identity. Such presumptions about ourselves and others, unless a person is ill or disturbed, are at the root of our cultural life. The view that there is some such fundamental 'core' of selfhood has, of course, been central to the Enlightenment's basic understanding of humanity. The Cartesian understanding of the self as a fixed, indivisible, and permanent whole ('I think, therefore I am') has underpinned existing notions about consciousness and reason. Indeed, as Dennis Wrong comments, the human sciences have for the most part operated with a wildly 'over-socialized' conception of the self; a conception which sees the individual as essentially rational, unified, and conflict-free.[1]

Psychoanalytic theory radically challenges such evaluations of selfhood. The self, which seems so obvious at one level, is deconstructed by psychoanalysis as only one region of subjectivity, a region that is merely the tip of the iceberg. The self, or 'ego' as it is termed in some versions of psychoanalytic theory, is shown to be a dimension of subjectivity which is *made* in fantastic form, constituted through the unconscious operations of desire itself. In this respect, psychoanalysis posits a *basic split* at the centre of psychical life between *consciousness of self* and that which is *unconscious*. Lurking behind all forms of self-organization – that is, our day-to-day fashionings of self-identity – there lies a 'hidden self', a dimension of subjectivity which produces itself through fantasy, drives, and passions. Significantly, this hidden self, however we may choose to act or express ourselves, constantly disrupts and outstrips us through displacing and condensing our conscious experience and knowledge. This splitting between waking consciousness and the unconscious is evident in the very act of self-reflection. For example, I might reflect on the nature of my own selfhood, thinking about the attributes of my personality and the nature of my emotional involvement in human relationships. However, a difficulty which inevitably arises is that this sense of self, on which I am reflecting, is actually located within myself as a human subject. On this line of reasoning, then, there will be aspects of what I desire, think and feel which arise outside and beyond the confines of my own organized sense of selfhood. And it is precisely at this point, the splitting of conscious intention and unconscious desire, that psychoanalytic theory installs itself, seeking to uncover repressed or overdetermined aspects of self-organization.

We can get a better idea of the importance of this notion of a 'hidden self' by considering the subtle emotional knowledge that people display in everyday life. For, in contrast to intellectual evaluations, our everyday accounts of ourselves, and of others, are often quick to highlight the affective dimensions of human subjectivity. Consider the following. What does it mean when someone during a dinner conversation makes the following remark about a friend who is in the process of ending his marriage: 'Peter is just not himself at all at the moment – he's got a lot of emotional stuff he's trying to work out.' To say in ordinary conversation that a person is 'not himself' is to indicate, implicitly, an awareness of the diversity and complexity of emotional life. This does not mean, of course, that such a comment appreciates the psychoanalytic distinction between self or ego and the unconscious dimensions of subjectivity. But this comment does recognize the centrality of conflicting emotions, the interplay of love and hatred, as well as the importance of a person's concrete emotional history in the development of their selfhood. It recognizes that the ending of a relationship, and especially an intimate sexual relationship, will bring into play complex, contradictory feelings of pain, hurt, and loss. And herein lies the significance of everyday talk: the implicit recognition that selfhood is shaped by broad emotional influences. At a theoretical level, these are the influences with which psychoanalysis is most directly concerned, tracing the fluid and multiple psychodynamics of emotional life on the construction of the self, and of human social relationships more generally.

Consider also the links between psychical life and the contemporary social world. In recent times, there has been a great deal of debate about the nature of the late modern age in which we live, about the end of modernity itself, and about the possible transition to a postmodern social condition. In these debates, there has been a broad consensus that modern forms of life are increasingly marked by a kaleidoscopic variety of events, by social contingency, uncertainty, and ambivalence. The cultural and institutional processes of modernization which have launched the West upon a dazzling path of global expansion are said to have reached into the heart of selfhood and created new forms of personal identity. In postmodernism, particularly in its poststructuralist guise, contemporary cultural experience becomes permeated by fragmentation – an outcome of the dynamism and intensity of modern institutions. Significantly, one important consequence of this view is that human subjects, outflanked by a global network of communicational and computational processes, are now understood to inhabit a world in which meanings no longer have any real moral value. Social reality becomes a world of surfaces, images, and fragments. (For further discussion, see chapter 6: 'The Dislocating World of Postmodernism'.)

Psychoanalysis has made significant contributions to these theoretical debates on modern and postmodern identity, providing methods of analysis for thinking through the connections between these cultural trends and new patterns of self-organization. In these debates, as we shall see, psychoanalytic theory has been used to trace the fragile and precarious structures of psychic interiority engendered by the cultural conditions of our late modern age. To widen our sense of social and political reflectiveness about the modern experience, cultural critics have developed psychoanalytic concepts to trace processes of self-constitution in an era increasingly characterized by risk and uncertainty. For, if contingency, ambivalence, and instability of a threatening kind really do characterize the late modern age, then it is reasonable to assume that self-identity is also radically transformed. Indeed, according to the American cultural critic Christopher Lasch, our contemporary cultural condition promotes a 'minimal self', a self preoccupied with survival which has narcissistically turned back upon itself. This shrinking of the self, Lasch says, is directly connected to the waning of political life today and the lack of interest in the public sphere more generally. Alternative traditions of social thought are less inclined to link patterns of self-organization to contemporary culture in this way; instead they draw on psychoanalytic theory as a way of understanding the constitution and reproduction of our social practice. These accounts, as elaborated by theorists such as Erich Fromm, Cornelius Castoriadis, and Anthony Giddens, have developed a more sociological appropriation of psychoanalysis for analysing social life. That psychoanalytic theory has inspired such diversity in the critical development of the human sciences will form one of the central concerns of this book.

Psychoanalytic Portraits of the Self

Existing versions of psychoanalytic theory assess self-identity and the self in different ways. In order to explore their various meanings, let us at this stage list some definitions of the human subject to be found in contemporary psychoanalytic theory and critique:

(a) the structural division of ego, id, and superego;
(b) topological structure of consciousness, preconsciousness, and the unconscious;
(c) defence-mechanisms motivated by ego-organization;
(d) originary drives which are 'object-seeking';
(e) the conjuncture of 'true' and 'false' selves;
(f) the process of splitting ranging from paranoid-schizoid positions to depressive positions;

(g) an imaginary structure of misrecognition and illusion;
(h) a process of linguistic closure in which repression is constituted.

There are several important points about this list which should be noted at the outset. First, no overall definition of the self can be extracted from these conceptual strands of psychoanalytic thought. If, for example, rationality and autonomy are written in to the constitution of the subject, then clearly it fails to make sense also to speak of the self as a 'structure of misrecognition'. Accordingly, the gamut of meanings here is simply too broad in scope to nail down an all-inclusive definition of individual subjectivity. That this wealth of meaning is a positive gain for social critique, rather than something to be lamented, is a contention I will defend throughout the book. Secondly, all of these portraits of the self carry far-reaching implications for social, cultural and political criticism. In many of these approaches, the self is seen as fully anchored in social and historical contexts, with the development and enrichment of interpersonal relationships a political aim. Other definitions, however, view self-hood as an imaginary fiction, or as a repressive point of closure of human potential – and to this extent such perspectives carry rather different implications for thinking about social and political organization. Finally, it should be noted that these psychoanalytic portraits involve knowledge claims of different types. In some approaches, human beings are recognized as possessing the capacity for critical reflection and thus the ability for self-transfiguration. Other approaches, however, are more cautious about such humanist conceptions of autonomy, asserting that the best hope for social subversion arises from the mutations of desire itself. These points form a conceptual backcloth for the critical examination of psychoanalytic theory contained in this book.

The Legacy of Freud: Sexual Subjectivity and the Unconscious

The portrait of the self which has most dominated twentieth-century thought comes from the founder of psychoanalysis, Sigmund Freud. Working in the cultural and social milieu of Vienna at the turn of the twentieth century, Freud developed psychoanalysis as a field of investigation, method of inquiry, and psychotherapeutic practice. Freud termed this practice the 'talking cure', in order to describe the magical power of language in exploring unconscious life. Exploring undiscovered regions of the mind, Freud looks at the implications of sexuality and the unconscious imagination for human subjectivity. The self, for Freud, is not something which exists independently of sexuality, libidinal enjoyment, fantasy, or the patriarchal cultural order of modern society. Indeed the very distinction between subject and object, self and world, necessarily involves a mind-shattering repression of the unconscious imagination. The human subject, in Freud's opinion, only comes into being through repression, splitting off libidinal desire permanently into the unconscious. Selfhood is thus fractured precariously between conscious and unconscious.) For Freud, all of our lives are carried on within this radical *otherness* of the unconscious, a realm of being which infuses three agencies of the psyche: id, ego, and superego. The id, lying at the root of unconscious existence, is that which cannot be symbolized yet constantly strives for expression. It is a hidden area of the self which knows no reality, logic, negation, or contradiction. The superego, an internal law of cultural prohibition, is founded in this id. Desire, according to Freud, thus infiltrates all human intentions, ideals, and imperatives. Similarly, Freud sees parts of the ego as bound to the force of the id, the self emerging as an outcrop of the unconscious.

Freud poses the question of the self in relation to human sexuality. He traces the genesis of libidinal desire to those early bodily experiences between the small infant and its primary caretaker – typically, the mother. At birth the human infant, says Freud, is wholly dependent on care from others for the satisfaction of its biologically fixed needs. The small child is incapable of surviving alone without the provision of care, warmth, and nutrition from other people. It is thus, one might claim, the emotional interaction between child and significant others which is central to the coming together of selfhood. 'There is no such thing as a baby' says the psychoanalyst D. W. Winnicott, thus underscoring the origin of self in relation to others. According to Freud, the small infant first experiences its mother within a kind of imaginary space, completely apart from everyday structures of time and space. At this point, the infant makes no distinction between inside and outside, itself and the maternal body. Rather, the infant lives within a world of plenitude, satisfying its natural self-preservative needs. Yet self-preservation, says Freud, goes beyond the biological. Needs are in fact bound up with the attaining of libidinal enjoyment (or what Freud called the 'pleasure principle'), even if the latter actually separates out from the former. Freud's exemplary case is the small child sucking milk from its mother's breast. After the infant's biological need for nourishment is satisfied, there is the emergence of a certain pleasure in the act of sucking itself; and this, for Freud, is the core of human sexuality: 'The baby's obstinate persistence in sucking gives evidence at an early stage of a need for satisfaction which, though it originates from and is instigated by the taking of nourishment, nevertheless strives to obtain pleasure independently of nourishment and for that reason may and should be termed *sexual*.'[2] In Freud's account, sexuality is not some pre-ordained, unitary biological force that springs into existence fully formed at birth. On the contrary, sexuality is *created*, not pre-packaged.

Freud's theory of sexuality, expounded in *Three Essays on the Theory of Sexuality* (1905) and elsewhere, grants to bodily, libidinal drives a fundamental role in the emergence of selfhood. Sexuality unfolds within a radically imaginary cast, Freud says, since libidinal drives can only achieve expression by being psychically represented, or put into 'images'. The concept of representation, or more commonly fantasy, is at the heart of psychoanalysis and is central to its interpretative strength. Broadly speaking, Freud's model of sexuality ties together two key realms – drives *and* fantasy, force *and* meaning. Sexual life is given meaning in relation to 'erotogenic zones'; that is, those parts of the human body, such as the mouth, the genitals, and the anus, which become the focus of sexual enjoyment. There is an originary bisexuality at the heart of psychical life – Freud speaks of the infant as 'polymorphously perverse' at birth. Bisexuality is therefore, to use a kind of shorthand, at the centre of all *pre-self* experience.

In the *Three Essays*, Freud catalogues many forms of human erotic attachment. Heterosexuality, homosexuality, sadism, masochism, exhibitionism, fetishism, paedophilia, coprophilia, necrophilia, sodomy; these are, says Freud, erotic pleasures created by the human imagination. Some fall within the ambit of acceptable sexual conduct in modern societies, yet many are regarded as deviations from 'normal' sexuality. For Freud, however, they all have one thing in common: their grounding in infantile sexuality. Indeed the dominant emotional conflicts of childhood are themselves, for Freud, secretly libidinal; from the retention of faeces to thumbsucking, the child's erotic feelings may become attached to any part of the human body. Freud looks at the implications of such infantile erotic pleasures as concern the individual human subject. Sexual subjectivity, as a unique organization of the libidinal drives, will always be carried on within the tangled frame of infantile sexuality. For Freud, all sexuality is polymorphously perverse, rooted in a pre-self experience of 'autoeroticism' of which we are not conscious. In this sense, the paradox or

contradiction of 'normal' sexuality, that is adult heterosexual inter-
course, is that it exists only through a specific ordering of the
inherently perverse libidinal drives.

Freud believed that the imaginary plenitude of the child/mother
dyad is broken apart through the intrusive impact of reality into the
pleasure principle. For Freud, the 'reality principle', which is experienced as the law of the outside world, imposes severe restrictions on
the pleasure-seeking drives of the unconscious. This opposition
between pleasure and reality, for Freud, is fundamental to human
life; and it is the task of the precarious ego, or the self, to attempt to
balance its unconscious demands for pleasure with the cultural
constraints of external reality. The constitution of a reality-ego,
rationality-testing, and self-control are, Philip Rieff comments, the
Freudian moral imperatives in the 'emergence of psychological man'.[3]
Freud's insight – that the self is differentiated from unconscious
pleasure through its contact with external reality – has been exten-
sively developed in contemporary social, cultural, and political
thought. One central lineage, from the Frankfurt theorist Herbert
Marcuse to the American Freudian-Marxist Joel Kovel, has been
concerned with tracing how cultural forms disfigure unconscious
pleasure in ways which produce 'surplus-repression'. By contrast,
other traditions of social thought, from poststructuralism to postmodernism, have sought to deconstruct the opposition of pleasure
and reality back to the mutations of desire itself. Both traditions offer
important insights into the connections between self and the social
world. These will be examined more closely in the following chapters.

We need, however, to look further at this painful intrusion of the
external world into the closed, imaginary world of the individual
subject. In positing a fundamental opposition between the pleasure
principle and the reality principle – or what is elsewhere termed the
'primary processes' of the unconscious and the 'secondary processes'
of consciousness – Freud's thinking indicates its affinities with
Enlightenment rationalism. The image of the self as purely pleasure-
seeking, which is subsequently brought within the regularized control
of society, certainly stretches back to classical liberal philosophy.
Most significantly, the ideological implications of Freud's theory
would seem almost entirely negative. For, as many commentators
have suggested, the victory of reality over pleasure in Freud's thought
is at one with the elevation of rationality over the irrational,
masculinity over the feminine, and reason over emotion. The extent
to which these ideological blindspots are actually rooted in Freud's
theory is a matter of ongoing debate. In my view, however, it can be

plausibly argued that Freud's work is more complex and subtle than such characterizations suggest. This becomes clearer once we consider Freud's argument that there are two sides to the surrender of the pleasure principle to the reality principle. According to Freud, all individuals must negotiate the shift from unconscious pleasure to external reality. Where this is not achieved, schizophrenic tendencies and related pathologies are certain to result. Yet here comes the twist in Freud's theory. In negotiating the dictates of external reality, the ensuing surrender of pleasure is itself a kind of decoy. Freud says unconscious drives only defer immediate satisfaction in order to achieve a more durable type of pleasure – that is, pleasure attained through the imaginary contours of selfhood. Pleasure is therefore not defeated; it merely takes new forms, via the imaginary tribulations of identity. And it is this insight that will lead Freud, in 'On Narcissism' (1914), 'Mourning and Melancholia' (1917), and *The Ego and the Id* (1923), to the view that selfhood is itself developed in fantastic form.

Our sense of selfhood, therefore, is not just magically assigned to us by the external world. Rather, identity has to be *made* or *created*. In this connection, Freud suggests that ego-formation occurs through the unconscious selecting or screening of objects by *identification*. Identification is a process in which the human subject 'introjects' attributes of other people and transforms them through the unconscious imagination. This identification with another is made a part of the subject by *incorporation*: the taking in of objects, either wholly or partially, to form the basis of an ego. In relation to the imaginary dyad of child and mother, for example, Freud comments that the subject has 'created an object out of the mother'.[4] Identification and incorporation are thus twin-boundary posts in the structuring of identity. For Freud, the identificatory process is engendered in and through painful feelings of loss. For it is the loss of a loved person which actually necessitates the introjection of that other into the structure of the ego itself. It is as if the hurt of losing somebody is so terrifying that the ego incorporates the lost love as an act of self-preservation. As Freud puts it, 'by taking flight into the ego, love escapes annihilation'. The links between loss and self-formation are made plain by Freud in *The Ego and the Id*:

> we succeeded in explaining the painful disorder of melancholia by supposing that [in overcoming this hurt] an object which was lost has been set up again inside the ego – that is, that an object-cathexis has been replaced by an identification. At that time, however, we did not

appreciate the full significance of this process and did not know how common and how typical it is. Since then we have come to understand that this kind of substitution has a great share in determining the form taken by the ego and that it makes an essential contribution towards building up what is called its 'character'.[5]

It is clear from this statement that the libidinal drives can take the self as an object of desire in just the same manner as 'external' objects. This significantly complicates traditional understandings of the relation between the individual and society, inside and outside, private and public. For it underscores the point that, in the formation of the human subject, identity is built up through picking out, and taking in, certain parts of other persons and objects in fantasy form. From this angle, the rational ego of the Western philosophical tradition is shown to be constituted to its roots through unconscious mechanisms of fantasy, drives, and desire. Significantly, it follows from this that the relation between self-identity and modern social processes will be more complex and contradictory than is commonly assumed. For if structures of identity are formed in relation to others (and particularly our affective images of others), then so too will changes in social relationships affect the nature of the self. In this connection, the nature of social transformations this century are palpable. Modernity – with its global economic mechanisms, its restructuring of time and space, its capitalist commodification, its phantasmagoria of mass media – brings into existence new forms of personal identity and social relations. The impact of these social and cultural transmutations upon self and identity-formation are at present controversial. Some critics find new possibilities for self-actualization in the late modern age; whereas other commentators take a more pessimistic view of the expressive cultural possibilities for the self. These debates will be explored in later chapters.

We have seen that, for Freud, self-constitution arises as a consequence of loss. Selfhood is formed under the sign of the loss of the object, in an attempt to *become* like the lost love. Yet identificatory processes carry serious implications not only for self-organization but also for gender as well. The links between the pain of loss and gender consolidation are to be found in Freud's theory of the Oedipus complex – a theory which conceptualizes the psyche's entry into received social meanings. For Freud, the Oedipus complex is the nodal point of sexual development, the symbolic internalization of a lost, tabooed object of desire. Sexuality, from its starting point of being polymorphous and bisexual, is reordered within the cultural framework of instituted gender relations. In the case of the young boy (the model in which Freud first theorizes the Oedipus complex), the child develops sexual knowledge of the penis and fantasizes sexual union with the mother. This fantasy of sexual union, however, is subsequently to be broken from outside the child/mother dyad, by the father. Consequently, the boy comes to hate his father's superior control of the maternal body and, as passion reaches fever-pitch, fantasizes his death. But recognizing that he cannot compete with the phallic authority of the father, and faced with the imagined threat of castration (the castration complex), the boy must renounce his primary erotic investment, repressing sexual desire for the mother permanently into the unconscious. Clearly, as far as culturally sanctioned heterosexuality goes, so far so good. However, there are certain difficulties in this psychoanalytic narrative of male sexual development. In his late writings, Freud notes that the child's originary bisexuality significantly complicates any forging of sexual identification, in which gender affinity is undermined by sexual ambivalence. This libidinal ambivalence can link to either the mother or the father, or both, as erotic objects.

The trajectory of the girl's passage through the Oedipus complex is a good deal more complex. Freud contends that in the case of female sexuality the Oedipus complex works in reverse fashion: instead of instigating the repression of Oedipal desire, the castration complex actually *produces* incestuous desire in the little girl. Several features of Freud's thought are relevant here. First, a masculine sexuality is the starting point of reference – 'the little girl is a little man' according to Freud. Second, sexual difference is founded upon 'the discovery' of the absence of the penis. As Freud puts this, 'She has seen it and knows that she is without it and wants to have it.'[6] This sets in train a series of sexual identifications. The discovery by the small girl that she lacks a penis with which to pursue her active sexual drives leads her to imagine that she has been castrated. As a consequence, she turns away in horror from her similarly castrated mother. In this connection, Freud believes that the girl's wish for a penis is so strong that it is subsequently transferred to a substitute, the desire to bear the father a child. It is this reversal from mother-love to father-love that establishes gender affinity for the girl. Through penis-envy, the girl renounces the more active elements of her sexuality and 'consolidates' feminine sexual passivity. In Freud's view, then, the development of heterosexuality in the girl is dependent upon an earlier sense of failed masculinity.

This description of sexuality as resting upon a male norm, with its consequent devaluation of the feminine, has been at the heart of the feminist debate with Freud. In short, Freud's ideas have come under fire for their perpetuation of the misogynistic view that femininity is little more than a negation of 'normal' male sexuality. However, there are two quite divergent interpretations of Freud's ideas on female development in the current literature. The first ascribes to Freud the view that it is the *moment of actual perception* of sexual organs which is fundamental to the psychical structuring of sexual difference. Yet the difficulty with this position, as many commentators have pointed out, is that it involves biological reductionism, and thus undercuts the critique of gender hierarchy. For if the 'inferiority' of the female sexual organ arises through such a 'sighting', then clearly the possibilities for restructuring gender relations also vanishes. The second interpretation, by contrast, argues that in Freudian psychoanalysis the child's sexual knowledge is only given meaning within the *structure* of gendered, social relations. That is, sexual difference and identity is given meaning with reference to the patriarchal sexual and social systems of modern culture. At this stage, it is important to note that Freud's work deeply problematizes female sexuality. Unlike the boy's strong repression of incestuous desire, the girl's Oedipal stage is understood to be relatively unstable, forever shifting between maternal and paternal identifications, and thereby always incomplete. Freud's own work, however, fails adequately to trace either the girl's ambivalent affinity with the feminine gender-role or how the Oedipus complex dissolves, if indeed it does.

A good deal has been written about the patriarchal nature of Freud's discourse. Certainly the notions of a primary masculine sexuality, penis-envy, and feminine sexual passivity suggest a widespread male bias in Freud's thought. The issues which arise, therefore, are these. Can psychoanalysis be defended as a progressive theoretical scheme for analysing sexist practices? Or is psychoanalysis simply the prisoner of the sexual and cultural assumptions which it seeks to investigate? The answer to these questions varies considerably in contemporary psychoanalysis and feminist theory. One line of argument is that Freud's thought about women is descriptive, not prescriptive. That is, psychoanalysis is something like a 'thick description' of what actually takes place in relations between the sexes. A major feminist defence of Freud along these lines is Juliet Mitchell's best-selling work *Psychoanalysis and Feminism*, which uses psychoanalysis to sketch a general critique of patriarchal culture. Similarly, Nancy Chodorow, Jessica Benjamin, Jane Flax, and Madelon Sprengnether have suggestively used psychoanalytic theory to analyse asymmetric gender-relations. An alternative tradition of thought, largely developed in Lacanian and post-Lacanian circles, has employed core concepts of psychoanalytic theory (the unconscious, displacement, identification, and the like) to deconstruct the ideological fiction of 'stable gender-identity'. This line of enquiry has been central to the French radical feminism of Luce Irigaray and others. Similarly, the work of the French psychoanalyst Julia Kristeva has sought to undo repressive gender norms by reconceptualizing human subjectivity within a primary realm of libidinal identification (known as the 'semiotic') as a means for rethinking identity. These different ideological perspectives in psychoanalytic feminism will be discussed in chapter 5.

Freud himself is clear that the Oedipus complex is at the foundation of civilization; it ushers in the structure of relations which prepares men and women for the repressions and sublimations required by culture. Significantly, Freud looks at how received social meanings are underwritten by the forces of unconscious desire, tracing the inscription of power and domination within the primary erotic attachments of the human subject. Accordingly, Freud's work provides us with conceptual tools for understanding why individuals should come to have a positive psychic investment in social arrangements which are in fact oppressive and restrictive. (For further discussion, see chapter 2: 'Modern Culture and Its Repressed'.) Yet there is a fundamental ambivalence at the heart of identity, says Freud. The internalization of cultural norms is at best a partial, contradictory affair, if only by virtue of the fact that such norms are shot through with the displacements and distortions of the unconscious itself. For example, the post-Oedipal child's connection to the mother as a separate, caring agent is always interwoven with its prior relation to the mother as an erotic object. Beyond the realm of social signification, as Slavoj Žižek points out, there is always a kind of leftover of unconscious desire which resists the basic dimension of ideology;[7] and it is this kernel of desire which serves as a support for 'reaction-formations' to the social and political fields.

This point can be put in another way. There are strong ambiguities in Freud's account of culture and its encoding of unconscious desire. Indeed we could say that there is a modernist and postmodernist Freud on the powers and limits of cultural ideology. Freud, the modernist, views culture as incorporating our libidinal drives in that psychical act known as 'sublimation', the embedding of libidinal enjoyment within the framework of social significations. This is the Freud who believes that psychoanalysis can confront the power of the unconscious in the governing of the soul. In this sense, Freud's enlightenment slogan 'Where id was, there ego shall be' refers to the possiblity of making the unconscious conscious. The pain caused by paralysing unconscious feelings is to be undone through the rational mastery of self-reflection. Yet there is another Freud, who is perhaps more postmodern in political sensibility. This is the Freud who stresses that unconscious desire is intimately bound up with everything we do, who stresses that fantasy is a constitutive and creative feature of the human imagination, and who underscores the point that analysis is itself interminable. As Cornelius Castoriadis puts this: 'Freud's proposition can be completed by its inverse: "Where ego is, id must spring forth." Desire, drives . . . have to be brought not only to consciousness but to expression and to existence.'[8] Significantly, both of these emphases in Freud's texts, the modernist and postmodernist perspectives, are elaborated and reconceptualized in contemporary psychoanalytic theory.

Post-Freudian Psychoanalysis: the Self and Others

The portrait of the self now found in psychoanalysis has undergone dramatic change since the time of Freud. In this period, clinical and theoretical developments in psychoanalysis have significantly recast the notion of the self, as well as the broader connections between individual experience and society. Roughly speaking, attention has shifted from the intrapsychic world of object representations to the relationship between the self and others. That is, post-Freudian developments focus on the psychical relations *between* human beings rather than the inner world of the individual subject alone. From this *intersubjective* angle, the dynamics of personal and social conflict appear in a new light. The reproduction of the patriarchal and social order of modern societies is no longer understood as merely rooted in sexual repression and the denial of deep inner passions, as in the classical view of psychoanalysis. Rather, repressive social conditions are traced to various pathologies that underlie human relationships, and of their impact on psychic life, selfhood, and gender-identity. Much of the impetus for this conceptual shift of focus has come from the failure of classical psychoanalysis to make sense of the sufferings of the modern clinical patient. In the post-Freudian period, the clinical picture of typical analysands has been, not one of individuals suffering from disturbances in sexual repression and self-control, but rather that of individuals experiencing a deep emotional poverty in relationships with others, coupled with a more general estrangement from the self. Moreover, recent psychoanalytic accounts converge on the point that modern social conditions drive a wedge between self and others, generating in turn a waning in social ties and the sense of political community.

The study of the self *in relation* to others carries important implications for understanding psychic life. For many modern theorists, social relationships do more than just influence the development of subjectivity. Rather, the human subject's inner world is *constituted* through these relations. That is, the nature and meaning of a person's subjective and sexual experiences are actually formed in relationship with others. Such a recognition of the intersubjective foundation of the self has led psychoanalytic debate away from issues of Oedipal conflict and sexual repression to a concern with the earlier pre-Oedipal period, the imaginary dyad of child and mother, and of psychic disturbances in ego-formation. Specifically, there has been a fundamental revision of Freud's atomistic and mechanistic language of unconscious drives. Instead, the psychological dynamics underlying selfhood depend upon mutually engaged subjects.

These changes within psychoanalysis are registered in the American post-Freudian tradition and the British school of object relations theory in very different ways. Both traditions of thought share the view that classical Freudian metapsychology is unable adequately to comprehend the nature of human motivation, problems of selfhood, and contemporary difficulties in living. They also share a common emphasis upon interpersonal processes in theorizing problems of selfhood and relationship difficulties. Yet there are also fundamental differences between these psychoanalytic traditions. The American post-Freudian tradition breaks into two schools of thought: (1) ego psychology and (2) the interpersonal (or culturalist) model of psychoanalysis. Ego psychology is generally concerned with the genesis, development, and adaptive capacities of the ego. The key figures in this school of psychoanalytic thought include Anna Freud, Heinz Hartmann, Ernest Kris, R. M. Lowenstein, Erik H. Erikson, and David Rapaport. The interpersonal tradition in psychoanalysis shares this focus on the rational capacities of selfhood, but also emphasizes the place of social and cultural conditions in its constitution. The key figures in this theoretical tradition include Erich Fromm, Harry Stack Sullivan, Karen Horney, and Clara Thompson. The British school of object relations theory, by contrast, focuses on the dynamics and structures of intersubjectivity itself, tracing the complex emotional links between the self and other people. The central figures in this school of psychoanalytic thought include W. R. D. Fairbairn, Harry Guntrip, Melanie Klein, D. W. Winnicott, John Bowlby, and Michael Balint. In order to provide ourselves with a map of these post-Freudian theories, let us now trace the general outlines of these positions.

For Freud, the powers of the ego are destined always to be outstripped by unconscious desire and external reality. As we have seen, the ego attempts to negotiate some sort of balance between inner desire and external necessity. As Freud puts this, the ego is like a 'man on horseback, who has to hold in check the superior strength of the horse'. In the reinterpretation of Freud developed in ego psychology, however, this steering capacity of the ego is shifted up a gear into a fully blown self-mastery. Ego psychologists emphasize the powers of the ego for masterful, rational action. We find an early theoretical outline of the ego as a powerful force in the psychic economy in Anna Freud's pioneering book *The Ego and the Mechanisms of Defence* (1941). In this book, Anna Freud advances the view that human development unfolds through the emergence of bodily needs and capacities in a context of a sharpening awareness of significant-other people. The earliest interaction between infant and mother consists of an original oneness, known as primary narcissism. In successive phases, the infant separates out from mother, transforming itself into an independent agent. This growing sense of the infant's independence, however, is seen as a *disengagement* from relationships. The ego's basic mechanisms of adjustment provide the psychic underpinning for a successive pattern of separations throughout the life cycle. In this connection, Anna Freud speaks of the ego as having a range of defences at its disposal against the unconscious. These defence mechanisms, such as an identification with the aggressor, are built up through human interaction and thus locate the ego within the wider frame of social relations. Accordingly, her work highlights the role of early interpersonal relations in the constitution of psychical life.

Anna Freud's work describes the mechanisms of ego growth and defence but it fails to document much about the psychic structure which promotes this functioning. In the writings of Heinz Hartmann, however, the constitutional basis of the ego is given explicit attention. Hartmann describes his psychoanalytic enterprise as a 'general developmental psychology'.[9] As such it is concerned with examining not only psychopathology, but everyday psychological functioning and associated processes of adaptation. Whereas Anna Freud sees the ego emerging from certain defensive mechanisms in the face of anxiety,

Hartmann argues that the ego is both primary and autonomous. The kind of ego autonomy that Hartmann has in mind encompasses a remarkably broad range of functions, including thought, language, perception, and memory. These ego capacities, Hartmann says, are essentially conflict free. By this he means that such functions can be smoothly performed in day-to-day social life in a way not anticipated by traditional Freudian theory, and which thus radically alters the potentialities for self-control and mastery. Free from internal distortion or unconscious compulsion, the ego is released, in Hartmann's scheme, to pursue an autonomous existence in its relationship with the external environment. For Hartmann, since the ego is largely conflict free, it can enter into an adaptive role with social reality, incorporating the demands of the external world and making them a fundamental source of human motivation. This enlargement of the ego's power, and of its direct links with the social environment, means that Hartmann's psychoanalysis can underwrite the rationalization of selfhood and everyday life. From this angle, social relationships are less significant than is a mastery of the inner world.

This focus on self-mastery and adaptation in ego psychology need not necessarily be taken as denying the importance of human relationships; it can be read as suggesting that autonomous selfhood is an essential precondition for equal interpersonal relations. By upgrading the powers of the ego in the face of its defensive struggles with external reality, Hartmann attempts to emphasize the capabilities of the individual subject for insight and reason. His emphasis upon adaptation shows that the external world has a major impact upon the strivings of the individual subject. However, the notion of 'adaptation' in this respect is not without its difficulties. As Russell Jacoby has argued, it leads psychoanalysis generally in the direction of social conformism, with every failure to 'adapt' being read as a sign of psychopathology.[10] Yet the nature of the dynamic unconscious surely suggests that the self is not really capable of such 'adaptation'. Hartmann's work also results in a neglect of the *quality* of social relationships to which human subjects have to submit. Since the only criterion of assessment is that of adaptation, Hartmann has no viable way of confronting social critique. From this standpoint, human autonomy depends on a successful introjection of the values of society, no matter how insanely exploitative or emotionally destructive they may be. Moreover, the primacy attributed to separation in ego psychology would appear to go hand in hand with the American ethos of individualism, thus promoting a narcissistic expansion of the would-be autonomy of the self. This is a limitation which will be discussed in later chapters, especially when we turn to consider the work of Erik Erikson and Erich Fromm.

Whatever the force of these ideological blindspots, ego psychology influenced the trajectory of psychoanalytic theory towards a deeper examination of interpersonal issues. This change in emphasis, from problems of drive regulation to those of relationship difficulties, is further expanded in object relations theory and related variants. Broadly speaking, object relations theorists view the self in an internal relation with others. Like ego psychology, object relations theory posits an initial symbiotic unity for the emerging infant with the mother. However, it differs from the former standpoint by rooting self-organization and development in socially situated engagement with other people – the capacity to force reciprocal relations between the self and others, while recognizing that such emotional connection depends upon the *mutual constitution* of subjectivity. The upshot of this is that the internal structuring of the psyche is seen as an outcome of interpersonal activity, reciprocity, and emotional exchange. Relations with other people, and particularly the mother, become part of the psychical economy of the self. The human need for connection and recognition leads to the incorporation of others into the self; and it is precisely such representations of others which are essential to the formation of psychical structure. Significantly, the other side of the coin is that any distortions or pathologies in social relationships will in turn be built into the structure of the self. In object relations theory, it is socially destructive relationships in the modern world which pervert the self's capacities for relating to other people. Thus, cultural conditions underpin problems of self-organization.

The theoretical premises which inform object relational approaches involve a fundamental re-evaluation of issues concerning self-constitution and the nature of psychical structure. In contrast to classical Freudianism, object relations theorists hold that human subjects want relationships with others for the intrinsic satisfaction of such connectedness, and not simply to reduce drive energy. In the words of Michael Balint, psychical life is itself characterized by a search for 'primary object love'. Relational needs are primary, and disturbances in self-constitution are seen as the result of a failure to obtain the love of significant others. In the view of W. R. D. Fairbairn, one of the pioneering analysts of the British object relations school, the psychic economy is object-seeking rather than pleasure-seeking. Pleasure is certainly still important, but in object relations theory unconscious enjoyment is itself regarded as a means of achieving emotional connection with others. From this angle, the understanding of unconscious drives as the underlying engine of human motivation and social interaction is too simple, since it obscures the complex processes through which the individual (ego) and social (objects) intersect. Rather, it is claimed that we should see the quality of interpersonal relations as structuring and transforming the libidinal drives themselves. For unconscious drives are only moulded into a distinct organization because they operate in the service of human relationships and circumstances. What this means for Fairbairn, in the words of his acolyte Harry Guntrip, is that drives 'can only operate satisfactorily when they belong to a stable ego, and therefore cannot be the source of the ego's energy for object-relating. It seems more conceivable that the energy of the ego for object-relating is the primary energy.'[11]

The starting point for the analysis of ego structure in the work of Fairbairn and others is the maturational environment, and specifically the quality of maternal care experienced by the small infant. In Fairbairn's view, the earliest months of life are characterized by a total merging between the infant and its mother, a mode of related-ness termed 'primary identification'. In this state, ego and objects are harmoniously linked since no differentiation has yet occurred. For Fairbairn, it is this primordial unity at the centre of psychical life which provides the basis for genuine interactions between the self and other people, from which self-organization becomes more or less integrated. This emphasizes that problems in selfhood stem from these early relationships with primary caretakers and, specifically, have their roots in infantile experiences of maternal failure and deprivation. Fairbairn argues that if parental availability and respon-siveness are low, the emerging child will attempt to overcome the pain of frustration by ego-splitting and internal fantasy substitutes. Typically, this involves splitting the pre-Oedipal mother into good and bad components. The inadequacy of real external relations leads the infant to create internal fantasy objects. Yet such compensatory fantasies limit the child's capacity for healthy development and real interpersonal interaction. Such external frustrations – that is, the mother's failure to meet the infant's needs – are thereby conceptual-ized as generative of splits and distortions in consciousness. Since object and ego only exist in connection with each other in this perspective, negative experiences in this early period will lead to distortions, as well as the formation of pathological defences, in the construction of the self.

From the foregoing considerations, it can be seen that the object relational perspective holds the promise for enriching our critical understanding of the interpersonal processes involved in the constitution of the self. By illuminating the subtle, yet profoundly important, interpersonal mechanisms of self-constitution, object relations theory suggestively reconfigures the relations between the self and social context. Significantly, its focus on the pre-Oedipal relationship between infant and mother provides a useful corrective to traditional Freudian theory, which tended to repress the role of the mother as an imaginary object, making the father the centre-point of object-internalization and thus self-constitution. This focus upon the pre-Oedipal infant/mother relationship also directs our attention to important dimensions of modern social experience. For object relations theorists, the late modern age creates severe disturbances in object relating. Particularly for Fairbairn and Balint, the destructive nature of modernity impacts upon the nurturing mother-infant tie too early, thus preventing the establishment of a core sense of self and trust in human relationships. This can lead, in turn, to a lifelong search for primary love through substitute fantasy objects.

However, there are also serious difficulties in object relations theory – problems that will be addressed throughout this book. A fundamental principle of the object relational perspective is that ego and object are inseparable. The ego is bound up with objects from birth, and disturbances in object relating arise through immersion in this interpersonal field. Yet Fairbairn's postulation of a unified, integral ego smacks of essentialism. It recalls the sort of ahistorical view of human nature that Freudian psychoanalysis explicitly challenges, privileging the consoling unity of personal identity over the split and divided dimensions of unconscious experience. The problem here is clear. If there really is a timeless core of personal unity, then surely the social, cultural, and political possibilities for transforming the self are also acutely delimited. It is this tendency to project self-development as the unfolding of a human essence that leads many commentators to conclude that object relations theory is conservative in political orientation; and this is a theme that will be examined in chapters 3 and 5. To be sure, there is an implicit assumption in object relational perspectives that the unconscious is an epiphenomenon, internal fantasy objects being merely derived from failures in real environmental relations. From this angle, fantasy arises not so much from internal necessity but rather as a consolation for, or escape from, external frustration. Rather than viewing the unconscious as a constitutive source and productive well-spring for selfhood, as is the case with Freud, the object relational approaches of theorists such as Fairbairn, Guntrip, and Balint find unconscious processes a distortion of human development. To this extent, they are in agreement with the German social theorist Jürgen Habermas, who takes the unconscious as a prime example of 'systematically distorted communication'.

Instead of bracketing unconscious processes in such a negative fashion, however, it might be more instructive to trace the processes through which the imaginary dimensions of selfhood interlace with those early object relations of the environmental surround. This line of approach is suggested by the work of the British paediatrician and psychoanalyst, D. W. Winnicott. Following Freud, Winnicott emphasizes that the newly born infant has to develop a sense of self from its original state of 'unintegration'. This struggle of the self for an individuated existence characteristically centres on the quality of object relation between child and mother. For Winnicott, the emergence of true and authentic selfhood is tied to a state of 'primary maternal preoccupation'. In this condition, the mother offers a special sort of presence, or devotion, which allows the child to experience itself as omnipotent and self-identical. The mother thus objectively provides support for connection with external reality, while at that moment the child is free to create a 'representational world'.

If all goes well during this process of maternal devotion, or what Winnicott calls 'good enough mothering', the small infant is able to develop a sense of independence in line with the exercise of her or his ego functions. In this connection, Winnicott suggests that it is vital for the mother not only to be responsive to her infant's needs but also to establish a kind of nonintrusive presence, a presence which allows the child to discover its core of imaginative selfhood. By offering nondemanding support, the mother leads the child to a positive experience of aloneness, thereby establishing a basis for 'going-on-being' in the world. Winnicott describes this as the child's move into 'transitional space', a concept which will be discussed in chapter 3. At this stage, it can be noted that Winnicott's portrait of the self underscores a key paradox at the centre of human development. The emergence of a stable core of selfhood, according to Winnicott, depends on establishing the kind of relationship which is at once liberating *and* supportive, creative *and* dependent, defined *and* formless. For it is within this interplay of integration and separation that Winnicott locates the roots of authentic selfhood, creativity, and the process of symbolization, as well as of social relations and culture. And it is precisely from this angle that Winnicott draws his infamous distinction between the 'true self', a person that is capable of creative living, and the 'false self', a person that cannot establish stable emotional relations with others. For Winnicott, the 'false self' is fashioned out of the loss of maternal sensitivity, as the small infant tries desperately to make some emotional connection with the mother by abandoning its own wishes and incorporating *her* demands, desires, and feelings. It is as if the child, unable to find an adequate representation of its own needs and psychic states, turns defensively against itself by internalizing the attitudes and reactions of others. Pathologies of selfhood thus screen real, authentic human needs; and this, for Winnicott, is the essence of the 'false self' as it operates 'to hide the true Self, which it does by compliance with environmental demands'.[12]

In Winnicott's version of object relations theory, then, other persons play an essentially facilitating role in the construction of the self. It is only if the mother, and later significant-others, are unable to provide a supportive, nonintrusive environment that a debilitating, unconscious fragmentation of the self arises. What Winnicott's model of development can be said to overlook, however, is that peculiar internal form of the unconscious which for Melanie Klein is known as fantasy. What is involved in fantasy processes, for Klein, is a kind of continual shuttling of inner and outer worlds, from which a sense of self emerges as an outcrop of unconscious 'internal objects'. Klein describes fantasy as an unconscious creation that emanates from within the self, yet it is also – and this is fundamental – a necessary accompaniment to any experience of outer reality. The self for Klein is originally caught up with, and dispersed within, a world of 'part-objects' – involving fantasies of the breast, for example. Adopting Freud's scandalous concept of the death drive, Klein posits certain primordial aggressive drives. She contends that these destructive drives are transferred to the earliest 'part-objects', from which the mother (or more accurately, at this point, the breast) is then experienced as persecuting and dangerous. These anxieties are in fact so terrifying, in Klein's view, that the infant must 'split' mother into good and bad objects, thereby displacing the pain of destructive unconscious fantasy. This splitting of the world into good and bad is what Klein calls the 'paranoid-schizoid' position. In order to get beyond these schizoid poles of paranoid displacing and projective idealizing, the infant has to integrate these conflictive feelings and come to grips with the fact that the mother is an independent and whole person. Klein argues that the main stumbling block in this respect is the child's fear that it has forever injured the object due to its violent fantasies about the maternal body. To transcend this, it is necessary for the infant to 'make reparation' through the experience of guilt and ambivalence – a process Klein calls the 'depressive' position. The negotiation of depressive feelings in the Kleinian framework carries a positive value, from which the creative and stable self emerges. Significantly, however, paranoid-schizoid mechanisms continually resurface in both personal and social life. And it is this interplay between destructive expression and creative reparation, as we shall see, that gives the Kleinian perspective a powerful critical edge for the analysis of self-identity and modern culture.

Before concluding this section, a few points should be made concerning the foregoing perspectives and their differing accounts of modern social life. In the object relations perspective, the emergence of selfhood is tied to the development of interpersonal relations. Because of this focus on the relational qualities of self, object relations theorists tend to see contemporary social experience as both opportunity and danger. There is a recognition of both the affirmative and destructive dimensions of modern life, as well as their impact upon the cultural sense of self. To the extent that contemporary culture restricts human relations, the object relations perspective argues that self-organization is stunted. Where this occurs, life becomes drained, society is experienced as dislocating, and superficial narcissistic relationships tend to predominate. By contrast, the Kleinian view of contemporary experience focuses less on relationships than affectively loaded internal objects. For Kleinian theorists, the psychic interpolation of paranoid anger and personal despair permeates all aspects of day-to-day social life. The key issue, therefore, centres on the extent to which modern culture provides opportunities for communal reparation and creative living. To the extent that cultural displacement swallows up personal strength, Kleinian theorists emphasize that self and world become disconnected, as paranoid anxieties prevail.

Post-modern Identities: Contemporary Psychoanalytic Strategies

So far we have examined a range of psychoanalytic portraits of the self. All of these portraits, notwithstanding their conceptual differences, are premised upon the guiding ethos of autonomous selfhood. In classical psychoanalysis, autonomy is conceived as the self which is emancipated from distorting unconscious drives and passions. This is best summarized in Freud's own profoundly Enlightenment maxim: 'Where id was, there ego shall be.' In this account, what used to be unconscious shall be reclaimed for individual control and rationality.

With the emergence of object relations theory, the psychoanalytic notion of autonomy undergoes significant transformation. The autonomous self can no longer emerge against the backdrop of an internal alteration of the individual subject, but rather depends on the reconstruction of emotional links with others. It is human relationships that matter, and the enhancement of the subject's capacity for interpersonal relations may depend variously upon the rational mastery of inner drives (Hartmann), stable internal objects (Fairbairn), creative human relations (Winnicott), or reparation (Klein). But, despite prescriptive variations, these standpoints offer a contribution to some future enlargement of the autonomy of the self. In psychoanalytic theories derived from semiotics and poststructuralism, however, there is a radical break with this search for self-coherence and autonomy. The distinguishing feature of poststructural psychoanalysis is the launching of a sustained critique on the very notion of 'self'. The problem of contemporary experience, it is argued, is not located in the failure of autonomy itself but rather in the idea that a stable, personal self is attainable at all. What this means, at least in its more thoroughgoing versions, is a complete deconstruction of the notion of subjectivity. In contemporary psychoanalytic perspectives, this deconstruction is characterized by unconscious contradiction, dislocation, and polyvalency – all of which make the goal of stable personal identity problematical. One important implication of all this is that the modernist belief in the would-be autonomy of the self is rendered little more than an ideological fantasy.

The links between poststructural psychoanalysis and postmodernism are complex in character, and will form a central thread of discussion in later chapters. At this point, it can be said that postmodern theory refers to certain social transformations ushered into being in the twentieth century, and examines a social condition characteristic of advanced contemporary societies. Central to these social and institutional transformations is what Jean François Lyotard has called the 'crisis of narratives'.[13] By this, Lyotard means that the lofty aims of the modernist epoch – rationality, emancipation, autonomy, and revolution – are no longer sustainable. By contrast, the new postmodern attitude welcomes the institutionalization of contingency, ambivalence and undecidability. This is so since postmodernists contend that we can have no global knowledge of the human predicament in the late modern age. Arguing against the grand ambitions of modernism, postmodern theorists suggest that we reject totalizing or unifying discourses and, instead, attempt to come to terms with the fractured and problematical nature of contemporary social experience. Significantly, it is at this point that the claims of poststructural psychoanalysis become most pertinent to postmodernism. For the emphasis on the illusory nature of the self and the polyvalency of unconscious desire in poststructural psychoanalysis fits neatly with the postmodern emphasis on surfaces, images, and fragments. This decentering of the self is, in brief, at one with the postmodern account of contemporary social experience – an experience in which the flows of libidinal desire mesh with an attitude of 'anything goes'.

For postmodern theorists, then, the concepts of self and self-identity are a fiction. Selfhood is an imaginary illusion, an illusion which serves to mask the painful reality that desire is itself insatiable. This deconstructive conceptual strategy is taken largely from the widely influential account of the human subject proposed by the French psychoanalyst Jacques Lacan. For Lacan, the narcissistic illusions of modern selfhood can be traced back to a very early stage in life; to a structuring event which Lacan calls the 'mirror stage'. This stage of human development comes about when the small infant, previously unintegrated and uncoordinated, finds its bodily image reflected in a mirror.[14] Whether the mirror stage is understood literally or metaphorically, the crucial point, for Lacan, is that the small infant is led to *misrecognize* and *misperceive* itself. According to Lacan, this is so since the mirror provides an illusory apprehension of self-unity that has not been objectively achieved. That is, the creation of an 'ideal self' – the self as it would like to be, self-sufficient and unified – is an imaginary construct which covers over the fragmentation of the psychical economy. The implications of this narcissistic construction of the self are far-reaching. Lacan and his acolytes claim that, whether or not one is actually fascinated with one's own image, the distortions and traps of the imaginary order shape all interactions between the self and others. This ranges from family interaction, through school, early adulthood, to the work environment, and human social relationships more generally. In Lacanian psychoanalysis, social relations and cultural association are themselves structured in and through infantile *images* of the imaginary order.

The Lacanian doctrine of the self as an imaginary illusion casts serious doubt on the question of autonomy as traditionally conceived. For if it is still possible to speak meaningfully of self-knowledge from this angle, then critical insight must shift to some other register than that of the narcissistic illusions of the ego. In Lacanian theory, as we shall see in chapter 4, this possibility is linked to the entry of the human subject into the symbolic order – that cultural plane of received social meanings, differentiation, and individuation. The anchoring point of this transition from imaginary distortions to symbolic meaning is language. Taking what we will find to be a typically post-structuralist turn, Lacan contends that 'the unconscious is structured like a language'. What this means, essentially, is that social, linguistic processes and the inner depths of the psyche are intertwined. To be a member of society requires a minimum level of linguistic competence, in order to adopt the position of speaker or listener. This demands the acceptance of a *subject position* in terms of the social conditions of culture, sexual difference, ideology, and so on. For Lacan, however, there is a fundamental contradiction at the heart of symbolization itself. Language certainly brings subjectivity into being as an 'I', separated from that which is 'Not-I'. Yet, from another angle, the social and cultural forms which structure linguistic definitions of self-identity are themselves constantly outstripped and overdetermined by unconscious desire. In the Lacanian view, then, the relationship between self and society is inherently problematic, as the oscillation of unconscious desire is refracted through the linguistic components of contemporary culture.

Lacan's linguistic reinterpreation of Freudian psychoanalysis has been taken up by literary, media, and cultural critics, and social theorists. What has been especially influential in Lacan's writings is the point that the imaginary and symbolic dimensions of psychical life are themselves the ideological carriers of culture and history. For, as we shall see, Lacanian theory offers a powerful account of the organization of personal life by the social institutions of modern culture. The Lacanian emphasis on the decentering of the subject grasps the inherent difficulties of forging a core of personal selfhood in the late modern age. Caught between the narcissistic traps of the imaginary and the structural positioning of the socio-symbolic order, the portrait of the human subject in Lacanianism is in certain respects an apt characterization of how personal life is globally outstripped by social, political, and economic mechanisms.

Lacanian theorists regard the symbolic order as that which orders the psyche into socialized form, at once ripping the infant away from the world of imaginary plenitude and referring her or him to received social meanings. The symbolic Law – that is, language – is the crucial means through which individuals are 'subjected' to the outer world. There is clearly a deterministic flavour to all this. The symbolic order structures the pyschical reactions of people in the face of social and political institutions. In this connection, Lacanian theory might be said to suppress unconscious contradiction as well as the profoundly imaginary dimensions of human experience. Indeed, it is just this binding of unconscious desire to the social order that Gilles Deleuze and Félix Guattari in *Anti-Oedipus* find as lying at the root of the Lacanian ideological position.[15] According to Deleuze and Guattari, psychoanalytic theory (both traditional and Lacanian) is politically reactionary in character. The psychoanalytic privileging of Oedipal identity, or what Lacanians call the Law of the Father, is at one with the imposition of repressive discourses on the free flow of desire. To combat this, as we shall see in chapter 6, Deleuze and Guattari emphasize the positive contours of unconscious desire, taking schizophrenia as their model for 'revolutionary action'. Whereas Lacanian theory regards desire as an impossible search for imaginary completeness, a search conducted under the Law of the symbolic order, Deleuze and Guattari argue for a primary desire resistant to closure, a desire that can be ideologically marshalled to overcome the repressive constraints of modernity.

A similar, though less dramatic, critique of psychoanalysis is to be found in the writings of the French philosopher Jean-François Lyotard. Like Lacan, Lyotard sees all discourse as traced through the structuring force of the symbolic. However, Lyotard questions the supremacy that Lacan attributes to the symbolic order in fixing meaning. For Lyotard, the unconscious is less an organized system of language than it is a 'libidinal band' of pure traces, intensities, and forms. And it is precisely from this angle, as we shall see, that Lyotard analyses the production of culture.

It follows from this view that psychoanalytic discourse might itself be a repressive component of contemporary society. We might say that psychoanalysis is a prisoner of rigorous binary codes (conscious/unconscious, pleasure/reality, love/hate, primary/secondary), codes which are used to impose a rigid theoretical grid upon the complexity of human experience in its entirety. In the postmodernist perspective, psychoanalysis is often charged with violently homogenizing the complexities and differences of social experience in terms of concepts such as the unconscious, castration anxiety, Oedipus, and the like. Thus, for the postmodern sociologist Jean Baudrillard, psychoanalysis functions as a 'mirror of desire', projecting its terms and concepts on to human subjects, and thereby, in the act of so doing constituting the unconscious and its effects.[16] Whether you find this sort of argument convincing or not depends, to a large extent, on how you evaluate the ontological conditions of desire and passion as well as the discourses we use to make sense of everyday life. It is, I

shall argue in this book, an intellectual sleight-of-hand to imagine
that discourse simply legislates into existence the concrete emotions
desires, and aspirations of human beings. This is not to say that a
reductive use of psychoanalytic categories does not limit our understanding of personal and social phenomena, nor is it to deny that
people in modern societies often draw on psychoanalysis in constitut
ing their daily activities and decisions. But it is to make the point that
psychoanalysis is not just a theoretical play of mirrors. Unless one is
willing to embrace the idea that individuals are just magically born
into the social network, or that desire is somehow always-already
true to itself, then one must concede that psychoanalysis provides
valuable insights concerning the imaginary world of selfhood.

   In contrast to the French anti-psychoanalytic claim that the intel
lectual fascination with Freudian theory is over, the enterprise of
psychoanalytic critique is developing at a faster rate than ever before
Indeed, it has been via a thorough-going revision of the whole
Lacanian framework that a number of theorists in recent years have
sought to rethink the relations between self and society, as well as
the possibilities for the socio-symbolic transformation of culture
This theoretical current is generally grouped under the banner of
'post-Lacanianism', though many of its leading figures tend to reject
this label. There are numerous common themes that surface in post
Lacanian theory, and in subsequent chapters we shall review the
influence of post-Lacanian motifs in contemporary theory. At this
point, the following key themes of post-Lacanian theory are noted
the re-evaluation of the creative power of the imaginary as it
intersects with symbolic processes; the rejection of a monolithic
symbolic Law; a profound questioning of the phallic, patriarchal
order of modern societies, together with a stress on the immanent
possibilities for alternative gender relations; and a peculiar concern
with social and political interests as the product of contingency, lack
and linguistic uncertainty. To date, post-Lacanian ideas have
attracted strongest interest in feminist quarters. The writings of Julia
Kristeva and Luce Irigaray, whose theories will be examined in
chapter 5, have provided feminism with a powerful reconfiguration
of feminine sexuality and the female body, urging women to reject
the prison-house of patriarchal language and to overturn it for an
alternative feminist vision of social relations. Significantly, though
post-Lacanian theory has also made important contributions to
rethinking human subjectivity within a general theory of ideology. In
this connection, the key emphasis is on social and cultural forms as
imaginary traps which paper over the impossible nature of desire

itself. In this sense, post-Lacanian criticism engages in a psychoanalysis of cultural objects, showing how people project desire into the social fabric of modern culture.

Summary

In this chapter, we have examined a range of psychoanalytic portraits of the self. In so doing, three fundamental themes have been developed: selfhood and its embedding in asymmetric relations of power; the links between personal meanings and the contemporary social world; and the relationship between psychoanalytic critique and individual and collective autonomy. These themes have been selected for their relevance to the central concerns of this book, and I shall seek to develop them in a substantive way in the chapters that follow.

In introducing these themes, this chapter has provided an overview of different psychoanalytic traditions. In the first part of the chapter, Freud's theory of the self as an outcrop of the unconscious was outlined. It was argued that in classical psychoanalysis the self, our relations with others, and with society, is fully shaped by unconscious drives and fulfilment. The chapter then reviewed various object relational accounts of the self. In these theories, it was stressed that relationships themselves are taken as primary and fundamental to self-organization. In this respect, it was emphasized that both classical and object relations theories adopt certain modernist assumptions about self-identity, pathologies of self and social relations, and their possible transformation. The chapter finally turned to consider contemporary psychoanalytic perspectives in the light of postmodernism, stressing the fragile links between unconscious desire and the self as an imaginary construct. It was argued that the self in postmodernism is seen as an alienating fiction, without psychic interiority of depth. Finally, some social and political implications of this general standpoint, as developed in Lacanian and post-Lacanian theory, were traced out.

We shall now turn to consider how these themes have influenced contemporary psychoanalysis and social-theoretical debates during the twentieth century. In the next chapter, I begin this examination by investigating various psychoanalytic interpretations of modern culture.

Table 1.1 The making of the self

Psychoanalytic model	Self and sexual subjectivity	Key terms
Classical psychoanalysis	Structural division of the psychical economy; self as outcrop of unconscious fantasy	Id, ego, superego, Oedipus and castration complexes
Ego psychology	Traced as the outcome of the separation-individuation scheme	Defence-mechanisms Adaptation
Object relations theory	Seen as the internalization of early environmental surround	Internal object relations
Kleinian theory	Understood as the product of love and death drives, from which ego-object relations undergo integration or disintegration	Splitting Paranoid-schizoid and depressive positions
Lacanian theory	Seen as an imaginary construct; structured by symbolic law of language	Imaginary, symbolic, and real orders Law of the Father
Post-Lacanian theory	Interplay of libidinal forces and symbolic codes; at once subject to and subversive of the law	Pre-Oedipal imaginary

2

Modern Culture and Its Repressed

From Freud to Lasch

Sexuality and repression: these are twin-boundary posts in the psychoanalytic interpretation of modern culture. In the wake of Freud's discoveries about human sexuality, a strong tradition of political radicalism has emerged which attempts to ground social theory in psychoanalysis. This brand of social-psychoanalytical criticism is concerned with the question of unconscious desire as it affects whole societies. The issues addressed in applying psychoanalysis to the spheres of social, political, and cultural life involves the following. How does the individual subject come to enter human society, to feel itself to be part of social reality? Do personal meanings merely 'reflect' social reality, or are they inseparably bound up with cultural life, and thus transformative of the social world? What is the location of unconscious desire in this relationship between self and society? And what of society itself? Does society play a facilitating role in human expression and development, or does it serve to restrict and deform the self? In exploring these issues, this chapter ranges widely across a variety of conceptual standpoints. Broadly speaking, one central lineage, from Freud's cultural diagnosis to Herbert Marcuse, is preoccupied with the idea of sexual repression as the key to understanding the modern period; whereas an alternative tradition of thought, from Erich Fromm to Christopher Lasch, is concerned more with interpersonal issues of sexuality, love, and emotional communication in modern societies.

The Ambivalence of Society: Freud's Social Theory

Towards the end of his career Freud wrote: 'I recognized ever more clearly that the events of human history, the interactions between human nature, cultural development, and the precipitates of primeval experiences . . . are only the reflection of the dynamic conflicts among the ego, id, and superego, which psychoanalysis studies in the individual – the same events repeated on a wider stage.' This statement captures the essence of Freud's cultural approach. The critical analysis of modern societies, like that of individual subjectivity, requires the application of psychoanalytic knowledge. This involves tracing the institutionalization of unconscious sexuality within the cultural social framework.

According to Freud, the central psychical mechanism which structures the precarious relations between the self and the world is *ambivalence*. The ground of all human thought, feeling, and action springs from a primordial ambivalence – an ambivalence which is vital to the complexity of social life itself. To be precise, Freud says, this ambivalence precedes society. Consciousness and the unconscious, reason and desire, primary and secondary process, self-preservation and sexuality, love and hatred: these are, for Freud, permanent dualisms of the human condition. Because the human subject was born 'polymorphously perverse', because psycho-sexuality is bound to bodily zones, aims, and objects, because unconscious desire is always clamouring for expression, the torments of ambivalence are no mere accident that might be overcome in a different social world. In this respect, Freud's social theory engages with some of the most painful and distressing aspects of human experience. Modern culture, Freud says, is repressive. Society imposes severe psychic demands upon individuals, demands that produce intense personal misery. But it is precisely from this painful ambivalence or unconscious anguish that Freud also detects the roots of psychic resistance. Too much repression, Freud says, leads to intense hostility and rage. At this point, the pressure of unconscious desire and passion can release the 'mental dams' of sexual repression in a far-reaching way.

Freud's earliest full-length consideration of the relations between self and society is ' "Civilized" sexual morality and modern nervous illness' (1908). The theory of society embodied in this text is usually interpreted as a one-way impress of culture upon the individual. However, as is so often the case with Freud, this essay is at once a polemical engagement with traditional views about morality and cultural order, and a preliminary outline of the immense conceptual difficulties in linking unconscious sexuality and social organization. Freud begins by considering the view that the emergence of modernity – the transition from pre-modern to modern culture – has produced a general condition of neurosis, of 'exhausted nerves'. According to

Freud, the competitive and materialistic quality of modern social life has given rise to serious emotional suffering. Indeed, the overall tone in the essay is that modern culture is lamentable. However, Freud does not wish to limit himself to only a socio-cultural explanation of modern anxiety. For the crux of the matter lies elsewhere: in those points of unconscious pleasure through which sexuality interlaces with extrinsic moral imperatives. For Freud, the ambivalence of psychical life rebounds as cultural ambivalence. What this means, essentially, is that the emotional conflicts which Freud uncovers in humans are shifted up a gear into the antagonistic structures of social and cultural life itself. Conflict, generated in and through the psyche, produces anxiety which is turned against culture.

In the same manner that the ego seeks to establish order and control over unconscious drives, it is essential for culture to incorporate the deeper psychical sources of the subject, pressing the pleasure principle into the service of the reality principle. This is so, Freud contends, for the very reproduction of social and cultural life. The development of civilization, social bonds, and the injunction to labour all depend upon self-control. However it is precisely at this point – the disjunction between individual desire and social necessity – that Freud locates cultural pathology, the initial 'manifestations of nervous disturbance'. The fundamental problem, in short, is that culture robs the individual subject of unfettered instinctual enjoyment, and places gigantic restrictions upon sexuality. Listening to the miseries and anxieties of his bourgeois analysands each day, Freud discovered a deep connection between personal, inner desires and the repressive social forms which engender excessive self-control. The denial of feelings, the structuring of sexuality into narrow paths of monogamy and marital legitimacy, the rigid (male) insistence upon genital monosexuality: these are, Freud argues, the oppressive repressions of modern selfhood. Imposing order on the free flow of unconscious desire, Freud comments, is certainly a key task of civilization. But when such an imposition results in a repressive closure, cultural life is condemned to self-annihilation. Authentic communal bonds are reduced to little more than a façade. Hence, Freud places 'civilized' in quotation marks in this essay. As he concludes, 'when society pays for obedience to its far-reaching regulations by an increase in nervous illness, it cannot claim to have purchased a gain at the price of sacrifice; it cannot claim a gain at all'.[1]

The ambivalence of the psychical economy, then, is the route by which Freud sketches the psychoanalytic interpretation of culture. Desire and control, pleasure and reality, sexuality and self-preservation: these are the dualisms, in the early Freud, through which individuals come to face social regulation. Central to this structuring process of prohibition and repression is the Oedipus complex. The intervention of the father into the child/mother dyad is of key importance in the institutionalization of extrinsic moral imperatives, since, as we have seen in the last chapter, the paternal position is primarily symbolic and thus prefigurative of the social order. The Oedipus complex plays a decisive role in splitting human passion and desire – prohibiting impulses for imaginary union with the mother – and thus establishes a symbolic transition to social life itself. Freud traced the origins of collective moral prohibitions back to a real, historical Oedipus complex. The theorem of an original parricide, of an actual murder of the father figure, led Freud in *Totem and Taboo* (1914) to reconstruct a collective Oedipal moral imperative. Freud paints a picture of a 'primal horde', a collectivity of 'brothers' dominated by an all-powerful father who monopolizes women. In anger and frustration, the brothers eventually kill and eat the father. However, due to ambivalence and guilt, the brothers come to feel remorse for the killing. This unconscious anguish induces the brothers to identify with the dead father as a 'totem', and to invent moral anchoring restraints against the free expression of sexuality. Like in the Oedipal fantasy itself, the terror of the father is now 'owned' on the inside and the regulation of society is instituted through the renunciation of desire, registered in the taboo against incest.

There is no need to rehearse here the grave limitations of Freud's account of the origins of social and cultural organization. For, in the light of subsequent anthropological knowledge this century, there are few advocates of this aspect of Freud's social account nowadays. Perhaps the most important point to note is that Freud's search for a real Oedipus complex displaces his crucial insights into the radically imaginary dimensions of selfhood. Seen in this light, Freud's collective Oedipal myth ascribes to real events what are in fact the imaginary tribulations of the unconscious: the ambivalence of love and hate, the mourning which accompanies object-loss, and the remorse and guilt which follows self-transgression. This emotional structure of ambivalence underscores the fact that the forbidden is desired precisely because it is outlawed. Yet, despite the limitations of Freud's account of the institutionalization of morality, there are still elements of considerable interest in this perspective. The problem of self and society, and their mutual imbrication, is fundamental in this respect. As Freud comments:

The asocial nature of neurosis has its genetic origin in their most fundamental purpose, which is to take flight from an unsatisfying reality into a more pleasurable world of fantasy. The real world, which is avoided in this way by neurotics, is under the sway of human society and of the institutions collectively created by it. To turn away from reality is at the same time to withdraw from the community of man.[2]

This passage underlines the essence of Freud's thinking about institutionalization. First, it stresses that reality is not pre-given or natural. Reality, Freud says, is structured by 'human society', by the social and technical frameworks fashioned by human beings. Second, it underscores the point that individual subjectivity and society presuppose one another. To take flight from reality involves rejecting or foreclosing social life. For Freud, social forms thus constitute the self at the deepest roots of its unconscious experience.

In his late writings, Freud comes to see human beings as living under the destructive force of a terrifying death drive – a primordial tendency within the psychic economy to return to nonbeing, to the inorganic. From this standpoint, psychic ambivalence is recast as the permanent co-presence of two drives: that of life and that of death, Eros and Thanatos. The hypothesis of the death drive served to account for a range of problems arising from Freud's clinical work. The issue of human aggressiveness, the question of sadism and masochism, the repetition of painful and traumatic experiences, the addictive character of neurotic suffering: these and other related phenomena could not be understood in terms of the pleasure principle of psychic functioning. Accordingly, Freud modified his earlier emphasis upon sexual pleasure and enjoyment. In *Beyond the Pleasure Principle* (1920), Freud proclaims that 'the aim of all life is death'. After 1920, psychical life for Freud still has its origins in sexuality and libido, but it is also shot through with aggressivity, sadism, and hate. As Freud notes of this new dualism: 'only by the concurrent of mutually opposing action of the two primal drives – Eros and the death-drive – never by one or the other alone, can we explain the rich multiplicity of the phenomena of life'.[3]

In retrospect, Freud's positing of the life-and-death drives can be seen as a preliminary cultural diagnosis, the essential underpinnings for his late global model of repression. For the new duality of psychic ambivalence entails a radical reinterpretation of the repressive character of modern culture itself. Human misery and oppression are no longer understood as the outcome of sexual repression alone. Instead,

Freud comes to equate culture with a fundamental constraint upon self-destructiveness. 'The main renunciation culture demands of the individual', writes Paul Ricoeur, 'is the renunciation not of desire as such but of aggressiveness.'[4] By incorporating this new dualism into his analysis of modern culture, Freud is able to rewrite the problem of self and society as a contest between love and hate. The Freud of *Civilization and Its Discontents* (1930) enfolds love and hate, Eros and Thanatos, in the following way:

> [C]ivilization is a process in the service of Eros, whose purpose is to combine single human individuals, and after that families, then races, peoples and nations, into one great unity . . . These collections of men are libidinally bound to one another. Necessity alone, the advantages of work in common, will not hold them together. But man's natural aggressive instinct, the hostility of each against all and of all against each, opposes this programme of civilization. The aggressive instinct is the derivative and main representative of the death drive which we have found alongside of Eros and which shares world-dominion with it.[5]

Modern society, and the pathological compulsions it generates, is rooted in a repressive structuring of love and hatred. To be sure, Freud remains faithful to his earlier view that the reproduction of society depends upon sexual repression. But in his late sociological vision this sexual repression becomes integrated into a deathly self-preservation, organized as a destructive assault on the human body, on others, and on nature.

The internalization of these repressive and deathly cultural norms is, for Freud, effected by the superego. Like the small infant in the Oedipal drama, human beings live out a relation to society through an unconscious identification with received social meanings and extrinsic moral imperatives. This is so, Freud argues, because human beings are born 'prematurely', and hence there is a dependence upon, and submission to, authority figures prior to the emergence of sexuality. What this means, in brief, is that human beings both desire and identify with the law at the level of the unconscious. From this angle, civilization is generally secure in enforcing a truce between desire and control. The sexual and aggressive passions of the libidinal economy are turned back upon the human subject with a vengeance by social institutions, thereby introducing a sense of guilt, anxiety, and unhappiness into the human condition. In this sense, the individual channels back 'unacceptable' desires into the psyche as the price paid for ordered social life. Yet, by mixing the death drive with erotic impulses, civilization also outflanks these goals of security and social order. The integration of the life and death drives increasingly supplants cultural order, as unconscious desire swerves onto destructive paths of social expression. Freud thus concludes: 'The fateful question for the human species seems to me to be whether and to what extent their cultural development will succeed in mastering the disturbance of their communal life by the drive of aggression and self-destruction.'[6]

Freud's signal contribution to social thought lies in the idea that culture is reproduced through a repressive structuring of unconscious passion. However, Freud's social thought has been fiercely contested, both inside and outside psychoanalytic circles. It has been argued, for example, that modern societies are far more differentiated and conflictual in character than is recognized in the Freudian model of repression. Such critics argue that psychoanalysis sees cultural order as necessarily involving the overpowering of chaotic passion and desire; and that, to this extent, Freud's theories are at one with the conservative-minded social thought of a Thomas Hobbes. This line of criticism involves a fundamental misunderstanding of Freudian psychoanalysis. I have already argued that it is mistaken to see Freud as equating culture with a one-way impress upon the individual. It is certainly the case that Freud finds modern culture repressive – often tyrannically so. But the fundamental tenet of his standpoint is that self and society interlock through ambivalence. There is a 'lack of fit', so to speak, between self and world; a disjunction which arises from the existence of psychic dualisms (unconscious/conscious, sexual drives/self-preservation, life/death) that prevents the individual subject from becoming fully integrated into society. That this is the case, Freud says, is positive news. For it is ambivalence that drives the self forward, generating in turn the complexity of social life. Significantly, the Freudian image of conflict between unconscious forces and social reproduction captures numerous aspects of modern social experience. Given the turbulence of modernity, Freud's social thought is in many ways an accurate reflection of the open, contingent, and fragmented world in which we live. Social upheaval is a crisis of human personality and of human relationships; and repressed desires and passions threaten (and often invade) everyday life, disrupting the world as it is.

There is indeed a problem in Freud's theory, however, about how repression and culture are interwoven. For Freud, heightened repression is intrinsically associated with the complexity of modern culture. However, this thesis looks increasingly untenable in the light of certain twentieth-century social transformations, such as changes in sexuality and gender power. Put simply, the repression of sexual and aggressive drives no longer appears to be the key issue in a world which has broken with moral constraint almost everywhere. Whether we speak of the mass media's fascination with sex or of the ideological turmoil of wars and revolutions, modernity incorporates (and indeed bolsters) the erotic and aggressive passions of human subjects. Such trends suggest that culture is at once an essential medium for the expression and repression of unconscious drives. Society may place restrictions on certain libidinal tendencies, but it also provides the means for self-representation through the constitution of social forms. In part, Freud's thought occludes this enabling dimension of the social network since it focuses primarily upon repressed passions of the self. This emphasis underscores the cultural repression of the drives, and of related problems of self-control, but only at the expense of diverting attention from the complex patterning of social relations and their intersection with personal relationships. By contrast, in object relations psychoanalysis and related variants, as discussed in chapter 1, the primary focus is away from the solitary language of the drives and towards the interpersonal dimension of desire and its embedding in the structures of social life. This psychoanalytical approach to the interpretation of culture will be critically examined in the following sections of this chapter.

Equally significant is the feminist criticism that Freud's account of social life and culture is unduly restrictive, centred as it is upon masculinist anchoring constraints. Here it is argued by critics that Freud is secretly held in thrall by the values of rationality and social authority that he seeks to disrupt. Though Freud is sceptical of Enlightenment reason, there is some truth to this charge. Civilization, in Freud's account, rests upon the repression of sexual and aggressive drives, itself the outcome of the Oedipus and castration complexes. In so far as Freud traces the psychic roots of Oedipal identity, it can be argued that his thought grasps the persistence of patriarchal domination. But there is also a defensive aspect here. By making Oedipus and the father central to his account of society and culture, Freud subordinates the role of the mother and pre-Oedipal experience as a whole. Paternal identification, for Freud, is the cornerstone of patriarchal culture, and the pre-Oedipal child/mother bond is cast aside as precultural. Society is equated with control, renunciation, organization, and commerce. The pre-Oedipal maternal realm, by contrast, necessarily threatens subversion to male-dominated language and culture. This is a point that has become of considerable importance to some feminists, particularly those associated with object relations theory and also some post-Lacanians. For these theorists, Freud's social account is essentially a theoretical replication of patriarchal power. A discussion of these trends in psychoanalytic feminism is offered in chapter 5. At this point, a related but diffferent point is made. By viewing the Oedipus complex as preparatory to individuation and social reproduction, Freud's theory underlines the importance of male rationality and self-control in modern societies. Such a psychoanalytic model grasps how restrictive cultural norms are internalized, and thus reproduced, by human subjects. However, there are limitations. By excluding the pre-Oedipal realm of sexuality, little is said in the Freudian scheme about love, empathy, and emotional communication.

Escaping Society: the Humanistic Psychoanalysis of Erich Fromm

We have seen that, for Freud, there is a fundamental ambivalence structuring the relations between self and society. Inner repression, Freud argues, is the price paid for social co-operation. It is just this conception of social repression that is challenged in the writings of the post-Freudian cultural theorist Erich Fromm. An early member of the Marxist Frankfurt School, and later an emigré from Nazi Germany, Fromm argues – in a series of influential books – that psychoanalytic theory must be reformulated better to conceptualize the place of social and historical factors in self-constitution. For Fromm, the key error of Freud's work is that it abstracts from a specific socio-political situation – the sexual repression of Victorian culture – and projects interpersonal conflict into the solitary world of the individual subject. In contrast to Freud's approach, Fromm is out to show, not how we suffer repression in order to join society, but how society itself inscribes deformation and isolation at the heart of human relationships. Indeed, Fromm sees modern culture as offering false solutions to human needs. As he puts this, society is our 'escape from freedom'.

In his early writings associated with the Frankfurt School, Fromm attempts an integration of Freud's theory of the unconscious with Marxist social theory. According to Fromm, Freudian theory is needed to supplement Marxism in order to grasp how social struc-tures influence and shape the inner dimensions of modern selfhood. The social system, in Fromm's reinterpretation of Freud, constitutes the identity of human subjects to fit the economic, cultural, and historical context. Feudal society produces subjects adapted to the roles of serfs and lords; market capitalism produces subjects as capitalists and workers; and twentieth century monopoly capitalism churns out subjects as consumers. Fromm calls this fashioning of subjectivity the production of 'socially necessary character types'. For Fromm, this fabrication of social individuals derives from the 'highly modifiable' nature of unconscious drives. Society affects a fundamental ordering of the psychic economy, projecting social values and processes into the deepest recesses of the self. The result, says Fromm, is human subjects 'wanting to act as they have to act'.

For Fromm, as for Freud, the family plays a key role in the emergence of repression. The winning of parental love entails the repression and denial of inner selfhood and the adaptation to socially prescribed patterns of behaviour. As Fromm puts this: 'The family is the medium through which the society or the social class stamps its specific structure on the child, and hence on the adult. _The family is the psychological agency of society._'[7] It is an institution that implants objective antagonisms at the heart of individual subjectivity, sustains economic conditions as ideology, and infuses perceptions of the self as submissive, self-effacing, and powerless. The central thread of Fromm's argument, then, is that the destructive effects of late capitalism are not only centred on economic mechanisms and institutions, but involve the anchoring of domination within the inner life and psychodynamic struggles of each individual.

If society, in Fromm's eyes, is a matter of sexual repression, libidinal renunciation, and pathologies of self, then it is really not all that far from the general tenets of Freudian social thought. In arguing that social and political relations affect self-identity in different and changing ways, Fromm enriches Freud's account of repression. Fromm's later writings, however, change direction quite dramatically. Increasingly sceptical of Freud's dualistic theory of psychic life, he became convinced that the Freudian drive model of human motivation could not adequately grasp interpersonal and social relations. In particular, Fromm rejected Freud's notion of the death drive, arguing that it only served to legitimate the increasingly destructive and aggressive tendencies of the late modern age.

In his major work _The Sane Society_ (1956), Fromm examines modern culture in terms of the pathologies it inflicts upon selfhood, considering the extent to which the social structure deforms human relationships. In that book, he argues that Freud underemphasized social and cultural relations, and also the general impact of culture upon human needs. Selfhood, says Fromm, is best understood in terms of interpersonal processes. From this angle, psychical life is composed of emotional configurations derived from relations between self and others. For Fromm, self-organization, though influenced by unconscious drives and passion, is reflexively organized through 'awareness, reason and imagination'. Fromm's theory of selfhood can be stated in five theses:

1 *Relatedness vs. narcissism* The human condition is rooted in an essential need for relatedness – a thesis with which Fromm challenges Freud's asocial account of the monadic psychical subject. The need for relatedness is not instinctual but arises from the separation with nature. Its flourishing depends upon creative social relations. Without such relations the self is impoverished, as in pathological narcissism.

2 *Transcendence-creativeness vs. destructiveness* Against the backdrop of biological need, the self-organization of creativity unfolds in both positive and negative forms. Creation and destruction, Fromm argues, 'are both answers to the same need for transcendence, and the will to destroy must rise when the will to create cannot be satisfied'.

3 *Rootedness-brotherliness vs. incest* Creative social life, Fromm argues, depends upon an interplay of masculine and feminine values. Arguing against the 'patriarchistic-acquisitive' logic of Freud's Oedipus complex, Fromm contends that human potentiality depends upon the integration of feminine qualities (such as care and nuturing) into the masculine realm of reason and reflexivity. In this connection, Fromm says, feminine qualities are dangerous in modern culture since they threaten incorporation back into a 'state of nature'.

4 *Sense of identity-individuality vs. herd conformity* The search for self-identity is intrinsic to the human condition, and modern societies play an essential role in structuring socio-economic possibilities for self-organization. The repressive transformation of this need, he argues, produces regressive ideologies such as fascism, racism, and the like.

5 *The need for a frame of orientation and devotion-reason vs. irrationality* The need for orientation and connection with the world is a precondition for human autonomy. Without this, symbolic forms become diffused, and the subject drained of ego-strength.[8]

Thus, the central feature of Fromm's theory is that helplessness, isolation, and aloneness are key building blocks in relations between the self and others. In this respect, the patterns of relationship that a person makes can be either progressive or regressive. Progressive

relations with other people involve a reflexive, rational understanding
of the human condition. The pain of individual isolation must be
confronted and accepted, in order for healthy intersubjective relations
to develop. By contrast, a regressive involvement with other people is
caused by denying individual separateness. In this mode of functioning, inner pain and emptiness are sidestepped by a neurotic immersion
in infantile illusions. An endless menu of regressive fantasies is offered
by mass consumer culture in this connection, fantasies which produce
narcissistic pathology and related disturbances. The key feature in
this neurotic, regressive zoning of the self is that other people are
used instrumentally in order to bolster self-identity, and thus to avoid
inner emptiness and isolation. Here Fromm's standpoint converges
on a crucial object relational distinction between self-development
and self-distortion – as in Fairbairn's formulation of good and bad
object relations, or Winnicott's account of the true self and the false
self. However, Fromm proposes a more open psychoanalytic theory
of the self by directly linking interpersonal relations and social
context. The core of his argument is that problems of self, which link
with social relationship pathologies, have their roots in already-
existing patterns of cultural domination. Because the spheres of
economic, political and cultural life are shot through with the sadistic
satisfactions of power and domination, regressive self-solutions are
reproduced in the individual domain.

Given that contemporary social arrangements so violently deform
and warp self-constitution, is there anything that can be done to
reverse this pathological state of affairs? Can human beings create,
and sustain, any kind of meaningful liberation? Fromm believes that
they can. Surprisingly, given the pessimistic tone of the foregoing
analysis, Fromm contends that it is still possible to face the painful
realities of life in a mature and rational way. To do this, Fromm
argues, it is vital for the self to *disengage* from the corrupting
influences of the contemporary epoch. To live authentically means
fashioning a creative and responsive selfhood, a self that can produc-
tively engage in intimacy and mutuality. Such a capacity, he contends,
depends on coming to terms with individual separation and aloneness
– realities that are usually experienced as isolation or emptiness in
modern culture. A shorthand way of describing this is that Fromm is
encouraging a more reflexive involvement with the self. But what
then of social conflict? In this context, Fromm attempts to develop a
moral dimension as an energizing vision for emancipation. The more
that human subjects reclaim the possibility of authentic existence

through introspection and self-reflection, the more a social order based on mutual respect and autonomous activity will develop.

Fromm's writings rank among the most important post-Freudian mappings of the relations between self and society. Indeed, his model has had a major influence upon the reception of psychoanalysis into social and cultural theory. There are, however, important problems in Fromm's humanistic psychoanalysis. It has been argued, for example, that his account of self-constitution and the social process leads to a form of sociological reductionism. What is meant by this charge is that Fromm reduces the complex, contradictory relations between self and society to a dull, mechanical reproduction of pre-existing social values. As John Cash has argued, Fromm's extreme conception of the malleability of the sexual drives has the effect of freezing the dynamism of selfhood into a 'general, trait-like, libidinal structure'.[9] The subject is repressively constituted through certain agencies of socialization, which stamp the prescriptive values of society into the human soul and thereby deform the essential needs of the self. Fromm thus presents an account of self-constitution that eliminates the profoundly imaginary features of unconscious experience, and leaves unexamined the diverse human possibilities for agency, creativity, critical reflection, and transformation. He reduces Freud's notion of the unconscious to a totalistic conception of libidinal malleability. The limitations of such an approach are plain. The ambivalence that Freud locates between self and society – the tension between psychical and social reality – is obliterated. Although wanting to compensate for Freud's focus on unconscious drives, Fromm's cultural analysis proceeds too far in the other direction – sociologizing psychical reality out of existence. Ironically, then, it is the *post*-Freudian Erich Fromm that ultimately speaks up for a *pre*-Freudian conception of the 'total personality'.

A related criticism is that Fromm evaluates society against some 'human essence' of a non-cultural kind. It is as if Fromm, having diagnosed modern selfhood as thoroughly ideological, has to safeguard some resistant kernel of the human condition in order to articulate an emancipatory claim at all. Rationality, individualism, transcendence: these ideals may be absent from modern society, but they underlie all human experience and will potentially transform the social world. But in arguing that there is a transhistorical, universal 'human condition', Fromm seems blind to the fact that ideals such as rationality and self-mastery are often quite explicitly oppressive. Many contemporary world problems – global warming, the risk of massively destructive warfare, the exploitation and pollution of nature – are intimately bound up with the expansion of Western rationality and mastery. As one commentator puts it: 'Fromm revives all the time-honoured values of idealist ethics as if nobody had ever demonstrated their conformist and repressive features.'[10] Significantly, the ideals which Fromm stresses are also those of a male-dominated realm. Little is said about gender or the repression of female sexuality in Fromm's work. His humanistic psychoanalysis, and its underwriting of the 'essential needs of mankind', thus reproduces at a theoretical level masculinist fantasies of omnipotent self-control. Seen in this light, the inadequacy of Fromm's belief that authentic living is possible through social disengagement becomes plain: to turn inward in the hope of discovering authentic existence represents not a 'radical endeavour' but rather an illusory wish to overcome domination and suffering by escaping society.

Marcuse's Freudian Revolution

For the Frankfurt School social theorist Herbert Marcuse, unconscious desire is at once subject to the social-historical process and also potentially transformative of that world. People suffer from too much repression in modern society, says Marcuse. Yet, by adapting Freud to radical ends, he argues that the liberation of repressed desire could produce social transformation of a far-reaching kind. Like Fromm, Marcuse sees psychological and political repression as interconnected. A critical reading of psychoanalysis is vital, Marcuse argues, for understanding how cultural domination penetrates the inner world of individual subjectivity, how monopoly capitalism and mass consumer culture shape personal desires, and for comprehending human passivity in the face of exploitative and destructive social processes. However, Marcuse does not accept that social forms repressively triumph over the individual subject completely. Critical of Fromm's humanistic psychoanalysis, Marcuse contends that the way forward is not through private disengagement, but through psychological and social transformation. From this perspective, Fromm's programme for 'authentic living' is fundamentally conservative since it implies accepting the world as it is. Whereas post-Freudians like Fromm graft society and culture on to psychoanalysis, Marcuse seeks to unfold psychoanalysis from the inside, in order to reveal its inherently critical edge. That is, Marcuse reads psychoanalysis as a critical theory of self-organization, one alert to the repression, domination, and suffering of modernity.

In his seminal *Eros and Civlization* (1955), Marcuse traces how modern social processes deform the self and social relationships. According to Marcuse, it is necessary to recognize that the contradictions of capitalism pass into individual subjectivity itself. Capitalist processes of mechanization and automation – and the oppressive, dull labour which they spawn – inscribe themselves within the inner world of the human subject through an intensification of repression. All social reproduction demands a certain level of repression, but in capitalist society the social organization of production institutes a crippling (though unnecessary) burden of renunciation. In this social-theoretical reading of Freud, the individual is, in fact, adapting to the interests of capitalist domination masquerading as the 'reality principle'.

Marcuse's cultural diagnosis proceeds from Freud's account of the conflict between pleasure and reality, sexuality and self-preservation. For Marcuse, as for Freud, conscious rationality depends upon the shift from the pleasure principle to the reality principle – a transformation that in fact safeguards the long-term interests of pleasure itself. According to Marcuse, however, the capitalist expansion of oppressive systems of technology and bureaucracy this century has led to a 'transubstantiation' of unconscious pleasure itself. What this means, essentially, is that pleasure has somehow become disconnected from the needs of the human body, being bent out of shape by the power interests of late capitalism. Indeed, this restructuring of the self has gone so far that the psychoanalytic division of the individual into id, ego, and superego is today obsolescent. The psychical economy, says Marcuse, no longer has these sharp divisions. The Freudian image of man is dead. In this connection, Marcuse emphasizes the interweaving of the personal, technological, and political spheres. Marcuse argues that by a perverse kind of internal logic, unconscious desire is now subjected to – and manipulated by – techno-science and the mechanical network of capitalist processes. The phantasmagoria of the mass media, the commodification of sexuality, and destructive warfare: these and other features of the modern world accompany a general *disorientation* in self-identity.

From this angle, Marcuse's interpretation of Freud has certain themes in common with Lacanian and postmodern psychoanalysis. Like Lacanian and postmodern cultural criticism, Marcuse argues that the modern world is experienced as dislocating. The more that the stable psychological features of self-identity break down, the more people experience the world as fragmented, as a field of fleeting surface images. In contrast to these standpoints, however, Marcuse believes that an excavation of the repressed unconscious will herald personal and social emancipation. (As will be seen later, some postmodern theories share this emphasis upon the truth of the unconscious, although their psychoanalytic base is deconstructive in orientation.) For Marcuse, repression and cultural domination are to be completely overturned by the disruptive forces of unconscious desire and passion.

For Marcuse, the Freudian interplay of repressed desire and self-control is expressive of a wider social conflict. In modernity, the unconscious is denied true expression in the interests of capitalist domination. In Marcuse's view, however, Freud's emphasis on the contradiction between unconscious desire and cultural order was pulled in an ahistorical direction, making it the self-same in all possible worlds. Seeking to recapture the historical dimension in psychoanalysis, Marcuse therefore distinguishes between two kinds of repression: 'basic repression' and 'surplus repression'. Basic repression refers to that minimum level of libidinal renunciation in facing social life. Marcuse uses this term to indicate that a certain amount of repression is necessary to produce a 'socialized subject', a subject capable of sustaining the business of social and sexual reproduction. Surplus repression, by contrast, refers to the intensification of self-restraint caused by asymmetrical relations of power. Marcuse described the monogamic-patriarchal family and modern work practices, for example, as cultural locations in which there is a surplus of repression. This repressive surplus operates through the 'performance principle', a culturally specific form of reality structured by the economic order of capitalism. According to Marcuse, the capitalist performance principle recasts repression as surplus in several key ways. It causes human beings to face one another as 'things' or 'objects', it replaces general eroticism with genital sexuality, and it fashions a disciplining of the human body (what Marcuse calls 'repressive desublimation') so as to prevent repressed desire from interfering with capitalist exchange values.

What of the possibilities for social change? Marcuse differs sharply from Freud as regards the nature of emancipation. Marcuse contends that the performance principle, ironically, generates the cultural conditions necessary for a radical transformation of society. What promises an end to surplus repression are the industrial-technological advancements of late capitalism itself. For Marcuse, the material affluence generated by Western capitalist industrialization and techno-science opens the way for an unravelling of sexual repression. The overcoming of cultural domination will release the repressed, creative unconscious forces of personal life, reconnecting the sexual drives and fantasy to the social network. Such a reconciliation between culture and the unconscious will usher in a new, sensuous reality – a reality Marcuse calls 'libidinal rationality'. Libidinal rationality, though abstract in character, involves a radical reversal of surplus repression. Liberation from this surplus will facilitate a general eroticism, not only of the body, but of nature and cultural organization. There are shades here of the sexual radicalism of Wilhelm Reich: sexual liberation as a foundation of social emancipation. Yet Marcuse's grounding of social theory in psychoanalysis stresses that emancipation requires more than just sexual freedom. It demands an integration of sexuality and love into transformed social, institutional life.

How are we to understand this notion of libidinal rationality? Is it just some emancipatory dream of the Frankfurt School theorist Herbert Marcuse, or does it unearth certain psychical tendencies that point towards an alternative social condition? As a resexualizing of social life, libidinal rationality can be interpreted as an encouragement of emotional communication and intimacy. Fantasy occupies a special place in this context, Marcuse says, since it contains a repressed truth value. As he puts this: 'Imagination envisions the reconciliation of the individual with the whole, of desire with realization, of happiness with reason. While this harmony has been removed into utopia by the established reality principle, fantasy insists that it must and can become real, that behind the illusion lies knowledge.'[11] Thus fantasy is itself a longing for reconciliation – between pleasure and rationality, desire and reality. For Marcuse, this recovery of unconscious desire will facilitate the resexualization of the human body, so as to create harmonious, libidinal social relations. Against the repressive structuring of 'sex' under the performance principle, the release of fantasy will eroticize all aspects of society, allowing for a spontaneous and playful relation to life.

Marcuse's influence over debates on sexuality has been immense in recent decades. What he has contributed in particular is the idea that sexuality, rather than being some 'private space' internal to the self, is a thoroughly psychosocial phenomonon which is transformative of the social world. It was this strong emphasis on sexuality as revolutionary that shot Marcuse to international celebrity as a prophet of the student and sexual liberation movements in the late 1960s. Because of this involvement, Marcuse's work has sometimes been represented as elevating the personal over and above the political. However Marcuse himself did not equate sexual liberation with a non-repressive society. The transformation of culture, he argued, 'involves not simply a release but a *transformation* of libido'. The transfiguration of sexuality presumes the flowering of emotional communication in social institutions. In this context, the conflict between life and death will diminish as Eros infuses social activity and culture.

Notwithstanding its sociopolitical importance, many psychoanalytic commentators would now agree that Marcuse's work is unsatisfactory in several respects. To begin with, Marcuse's account of the individual and repression is wanting. He tells us that repression is socially imposed, with no aspect of psychical life escaping the total penetration of cultural domination. However, this view sits badly with psychoanalysis and, indeed, Marcuse's own social theory. Repression, as we have seen, involves a dynamic conflict between unconscious drives and self-organization. In the making of the self, unconscious drives will be organized in a particular way, involving compromise formations as well as the exclusion and repression of unacceptable desires and passions. But the crucial point, as Freud and others affirm, is that *internal psychical conflict* underlies self-organization and social relationships. Yet Marcuse ignores these psychodynamic aspects of unconscious experience, focusing instead on the power of society to shape and control the individual. The result is an absolute conception of repression which destroys the existence of psychical conflict and turmoil, individual agency, critical self-reflection, and the capacity to act differently. Marcuse's focus is thus radically individualist: the complexity of self-identity and emotional life is evaluated simply in terms of how far society represses the drives. Many object relational and related psychoanalytic theories, by contrast, make the quality of relatedness, the sense of interpersonal bonds and community, and the extent of self-continuity central to evaluating the nature of repression in the modern epoch. The emphasis here is away from drive energies and potentials and towards interpersonal issues of social life – an approach that will be examined in the next section of this chapter.

Secondly, as a consequence of this totalistic image of repression, Marcuse is forced to round the individual back upon itself in order to find an escape route from the contemporary performance principle. The way forward is through the drives – which are ultimately beyond the scope of social domination, and thus prefigurative of an alternative society. Yet, despite the explicit aim to develop a new political vision, Marcuse has little to say about new forms of social relationship or improved cultural association. Rather, his vision of collective autonomy is one in which repressed drives are liberated and thus expressed. But such a vision of liberation is highly questionable. It tends to suggest that the drives themselves, and not people, are charged with transforming society. Human agency is reduced to domination, while the repressed unconscious is linked to emancipation. Yet, if the individual subject really is obsolescent and repression complete, who might possibly transform the truth of the drives into new social conditions? Who exactly would be capable of sustaining a liberation known as 'libidinal rationality'? The central problem here is clear. Marcuse's focus upon drive potentialities, although valuable in some respects, actually mirrors an individualist culture which constantly forecloses issues about cultural bonds and political community. Here comparison with Fromm is instructive. If Fromm is in danger of losing the unconscious by sociologizing the ego, Marcuse risks a reductive account of social and political life – society being refracted through drive energies alone. Significantly, Marcuse's argument in favour of the liberation of repressed drives also smacks of essentialism. It recalls a *pre*-Freudian view of human passion as somehow natural and timeless, outside and beyond the reach of the social structure. But the view that the repressed unconscious, or fantasy itself, will only gain expression in the non-repressive society fails to see that fantasy structures are already bound up with institutional life. It fails to recognize that the 'truth of the unconscious' is already interconnected with embattled human relationships, violent gender tensions, and ideological conflict.[12]

Finally, Marcuse's work raises serious difficulties for the interpretation of modern culture. His downplaying of human agency, and idealization of repressed drives as the basis of human liberation, does not allow students of psychoanalytic social theory to see how creative self-organization intersects with social processes, what goes into the making of interpersonal relations or politics, or of how individual subjects reflect critically on, and disinvest from, destructive ideological forms. Writing in the social context of the American cold-war period, as a refugee from Nazi Germany, it is perhaps not surprising that Marcuse holds a gloomy view of late capitalist consumer culture. Yet, however much this cultural diagnosis captured the dulling conformity of individuality at this historical time, it is plainly inadequate as a measure of the internally differentiated social formations that exist in the contemporary epoch. The emancipatory struggles of peace, feminist, and ecological groups, among others, clearly suggest the bankruptcy of Marcuse's thesis concerning the total penetration of the psyche by social forms. To find an account of creative self-organization, and its links with interpersonal relations and the social process, it is necessary to look elsewhere.

Narcissism: Sign of the Times?

The foregoing sections have examined the intricate relations between selfhood and culture. In the drive model of psychoanalytic theory, we have seen that unconscious ambivalence underlies the structuring of sexual and aggressive drives within culture at large. Libidinal and destructive unconscious forms are fused to make possible the reproduction of society. In relational psychoanalysis, by contrast, social context and relationships are not something just tacked on to the self, but are actually constitutive of personal identity. Here it is social relations themselves that constitute the fabric of self-identity and daily life. But what happens to self-identity when social relationships themselves go awry? What happens when cultural experience becomes permeated by a thoroughly global capitalist system, and social relationships are in the process of fragmentation and dispersal?

One major response to these questions in contemporary theory focuses on narcissism. The ever-increasing randomness and contingency of modern social life is said to have led to a shrinkage of the public world, thus promoting a defensive, yet painfully empty, search for self-gratification. The key image is one of 'dead' social experience – culture becomes thoroughly structured by media images, centred upon consumption and surface appearances. The self in this context becomes permeated by a deep sense of cultural emptiness, fractured by the repetitive life-rhythms of monopoly capitalism. In fact, for many authors the modern world has become so emotionally drained that human autonomy and creative social relationships are rendered redundant. Modern culture is simply unable to provide the emotional conditions necessary for autonomous social relationships – the self being left distorted, deformed, and brittle.

In this final section of the chapter, we will look at some painful emotional costs of modernity by examining this narcissistic void at the heart of the self. In particular, we will concentrate on the links between narcissism and contemporary cultural forms. To do this, the influential writings of Joel Kovel and Christopher Lasch will be examined.

Kovel: narcissism, de-sociation, and late capitalism

In an essay entitled 'Narcissism and the family' (1980), the American psychoanalytic Marxist Joel Kovel explores the connections between narcissism and advanced capitalist societies. Narcissism, Kovel says, is a location of desire in the self which underpins basic psychic functioning and self-esteem. In this potentially healthy mode, narcissism regulates all self and other relations – supplying the vital libidinal components for self-regard, ideals, values, and so on. In exaggerated form, however, narcissism becomes a character disorder, a disorder which produces a general estrangement from the self and from other people. To understand narcissism as a character disorder, Kovel returns to Freud's distinction between primary and secondary narcissism. Primary narcissism is constituted in the imaginary child/mother dyad, prior to the infant's distinction between self and other. In this fusion of desire with part-objects (specifically, the breast) the infant jubilantly feels itself to be self-identical, living in a magical world of omnipotence and fulfilment. Secondary narcissism refers to the break-up, yet continuation in new form, of this raw and primitive state of narcissistic self-unity. Secondary narcissism thus occurs with the first emotional separation of the infant from mother – a time in which the infant learns of mother as a separate person and thus forms a prefigurative sense of social reality. This gradual learning or finding of reality, however, is a painful experience since it is connected to a primary loss: the loss of that blissful imaginary state of self-unity. Yet, insofar as the infant forges a broader connection with mother and world, there is a kind of reflux of primary narcissism; but it is a reflux which is now securely centred within a human relationship and thus tempered by social factors. Secondary narcissism thus substitutes for infantile omnipotence; what makes the infant a socialized individual is this internalization of the other, an internalization that brings the child into the wider context of social and cultural relations.

Narcissistic disorders, Kovel says, have their origin in this transition from primary to secondary narcissism. The key problem here is that the child remains stuck within raw and destructive early omnipotence, thus preventing the development of healthy boundaries between the self and the external world. In modern social conditions, the internalization of the early parental relationship fails to provide a widening of social and cultural objects – deemed so vital for the emergence of individuality. Instead, the child remains a prisoner of primary omnipotence, the result being a narcissistically troubled relation to the self and to others. In fact, the narcissistic character can at best relate to other people only as suppliers of general approval and admiration. Lacking emotional connection with others, the narcissist inhabits an unintegrated world, a world in which persons and objects are split off, either powerfully idealized or arrogantly denigrated. However, there is another side to all this. Kovel, drawing on the post-Kleinian research of Otto Kernberg, argues that narcissistic states of grandiosity in fact hide deeper feelings of worthlessness and inadequacy. The narcissist's continual search for approval, and absorption in superficial pursuits, is in reality a defence against a painfully weak and fragile sense of self. The underside of the grandiosity of the narcissist is thus a ravenous rage, a rage which threatens to devour and destroy the self. This narcissistic rage, in Kleinian terms, is bound up with early paranoid-schizoid processes – such personalities simply cannot tolerate depressive feelings in which other persons are experienced as ambivalent. Instead, the narcissistic personality undergoes a process that Kovel terms 'de-sociation'. De-sociation, in Kovel's description, refers to the relation between all-consuming narcissistic rage and the social network. Cut off from realistic social engagement, and in the face of intensive feelings of powerlessness and inadequacy, the narcissistic self can cope with reality only through sadistic attempts at manipulation, control, and self-aggrandisement.

Advanced capitalism, with its colonization of social relationships under the sign of the commodity form itself, plays a key role in furthering narcissistic rage. Indeed monopoly capitalism, according to Kovel, replaces earlier enlightenment processes of subjective differentiation with a 'non-human other' – the commodity. Late capitalism creates a thoroughgoing commodification of the personal sphere, thus engendering an age of consumerism which tears wider social relationships apart. Kovel's central point here is that the loss of social texture generated by capitalism becomes deeply inscribed within self-organization. This can be seen, says Kovel, in the increasing tendency to treat human beings just like commodities in modern Western culture – and this is nowhere more clearly evident than in family life today. Suffering under the emotional impoverishment of modern culture, the developing child is said to encounter parents who themselves are on the brink of unthinkable rage and despair. In late capitalism, parents relate to their children primarily as 'investments'; an investment which might bring a future yield of narcissistic satisfaction. This distorted parent/child link thus reproduces narcissistic pathology, generating inauthenticity and rage within the wider social environment. According to Kovel:

> the bourgeois age is, among other things, that age of a family centred upon children. It is therefore the era in which childhood emerges for the first time in history as a distinct category of existence. Pathological narcissism is then fundamentally the outcome when the family, so to speak, is not merely centred on children but collapses upon them as well, crushing them beneath its weight. It is therefore a specific disorder for that phase of capitalist development in which such a collapse occurs. Pathological narcissism is a pox of late capitalism.[13]

Lasch: narcissism and survival

The American historian Christopher Lasch in two of his best-known books, *The Culture of Narcissism* (1979) and *The Minimal Self* (1984), utilizes psychoanalytic theory to explore the relation between narcissism and contemporary culture. Whereas Kovel sees pathological narcissism as an outcrop of capitalist relations, Lasch relates the phenomenon to the flux and unpredictability of modernity itself. Capitalist production and, perhaps more significantly, consumption, certainly play a key role in Lasch's analyses of the self in the modern world. As Lasch says, we live in a world in which mass production and mass consumption drives a wedge between creative self-other relationships; restructuring the self as a 'consumer' who measures everything in terms of market attractiveness and the approval of others. However, narcissistic self-distortions, in Lasch's writings, are shown to depend, not only on capitalism, but on fundamental social transformations which have arisen this century. Lasch thus links narcissism as a modern experience with globalization, mass communications, the end of history, the decline of tradition, and so on. Here contemporary identity formation is shown to be increasingly thin and precarious, as the self is outstripped by the dislocations and terrors of modernity. Against this background, selfhood and meaning begin to evaporate. For Lasch, the personal sphere starts to shrink in the face of an incomprehensible social environment – so much so that most people shut out this threatening external world, turning inward towards personal preoccupations in the interests of 'survival'.

Lasch, like Kovel, suggests that a deep sense of hatred underpins narcissistic self-organization. Locked into psychic splitting, narcissism brings into play an over-idealization of the object as a defence against infantile rage. This rage focuses on a complete inability to accept reality itself – with grandiose fantasies of omnipotence being used in the hope of returning to a state of imaginary self-unity. However such states of narcissistic self-regulation are only bound to disappoint, and processes of idealization are quickly overshadowed by devaluation. In this way, Lasch says, feelings of infantile grandiosity alternate with feelings of complete emptiness and abject inferiority in the narcissistic personality. Linking this narcissistic orientation to contemporary culture, Lasch argues that the modern self is: 'facile at managing the impressions he gives to others, ravenous for admiration but contemptuous of those he manipulates into providing it; unappeasably hungry for emotional experiences with which to fill an inner void; terrified of ageing and death'.[14] The general point is that an interplay of grandiosity and emptiness, idealization and rage, intersects with social processes. In the modern world, the subject is narcissistically dependent on others in the forging of self-identity. Yet, far from helping to provide a sense of meaningful identity, other persons remain cut off from the narcissistic self.

Lasch believes that it is social conditions which generate narcissistic pathologies; they do not arise out of any internal necessity. The unpredictability and dynamism of modern social life makes us narcissistically dependent on others in the making of our own identities. The problem, however, is that human beings are increasingly estranged and disconnected from each other since social life is itself fractured. Here Lasch concentrates on the breakdown of historical continuity in the public realm, and the subsequent emergence of mass-produced commodity images in the present age. He observes that the modern world is no longer one of durable objects. Instead, the high technology of mass communications inaugurates a world of fleeting images. These images take on a kind of hallucinatory character, spilling into everyday activities and the personal sphere. For Lasch, this dream world of media images not only restructures self-identity but also blurs the boundaries between the self and its surroundings. The self is today forged in a fantastic space of mirrors, divided between inner and outer boundaries. Yet this mirror-centredness of the self is deeply problematic. For just as the social world enters a phase of unprecendented flux and unpredictability, so too the self becomes structured by a deep sense of emptiness and despair.

Thus modernity for Lasch – with its commodified forms, its liquidation of intimate relationship, its globalization, its destruction of local historical meanings – makes the achievement of selfhood extremely precarious. Yet the self does not simply internalize these more terrorizing elements of the modern world. For Lasch, the interplay between the self and the social world is much more subtle than one of external intrusion into the personal sphere. Instead, the contemporary stunting of human relations involves the perversion of that intermediate realm between the inner world and the outer world, namely transitional space. Connecting this analysis to Winnicott's theory of transitional objects, Lasch observes that modernity downgrades cultural and aesthetic domains. Today, culture is patterned after the cold and detached images of economic calculation promoted through mass communications and consumption. As Lasch puts this:

> Instead of providing a 'potential space between the individual and the environment' – Winnicott's description of the world of transitional objects-[culture] overwhelms the individual. Lacking any 'transitional' character, the commodity world stands as something completely separate from the self; yet it takes on the appearance of a mirror of the self, a dazzling array of images in which we can see anything we wish to see. Instead of bridging the gap between the self and its surroundings, it obliterates the difference between them. Far from providing a creative bridge between self and world, then, our contemporary one-dimensional culture at once mirrors and intensifies an alienated subjective world, a world of inner emptiness.[15]

The contemporary narcissistic zoning of the self, designed to avoid the meaninglessness and emptiness of modern experience, connects directly to what Lasch terms our 'culture of survivalism'. In this argument, survival signifies both a loss of selfhood, but also a desperate attempt at self-management in a brutal and chaotic world. Lacking a framework of meaning for a fulfilling human life, individuals are forced to live one day at a time, in order to survive the conflicting processes that characterize modern life. Emotional disconnection from others, apathy, lack of concern about the future – these are the key features of Lasch's surviving 'minimal self'; a self turned defensively inward upon personal preoccupations in a world felt to be out of control.

Lasch, and also Kovel, provide detailed assessments of the prevalence of narcissism in modern societies. The analyses set out by them highlight the extent to which modern social processes promote unconscious feelings of despair and emptiness. Yet there are dangers to such characterizations of the modern period. Lasch and Kovel frequently demarcate narcissistic pathologies as the central dynamic of modernity. Such a standpoint, however, violently homogenizes the complex, contradictory cultural patterns of identity formation in the contemporary epoch. One consequence of this is a loss of critical perspective on the imaginary contours of self-formation as well as the dynamism and diversity of modernity. In this respect, I contend, it is better to read Lasch and Kovel as offering a description of narcissistic disorders, as a warping of the self which modern social life in some part promotes. However, in this perspective the forming of the self is not necessarily deformed by narcissism. For, as Marcuse has reminded us, narcissism is also an essential condition for a creative and autonomous engagement with the self, others, and the outside world.

Concluding Remarks

The cultural-psychoanalytic criticism examined in this chapter represents one of the richest traditions to have emerged from Freud's own theories. Sexuality and unconscious desire, as we have seen, are central to the reproduction of societies. In the drive-centred theories of Freud, and Marcuse after him, sexuality is pressed into the service of cultural reproduction, but it also retains a relative autonomy in respect of the social process. From this angle, emancipation presumes the undoing of sexual repression in conjunction with a transformation in social and political institutions. In cultural and interpersonal psychoanalysis, by contrast, it is social relations themselves which distort and pervert the relational capacities of the self. In the work of Fromm, Kovel, and Lasch, it is pathologies in social relationships which are constitutive of dislocations in self-organization, which in turn feed narcissistic and related conditions.

A few concluding observations might be useful at this point. The drive model of psychoanalysis underscores in a remarkably clear manner how personal desire is intricately interwoven with modern social processes. Yet, as I have suggested, an undue emphasis on libidinal enjoyment is unlikely to be of much help in tracing contemporary transformations in social relationships. In this respect, the various relational models of psychoanalysis examined offer alternative leads on the dynamics of repression and cultural life. We can learn from relational psychoanalysis that oppression and domination are deeply structured by a complex interpersonal pattern of emotional relations. This is not to say, however, that the analysis of unconscious passions and conflicts should be sidestepped in cultural analysis. On the contrary, we need to know more about the interlinking of drive configurations and the social context. The psychoanalytic tradition of social enquiry, I think, must confront structural processes of intersection between unconscious desire, interpersonal relations, and modernity. For the transformation of modern institutions, involving developments such as globalization and techno-science, are increasingly important in the constitution of selfhood and in social relations.

Table 2.1 Modern culture and its repressed

Theorist	Analysis of modern culture	Key terms
Freud	Self-society structured through ambivalence; culture reproduced through unconscious repression	Ambivalence Primary/Secondary process Life and death drives
Fromm	Modern societies deform human needs and relationships	Human needs Authentic living
Marcuse	Modern societies reproduced through surplus-repression	Surplus-repression Performance principle Libidinal rationality
Kovel	Narcissistic pathology outcrop of capitalism	De-sociation
Lasch	Narcissism connected to general social conditions of modernity	Survival Minimal self

Object Relations, Kleinian Theory, Self-Psychology

From Erikson to Kohut

In the previous chapter we examined the relationship between social and political organization in modern societies and the psychological repression of the individual subject. In this chapter, the focus is reversed. Rather than looking at social organization, we shall concentrate on personal life itself, examining the deep and pervasive psychical mechanisms by which repression and pathology are generated in everyday life. Such a shift in focus necessarily entails a concern with psychical structures of self-organization, as well as interpersonal relationships, and of how these structures become incarnate in day-to-day social life. From this angle, psychoanalytic theory is used to yield information about deeply layered human emotions and desires by which social activity and structures can be judged. In what follows, I shall review some of the major social-theoretical contributions that investigate these links between patterns of selfhood and contemporary social experience. I begin by examining certain concepts in object relations theory, and then link these concepts to issues of self and society in the late modern age. Following this, Kleinian psychoanalysis is critically examined, with particular attention given to the concepts of paranoid and depressive anxiety. In the final part of the chapter, I examine contemporary American self-psychology.

Object Relations Theory: Trust, Transitional Space, and Self

Object relations theory, as outlined in chapter 1, offers a powerful account of the interconnections between selfhood, gender, autonomy, and social relations. In classical Freudian theory, as we have seen, culture is largely evaluated in terms of the possibilities it offers for unconscious drive gratification. In object relations theory, by contrast, it is the form of relational processes that counts most in the assessment of the quality of cultural life. For object relational theorists, it is only through an intimate relationship with primary caretakers, and especially the mother, that a sense of difference between self and others is at all possible. It is *human relatedness* that generates a sense of selfhood; and thus relational processes are at the heart of individual experience and fulfilment. Furthermore, in mapping the relational processes that underpin the development or inhibition of the self, object relations theory has much to contribute to the formulation of desired social and political outcomes. That is to say, certain aspects of the object relations perspective can be used to assess how cultural activity and social institutions facilitate genuine communal relations.

The relation between self and other, for object relations theorists, is a dynamic one – a complex series of interactions and expressions that unfold through time. The key tenet in this perspective is that human beings are 'object seeking'. Whereas Freud's robust individualism describes self-organization in terms of the satisfaction of libidinal drives, object relations theory describes a fundamental linkage between self formation and the environmental and emotional provisions provided by significant others. Of course, unconscious enjoyment is inseparably bound up within this context of human interaction. But what object relations theorists stress is that libidinal gratification is never merely an internal affair, the regulation of drive tension alone. Rather the gratifications and frustrations that we first experience in life are fundamentally structured by the dynamics of human interaction. The small infant experiences 'being with' the mother in the opening out of a *shared reality*. And it is within this space of co-existence between the child and its providers that a sense of selfhood, as well as faith in others, gradually begins to emerge. The origins of this emergence of self, as portrayed by American object relational theorists, are rooted in feelings of trust. Striving to construct a core of meaningful selfhood, the small infant learns to trust in the reliability and responsiveness of the mother and hence, by extension, the external world. A sense of trust in the consistency of parental figures is deemed vital for psychological development. It is also fundamental in this perspective for the creation of meaningful social relationships.

Erik Erikson, who deeply influenced the development of American object relations theory, and whose views I have been sketching, provides a detailed account of the links between trust and social reproduction in *Childhood and Society* (1963). What Erikson calls 'basic trust' is a fundamental condition for the subject's binding of unconscious anxiety, and for the achievement of separation and autonomy in the network of social relations. Basic trust, Erikson argues, is forged against a backdrop of the presence and absence of the mother. In order to establish a degree of continuity of the self, the small infant must learn to cope with its mother's periodical absences, and to develop a sense of trust that she will return. To make such a commitment to trust, however, is emotionally very taxing. The infant has to mobilize its capacity for 'adaptation' to the mother's absence against a background of pervasive unconscious anxiety. The capacity for basic trust, Erikson says:

> forms the basis in the child for a sense of identity which will later combine a sense of being 'all right', of being oneself, and of becoming what other people trust one will become . . . But, even under the most favourable circumstances, this stage seems to introduce psychic life (and becomes prototypical for) a sense of inner division and universal nostalgia for a paradise forfeited. It is against this powerful combination of a sense of having been deprived, of having been divided, and of having been abandoned that basic trust must maintain itself throughout life.[1]

In discussing the formation of trust, Erikson stresses that self-organization is fundamentally tied to the adaptation or incorporation of cultural norms. I am not free, according to this view, to become merely anything I want. In order to create an 'ego-identity', I have to rely on certain trust networks, which involves incorporating what other people expect of me into my own sense of selfhood. It is this focus on questions of 'identity' that leads Erikson away from the usual psychoanalytic terrain of infancy to a broader focus on adolescence and adulthood. The human agent, for Erikson, has a basic need for identity. What this implies is that, in order to achieve separation and autonomy, human beings must enter into a kind of self-interrogation about their own needs and desires, as well as cultural meanings more generally. Provided basic trust is established in infancy, the individual will be relatively free in making its world. To Erikson, people pass through a series of transitions, or 'identity crises', which can only be resolved through synthesizing cultural contingencies into new patterns of self, trust, and meaning. Ideological world views are thus inseparable from mechanisms of self-adjustment. But what, exactly, are the connections between the creation of ego-identity and society? How is self-organization structured by modern social conditions? Erikson takes up these issues in *Identity, Youth and Crisis* (1968). What this book makes clear is the fact that the social world is in continual interaction with revisions of ego-identity. To Erikson, society is essentially beneficial for self-definition; it provides the ideological matrix of meanings for new definitions of identity. The child who visits the dentist, for example, subsequently takes to cutting up paper and sharpening pencils, redirecting aggression through an 'identification with the aggressor'. Or the student who learns of socialist ideas may now have an appropriate 'object' in which to pour his or her own repressed idealization and self-admiration. Though bordering on psychoanalytic reductionism, Erikson elaborates a complex account of identity formation and of their connecting tracks to society – including such notions as 'negative identity' (a fascination with certain self-other prohibitions), 'ego diffusion' (a reckless experiment with inner selves), and 'totalism' (wild mood swings between personal hope and despair). These ego-formations are linked to a broader social dimension, in Erikson's view, since identity is an active synthesis of inner and outer worlds. 'Identity', Erikson writes, 'is a process "located" in the core of the individual and yet also in the core of his communal culture, a process which establishes, in fact, the identity of those two identities'.[2] Erikson then, in contrast to both Freud and Marcuse, stresses the 'identity' between self and society. Or, to put the matter slightly differently, Erikson's liberal humanism leads him to rewrite psychoanalysis, appropriately enough, so that all belief-systems are incorporated within the cultural system. In other words, there is a kind of fit between creative and expansive identity on the one side, and patterns of cultural development on the other. 'For in all parts of the world', Erikson writes in modern-day liberal vein, 'the struggle now is for the anticipatory development of more inclusive identities'.[3]

Erikson's theory, as the reader might have gathered, contains some serious conceptual difficulties and ideological blindspots. His concept of 'identity' is premised on the belief that there is a fundamental essence of selfhood, an essence from which human subjects strive for greater cultural inclusivity and wholeness. Such a definition of self-identity, however, overly domesticates psychoanalysis, reducing it to little more than bland talk about personal concerns and anxieties. Indeed, Nathan Leites has suggested that this reductionism actually accounts for the popularity of Erikson's ideas in the United States; allowing everyone the use of a certain psychoanalytic terminology to talk about 'self', yet somehow managing to close things down just at the point where things start to get interesting.[4] As regards psycho-analytic theory, the problem in Erikson's work is that it brackets the split and fractured nature of psychical life and replaces it instead with a focus on 'ego-adaptation'. That the human subject is internally divided – repressing painful feelings, denying parts of the self through projection and splitting, investing distorting self-images through unconscious fantasy – is thus sidestepped in this perspective. This has serious consequences for Erikson's analysis of social life. His stress on identity as adaptive and unified leads to an uncritical linkage of subjectivity and society. It allows him to imagine that modern social conditions provide an all-inclusive framework for affirmative iden-tity, an ideological vision which is at one with much contemporary multinational advertising, such as the projected world unity of 'The United Colours of Benetton'. Here Erikson's positive gloss on society, while trying to account for personal development, change, and autonomy, becomes a way of underwriting the cultural values of late capitalism. From this angle, it seems to me, Freud's social thought registers more faithfully than Erikson's the pathologies and repres-sions of everyday life in modern culture. In this view, as we have seen, self and society are mutually interlocking, but their relation is not one of mere equivalence. Psychical reality, Freud tirelessly repeats, cannot become fully incorporated into the social field. That this is the case is positive news, politically speaking. For, contrary to Erikson's pronouncements, modern societies are not 'affirmatively inclusive'. Rather, they function through asymmetrical relations of power and force, relations that repress, exclude, and marginalize social identities. And it is against this background, I think, that the social and political relevance of the Freudian 'split' subject, a self that is dislocated but also a self that can creatively resist social domina-tion, should be located.

Not all object relations theorists see the self in such ideologically blinkered terms as Erikson. The work of D. W. Winnicott stresses that, even though selfhood is constituted through interaction, there are many things that can restrict or inhibit self-organization. Winni-cott, as we have noted in chapter 1, provides important insights into the connections between selfhood, creativity, symbolization, and culture. Whereas Erikson understands the self as entering into social interaction through adaptation, the relation between self and other, for Winnicott, is one of (possible) mutual understanding and recog-nition. That is, there is a *transitional realm* where minds can come together; enjoying authentic interaction while maintaining a separate and autonomous subjective space. But, as Winnicott shows, this postulation of intersubjectivity does not involve an overestimation of the harmony between self and other, nor of the quality of relationships in modern societies. For Winnicott, interpersonal processes foster many forms of self-pathology, or what he calls 'the false self'. Significantly, Winnicott's theory also implicitly raises the issue of how social life and institutional arrangements enhance or distort human relationships.

In his highly influential essay 'The mirror-role of mother and family in child development' (1967), Winnicott traces the processes of interaction between baby and mother which lead to the emergence of a sense of self. The starting point of this analysis is the primary unity of the baby/mother dyad; a time in which the small infant makes no distinction between inside and outside, itself and mother. Winnicott suggests that it is within this context that the mother objectively provides emotional resources for the infant to create and develop an inner world. In this account, the mother functions as a 'mirror', reflecting back to the infant its own experiences and gestures. What is significant about this mirroring is that it provides the infant with a shared experience of human passion. The infant learns of its own inner love and admiration, as well as its fear and distress, through the reflecting face of the mother. There are certain parallels here between Winnicott and Jacques Lacan's theory of mirroring, as we shall see in chapter 4. Yet whereas Lacan views mirroring as necesarily leading to a false self (since the mirror is no more than mere image), Winnicott understands it as an essential basis for creative, ongoing human relationships. The mother, as mirror, shows the infant that she understands emotional states of jubilation and distress, and that she accepts these feelings. This acceptance, in turn, permits the incipient self to begin symbolization of inner feelings and to make emotional connections with other people.

If all goes well at this stage, Winnicott says, the mother's mirroring permits the infant a 'moment of illusion'; an emotional experience in which the infant feels that it alone has created the loving object (i.e., the breast) which the mother objectively presents. The mother's emotional sensitivity to the child – what Winnicott calls 'primary maternal preoccupation' – allows an illusion of omnipotence, of magical feelings of control. This narcissistic illusion, according to Winnicott, is vital for the emergence and development of the self. For it is through experiences of good enough mothering that the child develops a sense of contact with the real world. As Winnicott puts this: 'The mother's adaptation to the infant's needs, when good enough, gives the infant the illusion that there is an external reality that corresponds to the infant's own capacity to create.' The importance of this can be seen in what occurs when emotional sensitivity is not established between mother and child. If the mother fails to mirror the infant, and rejects its needs, pathology will result through the 'annihilation of the infant's self'.[5] In this situation, the infant is left emotionally unable to make contact with other people. Lacking a sense of trust, human interaction is itself perceived as terrifying. Winnicott suggests that the emerging person will attempt to deal with such anxiety through withdrawal into a 'false self', a self that compulsively anticipates the reactions of others. This false self is at once a defence against the failure of the maternal object as well as an attempt by the infant to establish some form of object relationship, however frail or brittle. Accordingly, the small infant strives desperately to make human contact, but the absence of feelings of inner trustworthiness are inevitably projected on to an outside world; a world which, in turn, is perceived as uncaring and harsh.

A sense of mutual understanding and shared feeling is thus vital for the emergence of a stable sense of self. And all this depends, as we have noted, upon good enough mothering and the child's creation of a rich, internal fantasy world. It should be clear, though, that the infant at this stage is not yet capable of entering, let alone sustaining, fully fledged social relationships. Caught in an imaginary realm of illusory omnipotence, the small infant is unable to recognize that it does not create and control the world. How then does the child make the transition from a world of inner, illusory objects to the world of outer reality? For Winnicott, the child forges a connection with the outside world through actively discovering the characteristics of other persons. Unlike Freud, who posits a brute enforcement of the reality principle at the time of the Oedipus complex, Winnicott does not view the object-world as repressively imposed upon the individual. Rather, the child emotionally searches for certain boundaries between inner and outer experience. This orientation towards aspects of outer reality is forged, in Winnicott's terminology, through 'transitional objects'. The establishment of a transitional or 'not-me' object (such as a blanket or toy) is a bridging between the inner world of fantasy and the outer world of objects and persons. The child at once creates and discovers such objects. Yet they are neither subjectively nor objectively located; instead they exist in a transitional realm between these two worlds. For Winnicott, the child 'creates an object but the object would not have been created as such if it had not already been there'.[6] Transitional space is thus a paradoxical realm in which the infant feels it creates and controls the object, yet also perceives that this object belongs in the world of other people.

The capacity to use and play with transitional objects is fundamental to the child's construction of symbols. Winnicott calls this the opening out of a 'potential space', a space which links fantasy and reality, self and other. Potential space, Winnicott argues, is essential for a creative involvement with interpersonal relations and cultural life. From this angle, culture is not something which human beings just suddenly encounter at some stage. It is, rather, creatively made and remade through a transitional realm of learning, tradition, ideas, and invention. And it is within this space between subjects, the bridging of inner and outer worlds, that culture and social life arises.

It may be useful to review the key elements of Winnicott's view of self-organization at this point. The emergence of self depends upon a *primary maternal preoccupation* with the needs and gestures of the infant. By functioning as a 'mirror' to the child, the mother plays a central role in the development or inhibition of the self. This emerging sense of self links to a stabilized world of objects and persons through *transitional space*, the bridging of inner and outer reality. Transitional space is essential to both individual creativity and cultural experience. Winnicott thus characterizes psychical development in terms of a *true-self/false-self distinction*. In the case of the 'true self', development has led to the creative and spontaneous expression of human needs and feelings. In the case of the 'false self', there is an annihilation of personal integrity and subsequent emotional vulnerability in the face of social relations. Yet, significantly, Winnicott argues that personal continuity is a precarious and fragile phenomenon. There is always tension and anxiety in relating inner and outer realities – which is experienced in and through the symbolic world of transitional space.

Winnicott's focus on mothering, and specifically the mother/child dyad, draws attention to the importance of early pre-Oedipal relations in the formation of the self. Whereas classical Freudian theory sees selfhood as constituted through the Oedipus complex, and thus ties individuation to the intervention of the father, Winnicott's theory stresses the centrality of the mother/child relation to ongoing self-organization and social context. This emphasis upon mothering in human development has had important implications for critical enquiry. It has been especially influential in feminist theory, as we shall see in chapter 5, where object relations theory has contributed to a re-evaluation of the social context of parenting and gender asymmetries. However, there have also been severe criticisms levelled against this aspect of the object relational perspective. For some commentators, Winnicott's theory romantically idealizes mother-hood, and thus eliminates the complexity of maternal desire itself. In this respect, it has been suggested that the whole concept of 'good enough mothering' is politically regressive; a myth used *against* women as both fantasy and blame.[7] Another difficulty is that Winnicott's theory refers to, but ultimately fails to theorize, the role of general social relations in the constitution of the self. That is, Winnicott's work lacks a critical account of social structure as it affects the self and interpersonal relations as a whole. In this connection, a number of questions can be raised. How is the mother/infant relation mediated by contemporary social conditions? In what ways have recent social, cultural, political, and technological trans-formations affected self and self-identity? And how might the increas-ingly informationalized and globalized framework of modern social processes affect the transitional realm in which culture is embedded?

One of the most promising uses of object relations theory to address these issues is to be found in the recent work of the British sociologist Anthony Giddens. Giddens approaches the question of the self/society interface on a fairly grand scale, tracing mechanisms of self-formation to certain institutional transformations associated with modernity. To do this, Giddens develops in *The Consequences of Modernity* (1990) the concept of trust, by which he refers to the necessary confidence in the continuity of self and in the constancy of the surrounding social world. Drawing on the object relational theories of Winnicott and Erikson, Giddens argues that the forging of personal trust is a central element in the structuring of self-identity as well as the essential basis for a creative involvement with the broader institutional contexts of modernity. Trust, in Giddens's view, is a basic psychic mechanism for handling the demands and dangers of everyday social life; or for establishing what he terms 'ontological security'. It is because an individual learns a sense of trust in other people that feelings of inner trustworthiness come to predominate over anxiety. Trust established between self and others is fundamen-tal to creative, ongoing human relations; and it is what enables individuals to achieve a practical engagement with the open nature of modern social life.

Giddens analyses trust against the backdrop of a highly original account of modernity. The dynamism of what he calls 'high modern-ity' – with its globalizing tendencies, its mediation of human experi-ence by mass communication, its ceaseless technological innovation

– reaches into the very heart of self-organization. Arguing against the much-repeated claim that world history has entered a condition of 'postmodernity', Giddens contends that what we are currently witnessing is modernity coming to terms with itself: that is, modernity's radicalization. To experience these institutional transformations is to experience what Giddens aptly terms the 'juggernaut of modernity', a realm of mixed possibilities. Modernity for Giddens, although racked with contingency and uncertainty, empowers men and women in the search for individual and collective autonomy. To live in modern society, he argues, involves living with ambivalence. It means facing new opportunities and new dangers. Trust is of key importance in this context. Mechanisms of trust provide an anchoring point, not only for personal relations, but for an engagement with the abstract, institutional systems of modernity. Significantly, trust is a means of coping with certain 'high-consequence risks' of the late modern age, such as the risks of nuclear war, ecological catastrophe, global economic recessions, and the like. Yet, since modernity is essentially a risk culture, the self can never be entirely secure. Rather self and society intersect, according to Giddens's portrayal, through generalized states of trust and risk, security and danger.

But how is individual trust embedded in certain forms of social and technical framework? How do individuals face the disturbing and unsettling risks of late modernity? And how can such traumatic 'high-consequence risks' be experienced without a dislocation and dispersal of the self? In *Modernity and Self-Identity* (1991), Giddens concentrates upon the implications of these issues in terms of the transformation of the personal sphere. He argues that the forging of trust between an infant and its caretakers is pivotal for a subsequent handling of the potential risks of day-to-day social life. Drawing upon Winnicott, Giddens relates the creation of a transitional realm between infant and others to a broader interpersonal organization of time and space. The transitional objects that bridge the space between the infant and others are seen as a basis for 'going-on-being' in the world; the cultivation of a sense of self that, in turn, protects the infant from unbearable anxiety. What matters most in this forging of self, according to Giddens, is 'what goes without saying' – that is, the establishment of routines and habits. Unconscious anxiety leads the infant into a transitional realm of self and others; and it is through an early involvement with parental routines and habits that such anxiety is then contained. A sense of self, trust, and object relationships is therefore forged through a transitional realm of *routinization*. Thus, Giddens concludes that the child receives 'a sort of *emotional inoculation* against existential anxieties – a protection against future threats and dangers which allows the individual to sustain hope and courage in the face of whatever debilitating circumstances she or he might later confront'.[8] In this reading of psychoanalysis, trust and transitional space operate as screening devices against unconscious anxiety; they provide what Giddens calls a 'protective cocoon' for the self in its dealings with the social world.

The bracketing of anxiety by trust is thus essential to the formation of self-identity. Where this is achieved, the individual can approach social life through calculations of risk and opportunity. Where trust is not achieved, self-pathologies such as disturbed narcissism are likely to result. Giddens contends that the relation between trust and routine, which is so vital to early human development, is also of paramount importance in maintaining and revising 'narratives' of self-identity. What this means, essentially, is that trust intersects with routine individual activity as an emotional basis for a stabilized world of objects and persons. Trust in this context is invested in day-to-day routines as a way of creating a 'normal' and 'uneventful' world, from which an individual can pursue his or her own projects and activities. Yet, significantly, the investment of trust in routines also functions to bracket fear and unconscious anxiety. As Giddens develops this point:

> Awareness of high-consequence risks is probably for most people a source of unspecific anxieties. Basic trust is again a determining element in whether or not an individual is actively and recurrently plagued with such anxieties. No one can show that it is not 'rational' to worry constantly over the possibility of ecological catastrophe, nuclear war or the ravaging of humanity by as yet unanticipated scourges. Yet people who do spend every day worrying about such possibilities are not regarded as 'normal'. If most successfully bracket out such possibilities and get on with their day-to-day activities, this is no doubt partly because they assess the actual element of risk involved as very small. But it is also because the risks in question are given over to fate.[9]

In a nutshell, then, trust brackets risk; and this entails the containment of anxiety.

It is clear enough from what I have said so far that Giddens draws on object relations theory to decipher how modern selves negotiate the troubled waters of modernity. For Giddens, the postulation of a relatively stable, reflexively grounded self is a precondition for any lasting and meaningful engagement with the modern world. That is, a coherent sense of personal identity and self-worth is essential for navigating the dizzying risks and opportunities of the late modern age. This position puts Giddens in opposition to the theoretical currents of poststructuralism and postmodernism, which instead theorize a 'decentred subject', thoroughly fragmented in and through language. Yet Giddens's stress upon identity does not imply that the self is immune from dislocation and dispersal. The ambivalence of modernity, and of the global processes of modernization, reaches through to the very heart of the self. In this connection, the creation of new identity patterns within such fluctuating social boundaries can lead to emotional disquiet. As Giddens puts this, 'the narrative of self-identity is inherently fragile'.[10] However, it is true to say that Giddens's stance on self-definition is essentially affirmative. He argues that modern social processes integrate as much as they fragment. They provide opportunities for personal appropriation as well as generating feelings of powerlessness. In this context, Giddens offers the example of a person on the telephone speaking with someone on the other side of the world. To be sure, this is an electronically mediated experience. Yet, as Giddens points out, the person's inter-action with this 'distant other' may be more emotionally intense than his or her relationships with other people sitting in the same room.

What are the gains and losses of Giddens's appropriation of psychoanalysis for understanding modern self-identity? To begin with, the constructive side of Giddens's work is that it alerts us to the necessary emotional capacities that are required to engage practically in modern social life. Reconceptualizing the object relational view within a comprehensive social theory of modernity, Giddens is able to demonstrate that anxiety, trust, and transitional space are funda-mental psychical mechanisms which lie at the root of social interac-tion. Significantly, this shows that individual development and relational processes are not closed off in an asocial world (the imaginary dyad of child and mother), but are intimately bound up with general social relations. The learning of self and other in a transitional realm involves a good deal more than merely adjusting to social reality; it is actually constitutive of an emotional acceptance of the socio-symbolic world of other persons and objects.

However, while accounting for the social context of self-organiz-ation, there are difficulties with Giddens's work. For one thing, Giddens's whole vocabulary of self-organization – 'bracketing anxi-ety', 'emotional inoculation', and 'protective cocoon' – has a very different intent from that proposed in object relations theory. For Giddens, as we have seen, human beings must be capable of trust, relatedness, and routine in order to go about day-to-day social life. And we may recall that, once these emotional capacities are secured, the individual is deemed to have met the basic requirements for generating self-coherence and consistency. Yet psychoanalytic theory, including Winnicott's variety, radically questions whether the self can ever be 'normalized' in this way. It stresses, on the contrary, the fractured and divided nature of self-experience – a product of unconscious sexuality itself. In Winnicott's theory, as previously noted, the self is never free from the task of relating inner and outer worlds; and, significantly, the self is always subject to dissolution through unconscious fragmentation and dread. Yet Giddens offers no account of this. Instead, the realm of the unconscious is generally 'bracketed' by social routines. What this standpoint fails to acknowledge, therefore, is that social routines may be constituted to their roots by unconscious desire; involving pathological, obsessional, or narcissistic forms. A person may 'live' a consistent self-identity, for example, following the routine of staring at his or her reflection sixty times a day in a mirror. Clearly, an obsessional routine such as this has direct links with the narcissistic overvaluation of appearances and images in late capitalism. Yet it is unclear whether we could critically interrogate the psychical contours of such self-pathology from Giddens's model. A central problem, then, is that Giddens's theory pays too little attention to the ways in which social systems of modernity disfigure and warp the unconscious constitution of the self. And, so too, it fails to examine how unconscious desire intersects with social symptoms – symptoms which distort the transitional realm of cultural experience.

The Kleinian Condition: Paranoid and Depressive Anxiety

In object relations theory our deepest unconscious needs, feelings, and desires are seen as embedded in *relationship*. Human social activity, and the boundaries of the self-other connection, are founded in emotionally dynamic relations – relations that constitute our daily life. Social context figures in this account as a backdrop either for the integration or fragmentation of self-organization. That is, society is seen as either enhancing or deforming the inherent relational capacities of human subjects. But if the link between supportive social contexts and the relational self is obvious enough in the object relational view, it is rather less so in the radical version of this case presented by the psychoanalyst Melanie Klein. Like all object relations theorists, Klein sees the emergence of self as tied to human relationships. The small infant depends on the mother (or primary caretaker) for both its physical needs and the development of its sense of self-identity. However, by translating Freud's theory of unconscious drives into the object relational account, Klein radically undermines the assumption that there is an essential unity to the psyche, or that self-unity can be established *through* social context. For Klein, rather, the psyche is in a state of constant flux, a primary condition of fragmentation, diffusion, and intolerable anxiety. At a very early stage of life, says Klein, the infant experiences violent and intense feelings of aggression in its imaginary relation to the mother. The infant, in brief, is caught up in fantasies of attacking and destroying the maternal body, and in turn suffers paranoid anxieties that it too will be destroyed. In Klein's picture of human development, the infant undergoes a position of paranoid anxiety, in which other persons become invested with persecutory powers, and gradually shifts to a depressive position, which involves feelings of loss, guilt, and ambivalence. In what follows, Klein's theory of the self – the 'paranoid-schizoid position' and the 'depressive position' – will be examined. We will then turn to explore how Kleinian concepts have been used in contemporary theory.

According to Klein, the infant begins life under the sign of the death drive. The anxiety produced by the death drive leads inevitably towards dissolution and disintegration. Indeed, the fear of death is so intense that the immature ego of the infant is threatened with complete annihilation. In seeking to handle this trauma, according to Klein, the infant deflects the death drive away from itself and projects it into the outer world – specifically, towards its mother's body. This is immediately soothing for the infant, as aggression is no longer felt to be inside and bad feelings are installed outside the self. This anxiety-reducing strategy, however, is of short-lived value. Since it is now the mother's body which is felt to be bad, as it contains the projected components of the infant's death drive, her presence becomes in turn an object of fear. That is, the child's fear now rounds back upon itself, giving rise to intense feelings of persecution and dread. Thus, Klein argues that the child fears the maternal body, entertaining fantasies that the breast will devour it, cut it into bits, destroy it, and scoop out its insides. Hence, there is a kind of 'eye for an eye' mentality at this stage of psychic development. If I sadistically attack you, then I can only expect retaliation in return.

This attempt by the infant to rid itself of bad things inside, that is hatred, not only rounds back upon itself but also leads to self-disintegration. For so precarious is the infantile ego, says Klein, that the infant simply cannot tolerate the return of these destructive feelings. In order to break from this destructive cycle the child is led to psychical *splitting*, a splitting of the object into good and bad dimensions. The pre-Oedipal mother is thus first experienced by the child as radically divided. Originally, the child constructs the mother as an ideal, 'good' breast. In this blissful state, the breast is a central symbol of goodness and perfection; and the child jubilantly feels itself to be self-identical. But these good feelings, Klein says, are only half of the story. The pressure of the death drive, coupled with real experiences of maternal deprivation and frustration, generates intense paranoid anxiety. In this state, a 'bad' breast predominates, and the child's internal world is coloured by persecution fantasies. Under the influence of the bad breast, the infant is beset by fears of annihilation. Good experiences are lost and the ego depleted. The crucial task for the infant in this 'paranoid-schizoid position' is to keep the persecutory powers of the death drive at a distance, to keep the bad breast on the outside, through a taking into the self of the more positive and loving aspects of the object, the good breast. 'The leading anxiety of the paranoid-schizoid position,' writes the Kleinian commentator Hanna Segal, 'is that the persecutory object or objects will get inside the ego and overwhelm and annihilate both the ideal object and the self.'[11] Thus, at this early stage of development, the infant splits its world: into good objects and feelings and bad objects and feelings. The split object, at this point, is of course a single entity, the pre-Oedipal mother. But Klein's central point is that the mother is fantasized by the infant as two separate objects.

Klein argues that splitting is a self-protective manoeuvre; a strategy by which the fragile and precarious ego strives to keep idealized and persecutory objects as far apart as possible. What characterizes this phase of paranoid splitting are the defence mechanisms of *projection* and *introjection*. The infant projects both positive and negative feelings outside into the external world; and introjects good and bad objects from outside into the self. In this respect, Klein essentially follows Freud. However, Klein says that the dynamics of projection and introjection operate in and through *fantasized identifications*. That is, Klein argues that the psyche is a constant flux of fantasies, fantasies that structure relations between the self and others. The implications of this for psychoanalysis are significant. Whereas Freud understood projection as involving a channeling of unconscious drives towards objects, Klein argues that it involves a fantasized insertion of *actual parts of the self* into others and the external world.

To capture this more interactional view, Klein speaks of 'projective identification', getting rid of parts of the self into others, and 'introjective identification', taking attributes of others into the self. In projective identification, for example, bad parts of the self may be attributed to others so that destructive feelings can be safely expressed. Alternatively, good parts of the self may be projected on to others in order to keep these feelings safe from bad and destructive fantasies inside. But in all of these schizoid mechanisms described by Klein – splitting, idealization, denigration, and projective and intro-jective identification – the key psychical task remains the same: to limit the pernicious anxiety generated by the death drive.

Klein's theory of the earliest stages of psychic life develops and deepens Freud's insight into human aggression and destruction. Modern culture, Freud said, constructs human subjects who are seething with rage, a specific elaboration of the death drive that is continually on the brink of complete self-destruction. This rage is mobilized and reordered by modern societies into social order through repression; a repression which is the key source, Freud argues, of cultural unhappiness. Klein's work, however, allows us to see that it is not only a repression of rage – or its potential return – which is at issue. When aggression is projected outwards, and deflected onto others through identification, it rounds back upon itself in a persecutory manner. And the typical defence against persecutory anxiety, Klein contends, is schizoid splitting. This view has considerable explanatory power with regard to social and insti-tutional life. From this angle, the paranoid-schizoid position of psychic functioning can be seen as institutionalized within whole sectors of modern culture. The spheres of social, political, and cultural life become structured by a kind of perverse splitting, between the narcissistic, idealized 'good' and the denigrated, hated 'bad'. The imaginative life of the pre-school infant, for example, is bent into a two-dimensional fantasy world by television, as numerous images of good heroes and bad villains, strong men and submissive women, fairytale loves and protracted violences, are disseminated. Such images reinforce a fabric of memories, fantasies, and feelings in the small child which become recurrent psychological themes in adult life. One can see how such splitting, when institutionalized, can lead to acute ambivalence in sexual relationships; as the desire for the perfect Other leaves deep fissures within gender relations. Or one can see how mechanisms of splitting, idealization, and denigration take hold of entire nations – fuelling terrors of real and imagined security threats, or underwriting a position of nuclear self-destruction. Indeed, one of the most striking aspects of the risk of massively destructive warfare in the contemporary age has been the response of general public apathy, a kind of psychic *denial* that comes to the fore under states of extreme splitting.[12]

Before proceeding too far with cultural diagnosis at this stage, however, it is necessary to stay with Klein's clinical picture of human development. For while schizoid mechanisms certainly underpin individual and social pathologies, Klein emphasizes that other aspects of splitting play a facilitating role in human affairs. From this angle, it is stressed that paranoid-schizoid mechanisms are a normal defence against early anxieties of the infant. For example, the splitting into good and bad allows the primitive ego to emerge from its primary condition of fragmentation. Splitting also lies at the basis, says Klein, of our capacity for judgement and discrimination; and, through idealization, it underpins human empathy and love. However, Klein argues that, when constitutional hatred is excessively strong, splitting is likely to occur in exaggerated form and thus distort human capabilities. This means that splitting into good and bad becomes excessive, with objects being either narcissistically idealized or destructively denigrated. In this condition, the infant feels that persons and objects are intensely persecuting, which in turn generates further splitting and overwhelming anxiety. Such excessive persecutory anxiety leads to perpetual dread and feelings of unreality, and sometimes into psychosis and infantile schizophrenia. Klein emphasizes, however, that in 'normal' psychic development good objects and feelings predominate over bad ones. In this connection, Klein's argument is that the paranoid-schizoid position, although underpinning all subsequent schizoid functioning, is essentially a preparation for psychic integration. Provided there is a predominance of good experience over bad experience, the ego gradually *gains* in strength, as the threat of the bad object diminishes. This means that persecutory and idealized objects are no longer ruthlessly split. By allowing good and bad objects to come closer together, the ego becomes increasingly capable of integration since it no longer deals with anxiety through violent, schizoid mechanisms of defence.

From this tendency towards integration, the small infant is led in the second half of its first year to perceive others as whole people. For Klein, this involves an emotional shift from part or split object relationships to object relations proper. That is, the infant no longer relates exclusively to part-objects of the mother's body (such as her breasts, eyes, skin surface, hands, and so on) but rather forges a connection to the mother as a *whole person*. At this point, the infant revises its previous split perceptions of mother, and comes to see that there is only one mother, a mother with good *and* bad human qualities. The construction of mother as a whole object, says Klein, is crucial to psychic organization. For the recognition that mother is a whole person, a person who is independent and who has separate relationships with others, is pivotal to the child's emerging sense of selfhood. Significantly, this new phase also results in a decrease in persecutory anxiety, as the child comes to learn that the same mother is a source of its good and bad feelings, and not a separate 'bad mother'. However, in the same way that a picture of the mother as a whole person is developed, so too the child will come to see that it is the same person – namely itself – that loves and hates the mother. That is, the child gets a kind of return dosage of the emotional pain and anger that it displaces on to 'bad objects'. The child thus comes to realize, at an unconscious emotional level, that such fantasized attacks are actually directed at the beloved mother. This leads to intense feelings of guilt and sorrow, and is termed by Klein the 'depressive position'. Whereas anxiety in the paranoid-schizoid position involves a fear of self-annihilation from outside objects, anxiety in the depressive position involves fears about the fate of others, the result of destructive fantasies generated by the child's own hatred. Having transcended schizoid splitting of the mother, it is as if the child realizes that others are no longer simply a receptacle for its own destructive fantasies. Instead, the child's connection to others becomes intensely social in form; and the emerging ego will respond to any damage inflicted upon others through feelings of guilt and depressive anxiety.

To sum up briefly: Klein posits a primary mode of psychic functioning in which child and mother interconnect through an unconscious communication of violent, destructive fantasies about part-objects and split-objects. In this paranoid-schizoid position, the splitting of mother into good and bad facilitates the containment of the child's destructive drives and allows for a creative development of projective and introjective processes – deemed vital by Klein for successful self-organization. If constitutional hatred is excessive, the lure of paranoid-schizoid processes will be deformed and self-pathologies will result. If all goes reasonably well, however, good experiences predominate over bad experiences and the child is led to withdraw projections of its own destructive urges and to construct the object-world in more realistic terms. In this depressive position, the child develops the capacity to form emotionally durable relationships and to experience the other person as a separate, and ambivalent, object. Feelings of guilt, loss, and reparation are crucial to this mode of psychic organization; and are connected to an interplay of destruction and reintegration which underpins mature self-organization. Responses to Klein's work in social, political, and cultural theory have taken a number of directions. Kleinian doctrine initially made its deepest impact in England, at the Tavistock Institute of Human Relations, where it was employed to trace unconscious mental processes in social relations. The Kleinian analysis of social institutions in the UK was developed especially in the work of Isabel Menzies Lyth and Elliott Jaques, whose research traced institutional defences against emotional pain and other related social aspects of splitting. But Klein's theories have also been significant in European and American contexts, and have been used for rethinking the nature of our social practice more generally: in the philosophical writings of Richard Wollheim, the feminist analyses of Dorothy Dinnerstein, the work of the French social theorist Julia Kristeva, the art critic Anton Ehrenzweig, and by Hannah Segal in drawing attention to the unconscious dynamics of warfare and the nuclear arms race. Kleinianism, in these differing conceptual contexts, is invoked to examine the existence of pain, destructiveness, and loss in human social relationships. It is also used to assess the social costs of generalized paranoid-schizoid mechanisms, and for developing political critiques of modern culture.

A useful way of charting the relevance of Kleinian thought to contemporary cultural criticism is by looking briefly at Michael Rustin's *The Good Society and the Inner World* (1991). Rustin wants to show the wider cultural meanings of psychoanalysis, and in particular to demonstrate the importance of the Kleinian tradition for the analysis of social and political relations. A prime instance of Rustin's application of Kleinian thought to politics can be found in the phenomenon of racism. For Rustin, racial antagonisms, as destructive forms of cultural oppression, are not only institutionalized within the social world but are deeply inscribed at the heart of self-experience. Rustin uses psychoanalysis to argue that racist ideology goes beyond the institutional structures of modern culture; it penetrates deeply into unconscious modes of desire and feeling. The relevance of Kleinian thought to understanding the phenomenon of racism, Rustin argues, derives from its account of the emotional, unconscious structures in which hatred, envy, and paranoia are expressed in human relationships. Klein's account of paranoid-schizoid and depressive anxiety offers a significant purchase on how destructive, negative feelings intertwine with socially valorized racial attributions. The key psychic mechanism fuelling racism, says Rustin, is splitting. From this angle, racism is a displaced expression of persecutory anxiety. The racist splits the world into rigid categories of good and bad, white and black, the in-group and the out-group. Unwanted feelings are projected into others, who are then seen in objectified form. Yet racial domination involves more than just fantasy projection. According to Rustin, the ideological attribution of hatred through projective identification is an *interactive process*, in which the victims of antagonism regularly absorb the fear, anxiety, and guilt of the persecuting group. There is a self-reinforcing logic here: the emotional damage caused by projections of persecutory anxiety and hatred are such that victims more neatly fit the delusional worlds of their oppressors, thus serving to bind unconscious fantasy and to intensify the fear of racial retaliation. It does not take much imagination to see that whole societies may find themselves acting out emotions which in part derive from such racial categorizations. Think, for example, of the problems, mysteries, and implications of race relations in South Africa, in which hatred, anxiety and aggression are formed around such fantasy scenarios.

Emotional pain is thus a central theme in Rustin's work. There is a continual spilling of hatred and destructiveness in the social and political world. Yet, for Rustin, however distorted unconscious passion may be, it does not mean that we should give up in our collective attempts to foster more caring, empathic social relations. For the most important feature of social life is the essential relatedness between human beings; and it is through the fostering of this emotional relatedness that Rustin believes we might realize alternative social futures. In this connection, Rustin contends that the Kleinian framework provides a *moral energizing vision* for the radical transformation of society. For Rustin, Klein's exploration of unconscious pain, guilt, and anxiety, as lying at the root of our moral concern for other people, provides an ethical norm for the assessment of political life and cultural organization. Whereas Freudian theory sees culture as repressive of individual desire, and thus focuses on the emancipation of the self from sexual repression, Klein's emphasis on emotional relatedness highlights the *primacy of social relationships*. Kleinian thought stresses that individuals are first and foremost social beings, capable of intense moral relatedness. As Rustin puts this:

> Innate concern for the well-being of the other, at a very deep level, appears in [the Kleinian standpoint] to arise from the earliest lack of

differentiation between self and other, and from the process whereby this differentation comes about. Pleasure and pain are only slowly located in space and time, and in relation to whole persons. This intense experience of pain, as given and received, and this deep involvement with the caring person as the perceived source of all well- and ill-being, gives rise to the capacity to experience the pains and pleasures of the other with an intensity comparable to the pains and pleasures of the self.[13]

The Kleinian account of human experience – of unconscious intersubjective transactions of love and hate, anger and envy, pain and anxiety – thus brings *social relatedness* to the fore.

Rustin presses this account of human development into a social theory with utopian intent. Society, and the task of improving social conditions, can be assessed in terms of concrete emotional experiences: of the signal importance of love and care for others; of the quality and intensity of emotional relationship; of institutional support for creative human development; and of membership from birth to a social community. This constitutes what Rustin calls a 'critical humanization' of the personal sphere. The reconstruction of contemporary society demands attention not only to institutional processes but also to the quality of emotional, interpersonal structures in which people interact. The principal link between emotional and institutional processes for Rustin is the family. The family provides a relational context, according to Rustin, that is usually absent in society at large. The critical point here is that familial life, notwithstanding internal distortions, can be located as a carrier for altruistic and caring values. As the emotional site of compassion and understanding, the family might potentially be harnesssed to rebuilding cultural life under an ethic of mutual help and development. At issue here, Rustin says, are new definitions of self-identity, gender, and interpersonal relations.

What are the contributions and limitations of Kleinian theory and cultural analysis? To begin with, Kleinian theory significantly enhances our understanding of the relation between self and society. As we have seen, the human subject in Kleinian thought is not only internally divided, split between consciousness and the unconscious, but is also caught up in fantasies of identification with surrounding objects and people. In this view, the relation between self and society is extremely dynamic and fluid; with aspects of the self being both deeply lodged in external objects and also potentially reintegrated into personal life. The concepts of projective and introjective identification offer a significant purchase on this mixing together of reality and fantasy in much phenomena of contemporary culture. For it is certainly arguable that a good deal of the imagery of modern culture – the superficial gloss of flashy commodities, seductive advertising images, and the like – are shot through with powerful paranoid feelings and idealized aspects of the self. In this connection, media responses to a range of social issues – terrorism, racism, sexual crimes, poverty – also reflect the unconscious dimensions of these processes, by lapsing into dichotomous evaluations of the good and the bad. The consequences of such excessive projections and denials, as already suggested, are that the victims of aggression become infused with persecutory feelings, which in turn leads to a perception of such persons and groups as even more menacing and threatening. In its crudest manifestations, this spiralling of projection and splitting can lead to delusional social feelings of persecution. At such a point, society as a whole starts to trade in stereotyped emotional responses.

The Kleinian view of destructiveness and hate is also of paramount importance, especially in the face of ameliorist psychoanalytical theories (such as ego-psychology), which put an optimistic gloss on the potential harmony of self and society. Klein's theory, by contrast, addresses the existence of human pain, anger, and despair. The implications of this for critical social analysis are considerable. That envy, hate, and destruction are prime components of modern culture is obvious from the amount of violence generated in social relationships, as well as from the fascination with violence throughout the population as a whole. The Gulf War in 1991 was a powerful indication of just how far contemporary political violence interconnects with inner hate, as was shown by our perverse interest in high-technology military destructiveness, encapsulated in the television presentation of the war. Viewed sociologically, the unlimited destruction of the Gulf War went beyond any mere unleashing of the Freudian death drive. Rather, the war was a product of a complex interplay between military and political forces on the one side, and destructive paranoid fantasy states on the other. The contemporary world system, it can be argued in Kleinian terms, maintains itself less through an attempt to repress or control destructive drives *in toto* than through mixing destruction and reintegration, fragmentation and reunification. In this view, social meanings and cultural identities are forged and integrated only to be destroyed, and in turn are thereby open to renewal. And it is this interplay, between hate and love, and pain and joy, that takes us to the heart of the Kleinian position. An awareness of pain, despair, and anger is fundamental if

we are to confront successfully the implications of violence to the self
and to others. For provided reparation can be made for prior damage
and pain, then creative possibilities exist on both the personal and
social planes.

Kleinian theory thus offers a complex account of human interaction, of the psychical exchange between the self and others. And it
does this, as we have seen, through uncovering a complex interplay
of fantasy and reality in all human affairs. But if Kleinianism breaks
with the individualistic focus of Freudian theory, substituting human
relationships for the psychic energy of the solitary subject, it does so
only by working outwards from the internal world alone. That is,
Klein's privileging of the internal realm of fantasy leads to a crucial
neglect of the role of social and cultural factors in the structuring of
human relationships. Instead of examining how modern social conditions enter into the construction of the self, Kleinians see internal
fantasy processes as causative of the fundamental contradictions and
deformations of human interaction – even though such processes are
said to be installed in the outside world through projection and thus
'institutionalized' to some degree. But, as Cornelius Castoriadis
points out, the Kleinian view that social life is distorted by fantasy
leaves entirely open the question of *what* is being 'distorted' here.[14]
How does fantasy inherently distort the social world in the act of
constructing it? What about the role of social institutions, politics,
and gender relations in deformations of the self? How might political
conditions affect and determine the systematic distortion of fantasy
formations which underpin social life? What seems to happen to the
concept of fantasy in Kleinian theory is that, while it is correctly seen
as the crucial psychic underpinning of all social activity, it is not
recognized as being inseparably bound up with the material conditions of its making. Instead, fantasy as the basis of intersubjective
distortion is closed off from the social world and rounded back upon
the human subject itself. As Stephen Frosh puts this: 'Kleinians seem
to be responding to the terrors of modernity by theorising them as
necessary elements in human nature; it is then up to the individual,
mediated and supported by the containment which a caring environment can provide, to make reparation for them – to produce creative
and integrative acts and artefacts which symbolise the possibility of
recovery from loss.'[15] The critical point here is that, without attention
to the social context of fantasy formations, it is extremely difficult to
imagine how radical politics might reverse the emotional damage
produced by modern social processes. Of course, it is important to
recognize that certain phantasmatic dimensions of social relations

might be too deeply sedimented to be changed in present conditions. However, like Freud, the starting point for such an analysis should give due recognition to the mutual imbrication of desire and law, fantasy and culture, in the social network.

Self-Psychology: Self-Objects and Meaning

Object relational and Kleinian thinking examines psychical life in terms of relationship difficulties. In contemporary American self-psychology, there is a similar concern with the experience of social relationships. In this theoretical current, however, more emphasis is placed upon the manner in which the relationship affects the organization and coherence of the self. The vision of the subject's inner, psychic world in self-psychology is one of a complex interplay between self-creation and social connection, individuality and affiliation. Heinz Kohut, the major theorist of self-psychology, develops a powerful account of the expansiveness of the self as refracted through interpersonal processes. For Kohut, absorption in other people is the central means through which the self is established, its boundaries defined, its purposefulness articulated. Kohut says that narcissism is vital to the emergent self in its early relationship with others. Narcissistic idealization and grandiosity, if supported by significant others, is a basic prop to a sense of self-esteem and therefore to psychological well-being. However, if the child's narcissism is not underwritten by empathetic relations, self-identity can become severely warped, and disturbed narcissistic tendencies are likely to result.

For Kohut, the child is born with a need for relatedness with others. In the same manner that humans require air for their physical survival, Kohut argues, there is a pyschological need for relatedness and connection. This need is usually met through emotional contact with the child's own parents, who provide psychic security for the gradual development of the self. That is, Kohut views the child as naturally embroiled in adult experience of the world; experience which is 'lent' to the child, to use a kind of shorthand, in its creative involvement with others. Kohut calls this primary interchange of self and other 'selfobjects'. Selfobjects, though in reality drawn from the outside world, pass into the child's own psychic structure, providing the essential building blocks for imaginary experience. There are certain parallels here with Winnicott's notion of transitional space. Lacking any defined boundaries, selfobjects permit the bridging of inner world and external reality, a transitional realm from which the infant can take into itself parts of the object in order to secure identity. Significantly, this imaginary immersion in selfobjects also provides for a reflexive involvement with the self. As Kohut puts this: 'The child's rudimentary psyche participates in the selfobject's highly developed psychic organization; the child experiences the feeling states of the selfobject – they are transmitted to the child via touch and tone of voice and perhaps by still other means – as if they were his own.'[16]

Psychical life contains two types of selfobject: that of the mirroring selfobject and that of the idealizing selfobject. The mirroring selfobject arises through the child's sense of grandiosity and omnipotence. If we imagine the small child expressing its basic narcissistic needs in relation to an admiring, mirroring other, we can grasp how the child's first development of self begins to happen. Through a narcissistic immersion in imaginary experience, the child establishes an image of itself as perfect, confirmed by the mirroring mother. The idealizing selfobject, by contrast, confers worth on the emerging self through an investment in the object itself, an object which is experienced as seductive and all-powerful. To achieve such identification involves fusing the self with this separate, and hence Oedipal, other. The ego bolsters its identity through identification with the idealizing parental image, thus finding something of meaning in surrounding persons and objects. For Kohut, both mirroring and idealizing selfobjects can provide for psychological satisfaction and the creation of meaning. Either can be used in the making of the self, and for a creative involvement with others. A failure to invest in either type of selfobject, however, leads to psychological crisis, to chronic depression or schizophrenia.

What Kohut calls 'transmuting internalization' belongs to the kind of stable psychic structure, the self, which is derived from either mode of selfobject. Here, as it were, the subject transmutes mirroring and/or idealized selfobjects into a coherent self-identity and trust in the external world. The subsequent involvement in interpersonal relations and the social network depends on this core sense of self, which is connected in an essential way to purposeful adult life. If, however, parents fail to provide positive experiences necessary for the development of self, then the child's internal world never receives the positive colouring it requires in order to establish stable self-identity. The rejection of narcissistic desire and idealization, severe disapproval, or uncaring letdowns all carry fragmenting tendencies into the later life of the individual. According to Kohut, such damage to self-esteem constitutes unconscious pathologies and deformations, especially narcissistic disturbances. Core emotional connections cannot be forged because the infant experiences itself as under attack. In this respect, narcissistic inclinations are never realistically incorporated into the interpersonal world, and are squeezed to the sidelines as buried unconscious feelings. Kohut, in short, makes the unconscious identical with failures or disturbances in the self's relational landscape. In the words of Greenberg and Mitchell: 'Kohut stresses that drives are disintegration products that appear *only* as the result of the frustration of healthy narcissistic needs. Sexual and aggressive impulses are not fundamental human motivations, but distorted, disintegrated fragments.'[17]

This severing of all necessary links between creative living and unconscious passion, however, is deeply problematic. Kohut's argument that the unconscious is a secondary phenomenon, the outcome of a breakdown in the relations of the self to selfobjects, echoes the object relational work of Fairbairn, Guntrip, Balint, and others. The unconscious, according to this view, is a subjective *distortion* which it is the task of psychoanalysis to undo. However, as I previously argued, such a standpoint can have no proper grasp of unconscious desire as deeply inscribed in everything we do, as intimately interwoven with constituting, reproducing, or transforming our conditions of personal and cultural life. It fails to recognize that unconscious anxiety, depression, conflict, and shifting identifications are part and parcel of personal life, and that, far from always being a blockage to self-realization, they are also an imaginary wellspring of productivity, creativity, and reflexivity.

Rather, Kohut's original and lasting contribution to psychoanalysis lies in his unpacking of narcissism, and of how it affects the self-experience. Kohut's analysis discloses that unmediated infantile grandiosity and idealization poses acute problems in securing a realistic sense of self-esteem. He shows that the desire for empathic mirroring and parental idealization is fundamental in the making of a positive self-image. Because the narcissistic self develops in and through relational configurations, Kohut makes it necessary to think that intersubjective relations are always at the root of narcissistic pathology. Like Lasch and Kovel, then, Kohut extracts from narcissism a disturbing picture of interpersonal relations in modern culture. In this respect, Kohut discovers a world of uncertainty and risk, a world of such rapid social and cultural change that nothing has the feel of durability anymore. In our present-day world, Kohut says, it is increasingly difficult to find a stable relational configuration to guard against the various splitting and displacing operations of the self. The internalization of selfobjects that are built upon shifting and unstable forces can only hamper self-constitution. In the face of the more lifeless dimensions of modernity, narcissism for Kohut represents a last-ditch struggle for the survival of the self.

Against the fragmentation of modern culture, Kohut's work can be read as a modernist defence of our collective need for expansive identity and secure self-boundaries. The mobile world of modernity means that individuals require identity and stable selfobjects in order to create a rich and meaningful life.

Table 3.1   Object relations, Kleinian theory, self-psychology

Theoretical model	Self-society link	Key terms
Object-Relational Theory		
Erikson	Self-organization through basic trust and ideological adaptation	Basic trust Ego-identity
Winnicott	Personal continuity created through transitional space of culture and symbolization	Transitional space True self/false self
Giddens	Self-identity forged via trust mechanisms and routinization	Trust mechanisms Bracketing anxiety Protective cocoon
Kleinian Theory		
Klein	Self embedded in fantasy scenarios, structured by mechanisms of projection and introjection	Paranoid-schizoid and depressive positions Projective/introjective Identification
Rustin	Selfhood as instrinsically social; connected to alternative futures	Society as relational context Moral capacities of self
Self-Psychology		
Kohut	Relational world affects self-experience	Selfobjects Transmuting Internalization

4

Poststructuralist Anxiety:
Subjects of Desire

From Lacan to Laplanche

We left psychoanalysis at the end of chapter 3 after examining the cultural climate of the late modern age, and looking critically at the quality of interpersonal relations realized in the contemporary social world. The guiding thread in object relational, Kleinian, and self-psychological theories outlined so far concerns the extent to which social arrangements enhance or restrict the relational capacities of the self. In these psychoanalytic standpoints, the human subject is seen as self-interpreting, other-related, and creatively interactive; qualities that might be either bolstered or stunted by modern institutions and social relations. In the branch of psychoanalysis which is influenced by the French theoretical currents of structuralism and poststructuralism, however, this relational capacity for self-constitution is powerfully subverted and overturned. Devoid of any fixed reference point, the human subject, in French psychoanalysis, is radically 'decentred' through endless slippages of language, caught in narcissistic mirror images, indeed dispersed and outstripped by the insatiable force of desire itself. In this chapter, I outline and discuss authors writing in a Lacanian and poststructuralist psychoanalytic vein. My starting point is with the issue of the self, paying special attention to the thesis of *decentred subjectivity*. After this, I turn to examine Lacanian and poststructuralist discussions of the self and cultural experience in the late modern age.

Lacan's Return to Freud

One writer whose work has profoundly influenced contemporary theory is the French psychoanalyst Jacques Lacan. Indeed, Lacan's reconceptualization of Freud in the light of poststructuralist theory has completely transformed cultural debates about the development

of the individual subject in social and historical terms. For it is no
that Lacan is just sceptical of attempts to link psychoanalysis wit
the social realm. Rather, he thinks that any projected marriag
between psychoanalysis and social theory is fundamentally doome
to failure. The reason he holds this view is perhaps best summarize
in his aphoristic maxim: 'The unconscious is the discourse of th
Other.' What this means, essentially, is that human passion is itsel
structured by the desire of others. Our deepest unconscious feeling
and passions are always expressed, as it were, through the 'relay' o
other people. For Lacan, therefore, desire *is* an intrinsically socia
phenomenon; and psychoanalysis *is* a theory about the fabrication o
the human subject as refracted through the social field. Huma
desire, says Lacan, is expressed in language. Yet desire for Lacan i
not pre-given; and it certainly does not just magically fit wit
language for its own particular ends. On the contrary, it is in an
through language that the human subject and the intersubjectiv
space of desire are interwoven with cultural forms. In this sense
language and unconscious desire, for Lacan, are co-terminous.

Lacan's so-called 'return to Freud' develops a powerfully origina
reading of Freud's texts. Yet it is important to emphasize that Lacan'
interpretation of Freudian psychoanalysis is of a rather special brand
concerned mostly with the development of Freud's early theoretica
innovations – from *The Interpretation of Dreams* (1900) through t
the metapsychological papers of 1915. For Lacan, this period o
Freud's work is radical and subversive since it uncovers the dee
structures of unconscious desire and infantile sexuality – concept
scandalous to the Western philosophical tradition. Freud's earl
theories are said to show how the human subject becomes an 'other
to itself, split and fractured through the disruptive effects of uncon
scious repression. In Lacan's view, this perpetual fragmentation o
disintegration of the self wrought by the unconscious is *the* discover
of Freudian psychoanalysis. However, according to Lacan, the impli
cations of this discovery – that the subject is radically divided betwee
the conscious ego and unconscious desire – have been watered down
The troubled waters of unconscious desire have been sidestepped
both in Freud's late metapsychological revisions and in mainstrean
American psychoanalysis. To combat this tendency, Lacan repeatedl
criticizes as imaginary – as some kind of fantastic day-dream abou
the would-be autonomy of the self – those theories which portray th
ego as socially adaptive.

Lacan's self-appointed project, by contrast, is to return psycho
analysis to its founding concern, the nature of the unconscious. T

lo this, Lacan in his *Ecrits* reinterprets Freud in the light of a dazzling array of Continental theoretical traditions – including Saussurian linguistics, structural anthropology, and poststructuralist theories of discourse. Moreover, to decipher the mute realm of repressed desire, Lacan fashions his own writing as fully shot through by the distortions of the unconscious itself – as an opaque discourse of metaphors, puns, and contradictions. This, in itself, makes reading Lacan a difficult endeavour, perhaps more akin to reading James Joyce or Gertrude Stein than to reading the sort of psychoanalytic criticism we have considered thus far. However, whatever the difficulties of Lacan's own prose, it is necessary for us now to consider his unique blending of psychoanalysis and poststructuralist theory.

We have seen that, for Freud, the human infant begins life in a symbiotic relation to its mother's body. It is precisely because human beings are born 'prematurely', Freud argues, that all infants are fundamentally dependent on others for the satisfaction of their biologically fixed needs. According to Freud, as discussed in chapter 1, the key feature of this dyadic child/mother relation is that the small infant makes no distinction between self and other, itself and the outside world. At this point, the infant's world comprises a kind of merging of itself and the maternal body, a body that provides satisfaction and pleasure to the infant. Lacan calls this pleasurable state of existence the 'imaginary order'. The imaginary for Lacan is a pre-linguistic, pre-Oedipal state of being in which desire slides around an endless array of part-objects. Prior to differentiation and individuation, the imaginary is a peculiar realm of ideal completeness, merging all that is inside with that which is outside. And it is within this imaginary realm of being, Lacan insists, that the first part-objects of the mother's body – such as breasts, lips, gaze, skin-surface, and so on – are given an emotional investment by the child.

According to Lacan, this imaginary condition of being provides an essential basis for the first drafting of selfhood. Lacan discusses this early construction of the self by returning to Freud's theory of narcissism, and focuses especially on the impact of mirror-images in identity construction. In the essay 'The mirror stage as formative of the function of the I' (1949), Lacan describes the infant's moment of recognition of itself in a mirror, and of how this generates a narcissistic sense of unified selfhood. What happens when the infant sees itself reflected in a mirror, Lacan argues, is that he or she makes an *imaginary identification* with this reflected image. The mirror provides the infant with a gratifyingly coherent image of itself as a *unified* subject. Through the mirror stage the infant becomes aware

of itself for the first time. Perhaps not surprisingly, Lacan notes, th
child reacts to this discovery of its self-image with fascination an
jubilation. Watching its reflected gestures in the mirror, the chil
gleefully celebrates its newly found sense of selfhood and wholeness

But this mirror moment is not at all what it first seems. For Laca
the key feature of the reflecting surface of the mirror is that it distort
it deforms. For what the imaginary mirror filters out of view is tha
the child is still dependent upon others for its physical security an
well-being; and that its body is still fragmented, its movement
uncoordinated. The mirror stage is profoundly 'imaginary', fo
Lacan, because the consolingly unified image of selfhood which i
generates is diametrically opposed to the bodily fragmentation tha
the child experiences. In a word, then, the mirror *lies*. The reflectin
image, because it is outside and other, leads the subject to *misrecog
nize* itself. Imaginary misrecognition, says Lacan, 'situates the agenc
of the ego, before its social determination, in a fictional direction'.
In Lacan's theory, then, the mirror stage is a narcissistic process i
which human beings construct a *misrecognized* image of self-unity.

There is, then, a distinctly negative ring to Lacan's account of th
imaginary order. In this account, it is through the misrecognition o
self that the essential seeds of subjectivity are planted. Imaginar
misrecognitions shape our self-perceptions as well as our fantasize
connections with others. But, for Lacan, mirror misrecognitions ar
not simply some phase of human development, a phase transcende
by subsequent individuation. On the contrary, this imaginary realn
of traps and distortions is in ongoing relation to subjectivity,
relation that is continually rerun and played out with other persons
In this connection, Lacan's theory of the mirror stage is profoundl
evocative of certain phantasmatic, narcissistic phenomena of contem
porary culture. Lacan's theory of the imaginary underscores th
power of seductive media images and glossy commodities to drav
on, and refashion, illusory desires. Advertising, television, pop icon
ography, as well as the media commodification of politics itself, al
play a key role in structuring the identities, gender patterns, an
aspirations in which society reproduces itself on an imaginary plane
Hence Lacan's work, as we shall examine in the following section
has much to contribute to the study of contemporary capitalis
commodification, media image production, and social, cultural, an
political forms.

The imaginary order in Lacan's work can thus be described as
kind of archaic realm of distorted mirror images, a spatial world o
indistinction between self and other, from which primary narcissism

ınd aggressivity are drawn as the key building blocks in the formation of self. Yet if the imaginary is already an alienation of subjectivity – the small infant becoming an 'other' to itself in the act of contemplating its reflecting image – then the same is certainly true of what Lacan calls the 'symbolic order'. The symbolic is that domain of received social meanings, logic, and differentiation – in and through which the infant begins to represent desire and is thus constituted as a 'subject'. Reinterpreting Freud's theory of the Oedipus complex, Lacan argues that the break up of the imaginary child/mother dyad arises through symbolization. What this means, essentially, is that the infant's imaginary unity with its mother is torn apart due to the intrusive impact of wider cultural and social processes. For Lacan, as for Freud, this happens with the entry of the father into the psychic world of the child. In disturbing the libidinal relation between child and mother, the father effectively drives a wedge into this blissful, imaginary union; and thereby refers the infant to the wider cultural network and the social taboo on incest. Lacan's innovation, however, lies in his emphasis on the underlying symbolic relations here which order social life. According to Lacan, there is a good deal more at stake than just sexual prohibition with the advent of the Oedipus complex. In contrast to a reductive focus on the immediate family situation, Lacan contends that the function of the father is to enforce the cultural Law. Not only is the child severed from the imaginary fullness of the maternal body, it is now inserted into a structured world of symbolic meaning – a world that shapes all interactions between the self and others. Finding itself excommunicated from the imaginary, the infant must gradually learn to represent itself within this social network.

But how does this act of self-constitution come about? How, exactly, does this shift from imaginary plenitude to the pre-structured symbolic network arise? Not just by the entry of the father, says Lacan, but by the acquisition of language itself. For Lacan, language is the fundamental medium in which desire is represented, and through which the subject is constituted to itself and to others. Language, he describes, as an intersubjective order of symbolization, an order embedded within patriarchal culture, and thus a force that perpetuates that which he calls the 'Law of the Father'. Drawing from the work of Saussure in structural linguistics, Lacan argues that language is a system of signs. Signs in general are made up of a signifier (a sound or image) and a signified (the concept or meaning evoked). The distinction between signifier and signified does not refer to objects themselves, but to the *psychic representations* created by their interplay. From this viewpoint, words do not 'mean' the objects: there is no inherent connection between the word 'tree' and the material object with which we associate this word. By contras meaning is created through linguistic differences, through the play c signifiers. 'If a signifier refers to a signified', write Laplanche an Leclaire, 'it is only through the mediation of the entire system c signifiers: there is no signifier that does not refer to the absence c others and that is not defined by its position in the system.'[2] Meanin is thus defined by difference: it is only by means of linguisti difference that particular signifieds can be established and known For example, the cry 'stop' has meaning only in that it can b distinguished from 'go' in everyday talk. The relation between a sig and object is thus always provisional and arbitrary; and its usag depends upon historical and cultural convention.

Lacan seeks essentially to apply this linguistic theory to th unconscious itself. The human subject, for Lacan, once severed fron the narcissistic fullness of the imaginary order, is inserted into th symbolic order of language. Within this order, the subject attempt to represent itself. Yet this proves to be an impossible task since th subject has become an 'effect of the signifier', inserted into th spacings or differences which constitute language itself. Languag and the communication of information are therefore necessarily mask covering over the impossibility of desire. The unconsciou then, is less a realm 'inside' the human subject, than an *intersubjectiu space between people*, as desire sinks or fades into the gaps whic separate word from word, meaning from meaning. As Lacan pu this: 'the exteriority of the symbolic in relation to man is the ver notion of the unconscious'. Or, in Lacan's infamous slogan: 'th unconscious is structured like a language'.

To illustrate how the infant is constituted as a 'subject' in th symbolic order, let us briefly consider Freud's famous discussion c the *fort-da* game in *Beyond the Pleasure Principle* (1920) – a gam often cited by Lacan in respect of the ordering power of languag Watching his grandson playing with a cotton-reel toy one day, Freu observed that the infant alternatively threw the toy away, uttering a expressive *fort!* (gone), and would then pull the reel back, exclaimin *da!* (here). Freud analysed the *fort! da!*, 'gone', 'here', game as th child's emotional attempt to deal with the recurring disappearanc and reappearance of his mother. It was through the repetition of thi game of presence and absence that the child sought to separate itse out from the mother. In this connection Freud points out that th game enacts several symbolic interventions into the world of sexuality. It allows the child to express its libidinal renunciation of the mother; in turning a passive experience into an active one, it represents a symbolic 'mastery' over the unpleasant fact of the mother's absence; and the game also gives expression to the child's wish for revenge – 'all right, then go away! I don't need you I'm sending you away myself.'

Lacan's commentaries on the *fort-da* game focus on the child's shift from the imaginary world of fantasy to the new horizon of language. Stressing that subjectivity and sexualization are defined in terms of linguistic differences, Lacan argues that the phonematic opposition, 'gone', 'here', signals the child's entry into speech – into the symbolic field of culture. For Lacan, however, and in contrast to Freud, the child is not the agent of this symbolization. Instead it is the child that *receives* desire from the Other, in this case the mother, who implants signifiers at the heart of the child's psychic world. 'The child,' Lacan says, 'begins to involve himself in the system of the concrete discourse of his surroundings by reproducing, more or less approximally, in his *Fort!* and his *Da!*, the vocables he receives from it.'[3] What the child receives, in short, is the whole field of received social meanings. The *fort-da* game, in springing the child into language, leads him to recognize that meaning outruns the mother/child relation. Language and speech now constitute the child in relation to others; and this is a relation which is pre-structured by social, cultural, and sexual codes. The child, now severed from its full imaginary relation to the mother, must move along this linguistic chain in order to be part of the communicational situation of the social network itself.

To summarize Lacan's doctrines: the imaginary order, emerging out of the child/mother dyad and forged in the mirror phase, is a fantasized realm of wholeness and plenitude. For Lacan, ego formation is profoundly imaginary since it is based upon narcissitic misrecognition – and hence involves a denial of loss, fragmentation, and difference. It is the symbolic order which actually breaks up this imaginary hall of mirrors – without which the subject would enter into psychosis – by instituting differentiation, logic, and meaning. The Law of the Father, symbolized by his phallus, breaks up the imaginary child/mother dyad through the prohibition of desire. The space of unconscious desire is thus born into this pre-structured linguistic/sexual setting. Subjectivity and the unconscious are structured linguistically within the cultural and social Law.

Contributions and Limitations of Lacan's Theory

Lacan's theories rank among the most significant contributions to modern psychoanalysis. His emphasis on language in the construction of psychic life, and its intimate connection with unconscious sexuality, has been original and provocative. Lacan's placing of the subjective 'self' at the centre of imaginary experience has served as a balance against other psychoanalytic theorists, particularly those influenced by American ego psychology, which argue that the ego is at the centre of rational psychological functioning. Lacan, by contrast, has emphasized that the self is always alienated from its own history, is formed in and through otherness, and is inserted into a symbolic network which is on the outside. Lacan continually emphasizes that the 'I' is an alienating screen or fiction, a medium of misrecognition which masks the split and fractured nature of unconscious desire. He has added to our understanding of the intertwining of desire and language, showing that the communicational situation is itself a process of division, in which human subjects constantly repeat that elusive search for the missing object of desire. He depicts the unconscious as created by language, and locates the open-ended nature of desire within the linguistic interstices of the cultural framework. Moreover, his account of language powerfully deconstructs traditional theories of representation which presume that mind and reality automatically fit together. Lacan's analysis is in part radical since it shows that the production of meaning is embedded in the signifying chain itself. In Lacan's theory, the meanings engendered within language would not exist if it were not for the impact of the Other upon the self in the symbolic register. Language, as that which is outside and beyond, constitutively mediates our relation to the social and cultural world.

Lacan's articulation of a psychoanalytic theory of subjectivity within a linguistic framework has been greeted by many as of central importance to cultural enquiry. (We shall examine the Lacanian interpretation of modern societies, culture, and politics in the following section of this chapter.) The decentering of the subject; the loss, lack, and impossibility of unity in psychical life; the primacy of signifiers over what is signified in the unconscious; our fragile and always precarious relation to the Other: these are, in Lacanian psychoanalysis, issues of core importance. Lacanian analysis seeks to deconstruct the narcissistic illusions of the self, allowing the lack and fragmentation which the symbolic register ordains for the human subject to resurface.

However, Lacan's comprehensive reconceptualization of Freud has also come under fire. Lacan's linguistic doctrines have been severely criticized on a great number of grounds, both inside and outside psychoanalytical circles. The key conceptual difficulties in Lacan's work seem to me to be twofold: the first concerns the general way in which sexuality and the unconscious are theorized, and the second concerns the inadequacy of linguistics for the critical analysis of subjectivity.

To begin with, consider the Lacanian proposition that the imaginary contours of self-identity are traversed by illusion or misrecognition. Lacan himself was in no doubt, as we have seen, that the constitution of the self through reflection involves an inescapable alienation of the subject. From this angle, the imaginary is a *distorting trap*. It constitutes the infant as a unified self through consoling mirror images and thus screens out the dismal truth that subjectivity is, in fact, fractured and dispersed. However, there are serious conceptual difficulties with this standpoint. The argument that the 'mirror' distorts fails to specify the psychic processes interior to the individual subject which makes any such misrecognition possible. For example, what is it that leads the infant to (mis)recognize itself in its mirror image? How, exactly, does the individual cash in on this conferring of selfhood, however deformed or brittle? The central dilemma here is that surely for an individual to begin to recognize itself in the 'mirror' it must already possess a more rudimentary sense of self. For, to take up a reflected image as one's own must no doubt require some general capacity for emotional response.

Cornelius Castoriadis has argued that Lacan's theory of the mirror stage can offer no solution to this conundrum of how identity is derived from self-reflection. For Lacan's theory only makes sense if, according to Castoriadis, we recognize the profoundly *creative* nature of the imaginary register, a psychic creativity that is the precondition for the 'mirror' itself and its possible reflections. Castoriadis thus draws attention to a central limitation in Lacan's doctrine about the human subject: namely, its failure to theorize how the 'mirror' is perceived as real. In contrast, Castoriadis suggests that to understand how the individual subject responds to and recognizes itself and others requires an account of our emergent capacities for representation and identification. As Castoriadis writes, a critical psychoanalytic conception of subjectivity must presuppose the subject's 'emergent capacity to gather meaning and to make of it something for him/herself'.[4]

Equally serious is the criticism that Lacan's work actually supresses the subversive implications of Freud's discovery of the unconscious by structuralizing it, reducing it to a chance play of signifiers. From this angle, Lacan's theory effectively represses unconscious sexuality and desire. This complaint is aimed not only at Lacan's use of poststructuralist theory, but focuses more generally upon his claim that the unconscious is naturally tied to language. Many critics – including Paul Ricoeur, Jean-François Lyotard, Cornelius Castoriadis, and Jean Laplanche – have argued the Freudian point against Lacan that the unconscious is resistant to ordered syntax.[5] These critics, in differing theoretical ways, have argued that the repressed unconscious is a primary, scenic field of representational forms, drives, and affects; a field which certainly intrudes upon waking language but one that cannot simply be equated with it. Malcolm Bowie has expressed this well:

> It is our lot as speaking creatures to rediscover muteness from time to time – in rapture, in pain, in physical violence, in the terror of death – and then to feel a lost power of speech flowing back. One may be ready to grant that these seeming suspensions of signifying law are themselves entirely in the gift of the signifier, yet still wish to have them marked off in some way as events of a special kind. A long gaze at the Pacific may be taciturn at one moment and loquacious the next. Language offers us now a retreat from sensuality, now a way of enhancing and manipulating it. Yet to these differences Lacan's theory maintains a principled indifference.[6]

Significantly, the unconscious is in some ways even more refractory to language than this characterization suggests. For the unconscious, as Freud said, is completely unaware of contradiction, time, or closure. For Freud, language is explicitly located in the preconscious system and the secondary processes that characterize it. In so far as certain unconscious representations are structured by the force of repression, they have the power to stabilize the secondary processes of language. But it is the unconscious which is the precondition for language and not the reverse. As such, Lacan's reformulation of the conscious/unconscious dualism as a linguistic relation does not correspond at any meaningful level with Freud's theory.

There are also important political implications raised by Lacan's assimilation of the unconscious with a linguistic structure. A central problem left in the wake of Lacan's 'linguistic revolution' concerns the status of human agency, above all the subject's capabilities for critical self-reflection and autonomy. One reading of Lacan holds that, in presenting a model of desire as disembodied and pre-structured linguistically, the human subject is effectively stripped of any capacity for creative identity, change, or autonomy. This charge, however, is in fact aimed more appropriately at those poststructuralist thinkers that champion the 'death of the subject' than at the Lacanian school. For, in contrast merely to celebrating the disintegration of the subject, Lacan posits a 'subject of the unconscious', a subject located in the *spaces* of language itself. Another reading of Lacan is that although the 'subject of the unconscious' is constituted in terms of difference – oppositions that are structured linguistically – no theoretical room is given in this account to practical agency. In my view Lacanianism does indeed face a real problem in this respect, casting off the most vital questions of self and self-identity on to an abstract theory of language.

There are also important criticisms to be made of Lacan's account of culture. Most importantly, Lacan's equation of language with cultural domination grotesquely downplays the importance of power, ideology, and social institutions in the reproduction of the cultural, political framework. In Lacan's account, the structure of subjectivity is determined by the cultural Law. Yet although language certainly pre-exists us as individual subjects, it is surely wrong to suggest, as Lacan does, that the business of everyday talk in social life – the communicational situation of the symbolic order – is singular and authoritarian. The human subject is not constituted as 'self-divided' merely because of its insertion into language. Rather, the traumatic divisions and splits which people experience via the whole field of the socio-symbolic order are intimately linked to concrete relations of power and ideology. To understand this requires a theoretical framework more sensitive to the articulation of subjectivity as embedded in the social context – to the complex, contradictory ways in which selfhood is defined in the contemporary age of mass communication, global economic mechanisms, the risk of nuclear or ecological catastrophe, and the like. It is, of course, true that there must always be a mode of discourse to encode social interests such as these; but the critical point is that Lacan's work fails to consider what the cultural and political determinants of that code might be. Instead of focusing on the political forms of specific, socially created interests and institutions, Lacan dissolves their importance into some undifferentiated, ahistorical category of the signifier itself. This is a problem which has been addressed by post-Lacanian cultural theorists as well as psychoanalytic feminists in the analysis of contemporary social relations, and we shall examine certain responses to this problem later in the book.

Finally, these problems involve broader epistemological dilemmas. The Lacanian narrative which we have traced – that the self is narcissistic, the imaginary a specular trap, the law omnipotent, and the symbolic a mask for 'lack' – would appear to undo its own claims to critical status. For surely any political project concerned with enhancing freedom and autonomy must also be caught in the same imaginary networks of illusion as subjectivity itself? But if this is so, then perhaps the whole Lacanian framework might be deconstructed. For example, how can Lacan's discourse evade the distorting traps of the imaginary domain? Surely Lacan does not seriously believe that the only way of overcoming imaginary distortion is through comic word-play, puns, and irony? In failing to grasp that human subjects are capable of critical self-reflection and self-actualization, the issue of individual and collective autonomy remains repressed in Lacan's work. Yet it is precisely this pessimistic determinism about the self and the intersubjective world that will be taken over and extended in Lacanian and post-Lacanian cultural theory.

Lacanian and Post-Lacanian Contexts

At first sight Lacan's interpretation of Freud might seem unpromising for critical social research. To say, with Lacan, that we are prisoners of our own desire, caught within the distorting traps of the imaginary order, and unable to advance beyond symbolic Law, is surely to undermine what is most vital to the radical political imagination. Yet it is precisely this sense of political resignation that has been used by Lacanian-inspired cultural critics to put the skids on such notions as Self, Truth, Freedom, and Meaning. In Lacanian terms, to believe that these words might hold some absolute value necessarily involves accepting the world as it is. By contrast, Lacanian thought attempts to show that identity and meaning are inherently unstable, and that the oppressive function of social discourse lies in occluding the multiplicity of unconscious desire itself. Here it is not fanciful to detect similarities between Lacanian cultural criticism and the psychoanalytic criticism of Fromm, Marcuse, Lasch, and others, as discussed in chapter 2. For like Lacan, these psychoanalytic critics draw on Freud to uncover the repressive forces at work in the construction of the ego. In contrast to Lacan, however, the recovery of the unconscious for these authors also holds out a promise for social emancipation. In Lacanian and post-Lacanian thought, a radically different tack is taken. Lacanian-inspired cultural theorists do not evaluate society in terms of psychoanalytic theory, but rather explore the logic of desire as a social index. From this standpoint, subjective distortions, displacements, and repressions are treated as symptoms of the social and cultural field itself.

Consideration of the implications of Lacan's work for social, political, and cultural analysis has led to a number of fruitful approaches and strategies. The characteristic emphasis on problems of language and communication in Lacan's thought has made Lacanianism highly relevant to a variety of theoretical projects. Above all, Lacan's thought has been enormously important to feminist concerns with our unequal socio-sexual world. (Lacanian feminism, as well as the feminist critique of Lacan, is discussed in chapter 5). Lacan's thought has also greatly influenced debates in areas such as social theory, cultural studies, film theory, and criticism, and literary and Marxist theory. In order to approach some of the ramifications of these debates, I shall trace the trajectory of Lacanian and post-Lacanian psychoanalysis which has had the greatest impact on general theorizing about modern culture and politics.

Imaginary mirrors, ideological traps

In his 1957 essay 'The agency of the letter in the unconscious or reason since Freud', Lacan tells the following story, a story about the relation of a word to its image. 'A train arrives at a station. A little boy and a little girl, brother and sister, are seated in a compartment face to face next to the window through which the buildings along the station platform can be seen passing as the train pulls to a stop. "Look," says the brother, "we're at Ladies!"; "Idiot!" replies his sister, "Can't you see we're at Gentlemen".'[7] How much can we glean about sexuality and gender from this image of everyday life? Lacan says that language assigns to individuals the signifier of their sexual difference. What this means, essentially, is that language has a certain productivity in the construction of individuals as subjects. As the little boy and the little girl gaze out at the station platform, the cultural signifier *carves out a difference* between the identical doors, inscribing each child on one or the other side of the imaginary domain of gender, Ladies or Gentlemen. Ultimately, there is no sexual relation according to Lacan. Instead, there is only each individual's relation to the Law and to language, a relation that enables social relations to persist.

It is just this imaginary inscription of the subject within social and political meanings that Louis Althusser uncovers as the principal function of ideology. Althusser, a French Marxist who had been in personal analysis with Lacan, develops the project of integrating Marxism and Lacanian psychoanalysis in order to understand the positioning of the subject in ideology. In 'Ideology and Ideological State Apparatuses' (1971), Althusser traces how ideology functions by leading the subject to understand itself in a manner which supports the reproduction of dominant class relations. How is this achieved? The chief effect of ideology is that it provides an imaginary centreing on everyday life, it confers identity, and makes the subject feel valued within the interpersonal world. 'Ideology,' says Althusser, 'interpellates individuals as subjects.' Interpellation here is to be understood as the establishment of an imaginary relation to the social network, such that the individual comes to recognize himself or herself as a 'subject'. Like Lacan, Althusser insists that the cultural forms of ideology are produced, not so much in the public space of politics and history, as in the private realm of day-to-day life. In this respect, Althusser offers the following example of a person being 'interpellated' through a closed door: 'We all have friends who, when they knock on our door and we ask, through the door, the question "Who's there?", answer (since "it's obvious") "It's me". And we recognize that "it is him", or "her". We open the door, and "it's true, it really was she who was there".'[8]

How are these imaginary dimensions of ideology to be understood? Echoing Lacan, Althusser uses the notion of the mirror stage to deconstruct ideology. For Althusser, there is a duplicate mirror-structure at the heart of the ideological process, a structure which possesses all the unity and plenitude of Lacan's imaginary order. In fact, ideology is doubly specular, according to Althusser, since it grants to the individual an ideological mirror in which it can recognize both itself and others. What the mirror of ideology essentially does is to implant received social meanings at the centre of the imaginary relationship of individuals to their real conditions of existence. Thus, in constituting the self in relation to discourses of class, race, sexuality, nationalism, and the like, the individual comes to *misrecognize* itself as an autonomous subject, believing itself to be legally free and self-legislating. This misrecognition, Althusser says, is rooted in Ideological State Apparatuses, institutions such as the mass media, schools, trade unions, and the like, whose function is to interpellate subjects to different social positions in the terrain of class struggle. That human subjects should come to overlook the nature of their own *decentred subjectivity* is precisely the function of ideology, thus serving to reinforce the dominant power interests of late capitalism.

Althusser's linking of psychoanalysis and Marxism had a significant impact upon the human sciences at the time of its reception. His central thesis that ideology is an indispensable imaginary medium for the reproduction of social life was original and provocative, and it did much to discredit the notion of ideology as mere false consciousness. Like the unconscious for Freud, ideology for Althusser is eternal. However, it is now widely agreed that there are numerous problems connected with this theory of the subject of ideology. To begin with, Althusser's argument about the speculary structure of ideology runs into the same kind of theoretical dead-end as does Lacan's account of the imaginary. That is, in order for the subject to recognize itself in and through ideological interpellation, surely it must already possess certain affective capacities for subjective response. As Paul Hirst notes: 'the "individual", who is prior to ideology and whose pre-ideological attributes of subjectivity are necessary to its becoming a subject, cannot be erased in Althusser's text.'⁹ But if there is a 'real' subject hiding behind the ideological effects of interpellation, then perhaps individuals are not as passively centred within received social meanings as Althusser leads us to believe. Consideration of the Lacanian imaginary and symbolic orders underscores the point that there is a fundamental instability at the heart of selfhood. The problem here, in short, is that Althusser downgrades the split and fractured nature of repressed desire, and thus displaces the concept of the unconscious. Consequently, the place of the subject is left so empty in Althusser's theory that it is rendered fruitless for critical analysis. Subjects are serenely inserted into the process of interpellation, and the possibilities for individual and political agency in turn vanish. As such, Althusser is left unable to account for the complex interplay between split, desiring subjects and social and political relations in the modern age.

Nevertheless, whatever the limits of these theoretical deadends, Althusser's work enabled a more sophisticated psychoanalytic articulation of subjectivity with theories of the social and culture. Those that embraced the framework of the Althusserian/Lacanian system included Etienne Balibar, Pierre Machery, Stuart Hall, Fredric Jameson, Paul Hirst, and Barry Hindess. In this theoretical work, the Althusserian model was more finely developed, or reconceptualized, in order to address a range of cultural and political issues, such as race, ethnicity, nationalism, social class, and the like. Yet perhaps the most important meeting point of psychoanalytical and cultural theories occurred in film and media studies in the late 1970s and 1980s, as represented in the French journal *Cahiers du Cinéma* and the British journal *Screen*. This discussion of cinema and ideology proceeded from the conceptual cocktail of Lacanian psychoanalysis, Althusserian Marxism, semiotic poststructural theory, and certain aesthetic discourses. The most notable psychoanalytic thinking produced about film can be found in the work of Christian Metz, Stephen Heath, Laura Mulvey, Raymond Bellour, Teresa De Lauretis and Mary Ann Doane.

Film is analysed by these theorists as a process of ideological production. What is studied is, not so much the latent unconscious thoughts of movie spectators, but rather the *ideological framing* of the film itself. This framing is imaginary. As Christian Metz puts it: 'More than the other arts, or in a more unique way, the cinema involves us in the imaginary: it drums up all perception, but to switch it immediately over into its own absence, which is nonetheless the only signifier present.'[10] Metz's reference to absence here refers to the manner in which film represses the production of its own making, the way in which it passes itself off as natural, the presentation of complex image constructions as simply the reality of day-to-day life. In this respect, the psychoanalysis of cinema is an attempt to decode the ideological images produced in film, and to trace out how these images construct the spectator-subject. The construction of the subject in film, however, is not a fixed or stable affair. Instead, it is suggested that films *order and reorder* the subject in relation to cinematic images. Whether we're watching the evening news, or the fantasy exploits of *Batman*, the point is that we are always caught up within a complex process of ideological framing, linked to the implicit assumptions and ways in which reality is being shaped before our eyes.

The role of ideological framing, though ambiguous, functions in two central modes. The first is *structurally closed*. Imagine a typical Hollywood film which dramatizes its narrative through the reality of the image, recording action as the simple unfolding of what is happening. Here spectators are invited, as it were, to identify with actors in a closed imaginary space, something akin to the mirror stage. Cinema, in this sense, is fully imaginary, constructing spectators as unified, centred subjects who 'control' the image-object before their eyes. Yet cinema in this structurally closed mode can only present such symbolic scenarios by bracketing off its active involvement in narrative construction. That is, film represses its own framing and selective definition of social reality. The second mode of film is *structurally reflexive*. Imagine a film, perhaps an avant-garde film, which constantly frustrates spectator-subject identification; a film in which action and events are presented always from different cinematic angles, including an incorporation of the role of the camera itself in the shooting of the narrative. Through such reflexive techniques, the spectator-subject is made aware of the active role of cinema itself in ideological representation.

If the selective definition of images is the very function of mainstream cinema, it is possible to imagine that film is itself a socially dominant machine of the imaginary, seeking to master reality at a stroke. This, in essence, was the view offered by theorists associated with *Screen* and *Cahiers du Cinéma* in any case. Following Lacan and Althusser, it was argued that the nub of representation in film is the way in which spectator-subject positions are fixed, and rearticulated, in relation to systems of meaning. However, there are several difficulties with this account of the relation between subjectivity, cinema, and ideology. For one thing, it is not at all clear that psychoanalysis, even in its Lacanian form, is compatible with the idea of a socially determined consciousness or misrecognition. If the unconscious is the site of our fragile and precarious relation to the Other, a treacherous terrain of multiple, exploding desires, then how might subjectivity ever be 'fixed' through the image production of film? Are not the illusions of generalized mass communication in some sense connected to the phantasmagoria of the unconscious itself? Significantly, it is not at all clear what is meant by the notion of fixation in broader social and political terms. Is the fixation of the spectator-subject, for example, simply to be equated with imaginary misrecognition? Does such fixation imply false consciousness or ideological distortion? And what does it mean to say that truth lies on the other side of ideology? At this point, the Lacanian analysis of film reaches its limits.

The lack in ideology

The failures and inconsistencies in the foregoing articulations of Lacanian psychoanalysis and cultural studies are the outcome of a specific theoretical dilemma: the tracing of the split and fractured nature of desire as embedded in specific institutional pressures of socialization. The central impasse of the Lacanian-Althusserian framework, as we have seen, is that it ties the subject of language and the subject of ideology ineluctably together. Thus, what began as a psychoanalytic account of the misrecognition of the subject is shifted up a gear, into a fully blown theory of social misrecognition; a position which in turn implies the possibility of non-ideological knowledge.

Slavoj Žižek, of the so-called Slovenian school of Lacanian psychoanalysis, speaks in *The Sublime Object of Ideology* (1989) of going 'beyond interpellation', to the unconscious core of libidinal enjoyment around which every cultural network is structured. Reconceptualizing the Lacanian-Althusserian framework, Žižek looks at the ambiguous realm of unconscious fantasy as manifested in the social and ideological forms of modern culture. For Žižek, as for Althusser, ideology is an imaginary field which always implies a shared relationship to socio-symbolic forms, such as class, race, gender, and the like. In contrast to Althusser, however, Žižek contends that ideology can never be reduced to the cultural reproduction of meaning as such – to the signifying network of language alone. On the contrary, ideology always outstrips its own social and political forms; it is a realm *beyond* interpellation or internalization. In this respect, Žižek attempts to underscore the radical involvement of the self in the social context. Ideology, he says, is not something which just magically goes to work on individuals, assigning social identities and roles in the act of producing itself, but is rather an overdetermined field of passionate assumptions and commitments. The whole network of ideology, for a psychoanalytic critic like Žižek, is reproduced through the fantasy identifications of human subjects, identifications which bring into play the troubled waters of the unconscious. 'The function of ideology,' writes Žižek, 'is not to offer us a point of escape from our reality but to offer us the social reality itself as an escape from some traumatic, real kernel.'[11]

According to Žižek, the fundamental substance of psychical life is *enjoyment*. The enjoyment of which Žižek speaks, however, cannot be given a wholly positive gloss. In Lacanian psychoanalysis, Žižek says, enjoyment is intricately interwoven with lack. The human subject, once ripped away from the plenitude of the imaginary order, is *itself* constituted as internally blocked, marked by lack, alienated through fruitless searches for meaning and unity whose sole purpose is to repair this essential nothingness. It is here that Žižek describes fantasy as a compensation for lack. Fantasy is the very dimension of libidinal enjoyment, spinning off in both pleasurable and painful directions, covering over the empty space of the self. From this angle, fantasy is at once connected to the *ideological* and *pre-ideological*, the latter being a realm of non-meaning which for Žižek is the source of the power and failure of social signification. In *Looking Awry*, (1991), Žižek discusses, among other films, Terry Gillian's *Brazil* as demonstrating fantasy's fundamental ambiguity in ideology. *Brazil* is a black comedy about life in a crazed, totalitarian society. Žižek analyses the ideological manipulation represented in *Brazil* in the following way:

> 'Brazil' is the stupid song from the 1950s that resounds compulsively throughout the film . . . it seems that the idiotic, intrusive rhythm of 'Brazil' serves as a support for totalitarian enjoyment, i.e., that it condenses the fantasy frame of the 'crazy' totalitarian social order that the film depicts. But at the very end, when his resistance is apparently broken by the savage torture to which he has been subjected, the hero escapes his torturers by beginning to whistle 'Brazil!' Although functioning as a support for the totalitarian order, fantasy is then at the same time the leftover of the real that enables us to 'pull ourselves out', to preserve a kind of distance from the socio-symbolic network.[12]

Enjoyment thus lies at the root of ideology, driving the imagination of the self within the framework of received social meanings. Yet enjoyment is also something which *cannot* be fully incorporated into the symbolic; it is a hard kernel of desire, traumatic irrationality, the ultimate displacement at every point of ideological identification.

The political thrust of all of this is to demonstrate that ideological discourse, which operates in and through fantasy, supports that lack or antagonism at the heart of selfhood. Ideologies of nationalism, racism, sexism, and the like, function to maintain the fantasy coherence of cultural formations; with unconscious forms of enjoyment manifesting themselves as symptoms of antagonism. For example, the resurgence of racism and nationalism in Eastern Europe in the 1990s, Žižek argues, has led to a surplus of enjoyment being projected onto objects of antagonism. This eruption of enjoyment, directed at the Other, is an unbearable kernel of desire which is alleviated through its translation into an ideological symptom. The collapse of Soviet totalitarianism in Eastern Europe unleashed a surplus of fantasy, antagonistic desire that was too painful to acknowledge within certain cultural formations. Ideological xenophobias, such as nationalist or racist desires, thus involved the projection of pain onto something perceived as strange and Other.

Žižek's theories represent a suggestive blending of Lacanian psychoanalysis and contemporary cultural theory. His work demonstrates, in a sophisticated, theoretical manner, the precarious and shifting connections between desire and law, enjoyment and meaning, in social and political life. Žižek argues for the centrality of fantasy and enjoyment in any actual social process; and his work critically underscores the point that any political project that does not take account of the unconscious dimensions of ideology is unlikely to amount to much. But various objections can be levelled against Žižek's ideas. In the first place, if loss and pain are the fundamental anchors of desire as enmeshed in ideological forms, their composition would seem to be more internally differentiated than Žižek recognizes. According to his interpretation, ideology is a fantasy scenario filling out the lack of selfhood. Yet the problem with this view is that it flattens out the complex, contradictory reception of ideological forms by human subjects. Whether one is in the grip of sexism, full-blooded nationalism, engaging in ecological protest, or simply listening to Prince, these are for Žižek all pieces of ideological fantasy aimed at soothing the sour taste of our 'fundamental antagonism'. Lack, and its filling through fantasy, simply becomes the uniform measure of cultural domination. Yet, by taking this view, Žižek strikes the ideological world empty of meaning. The 'impossible kernel of desire' of which Žižek speaks, though offering a potential space for critical political resistance, ultimately drains away the core emotional, unconscious connections through which human subjects interact in daily life. It offers no basis for understanding the richly ambiguous links between desire and social action, nor any basis for discriminating between the differentiated ideological formations of the contemporary epoch.

Seductive presences

Lacan's account of the human subject operates on a fairly global level, tracing unconscious desire as located in a structure of linguistic interrelationship, whereas the contemporary French psychoanalyst Jean Laplanche is more concerned with examining the complexities of desire in relation to parental sexual signification. The internalization of the Other first arises from the moment in which an adult message is proffered to a child – what Laplanche calls 'primal seduction' – and which thus constitutes the dimension of unconscious fantasy. In *New Foundations for Psychoanalysis* (1987), Laplanche elaborates a theory of primal seduction, the status of which is defined as the condition of possibility for the unconscious, the ego, and its relation to the other, and processes of symbolization and intersubjectivity.

The term 'signifier' is central to Laplanche's work, but it is deployed in a radically different fashion to that of Lacan. He postulates not a language, but verbal and non-verbal human expression as lying at the root of unconscious childhood experience. Laplanche employs the term 'enigmatic signifier' to capture the seductive nature of this unconscious interaction between child and adult. Through adult dispositions, the child is lent, as it were, an unconscious framework of meaning in order to naturalize its place in the world. As Laplanche argues: 'The *enigma* is in itself a *seduction* and its mechanisms are unconscious . . . The "attentions of a mother" or the "aggression of a father" are seductive only because they are not transparent. They are seductive because they are opaque, because they convey something enigmatic.'[13] Signifiers are therefore constituted as enigmatic for Laplanche since adult messages both outstrip the child's capacity for affective response and because they are shot through with parental unconscious signification. The mother and the father, in brief, present that which they do not know about their own sexuality to the child. From this angle, what is on the outside, adult sexual messages, creates an inaccessible world of meaning on the inside, the repressed unconscious.

Laplanche argues that a prime instance of enigmatic signification, of the other's already repressed sexuality, can be found in the role of the maternal breast in infant development. According to Laplanche, the maternal breast is a site of transmission for various opaque sexual messages to the child. As Laplanche puts this:

> Can analytic theory afford to go on ignoring the extent women unconsciously and sexually cathect the breast, which appears to be the natural organ for lactation? It is inconceivable that the infant does not notice this sexual cathexis . . . It is impossible to imagine that the infant does not suspect that this cathexis is the source of a nagging question: what does the breast want from me, apart from wanting to suckle me, and come to that, why does it want to suckle me? (p. 126)

The child thus receives a sexually loaded message from the mother, a message which founds its own desire and emotional relation to the intersubjective world.

At this point a qualification must be made concerning Laplanche's claim that the constitution of repressed desire moves within the framework of seduction. Laplanche's theory of primal seduction was attracting attention within the psychoanalytic community in France at roughly the same time as Jeffrey Masson was attempting to destroy the intellectual and political credentials of psychoanalysis in America. In *The Assault on Truth: Freud's Suppression of the Seduction Theory*, Masson argued that Freud had seen into the terrible truths of patriarchal society, of child sexual abuse and incest, yet had closed his eyes to this state of affairs by interpreting his patients' stories as unconscious fantasies. Abuse, says Masson, was recast as the effect of children's sexual desires themselves. Masson's attack on Freud, however, entirely missed the point that what is at stake in the psychoanalytic perspective is the constitution of desire as refracted through the social network. Neither Freud, nor Laplanche after him, denies the existence of child sexual abuse and its suppression in modern societies. Rather, their focus concerns the profoundly imaginary dimensions of human sexuality and desire – of which incest and abuse are certainly one manifestation. From this angle, Laplanche's focus on seduction is an attempt to trace conceptually the formation of repressed desire, located as a relation to enigmatic sexual signification and the adult other.

Suggestive as it is, however, Laplanche's work is not without its problems. In Laplanche's account, people appear as essentially passive in relation to enigmatic signification. Indeed there is almost a complete separation of the world of enigmatic signification from the actual responses of human subjects. As Jacqueline Rose has argued, Laplanche's reinterpretation of repression means that the 'child receives everything from the outside', desire being inscribed in the internal world via the deformations of parental sexuality itself.[14] There is another way of putting this point. Laplanche, like Lacan, presents us with a structural model of the conditions of possibility for unconscious desire. Both theorists betray a poststructuralist distaste for individual subjectivity; and both in their different ways develop an inadequate account of psychic interiority and human creativity. The Other, in short, is elevated over and above the subject. Yet important as others are in the constitution of the self, they will always be internally shaped by the unconscious imagination of the individuals they affect.

Whatever these limits, Laplanche has constructed a valuable theory within which sexual representation is given its due. His work as a whole underscores the inescapable imprint of unconscious sexuality upon all structures of intersubjectivity.

Table 4.1 Poststructuralist anxiety: subjects of desire

Theorist	Subjectivity and the unconscious	Key terms
Lacan	Self as narcissistic misrecognition, represented through symbolic order of language	Mirror stage Imaginary Symbolic Unconscious structured like a language
Althusser	Individual as subject of ideological misrecognition	Interpellation Hailing
Žižek	Self decentred through pre-ideological lack of desire	Enjoyment Antagonism
Laplanche	Self constituted in and through primal seduction, an opaque realm of sexual messages from the Other	Enigmatic signifiers Seduction

5

Psychoanalytic Feminism
From Dinnerstein to Irigaray

In her pioneering *Psychoanalysis and Feminism* (1974), Juliet Mitchell boldly proclaimed: 'The greater part of the feminist movement has identified Freud as the enemy . . . [but] a rejection of psychoanalysis and of Freud's works is fatal for feminism.'[1] Mitchell's foray at this time into the possible convergences between psychoanalysis and feminism signalled an important departure for the resurgent women's movement. For, as the radicalism of the 1960s gave way to the political resignation of the 1970s, and as memories of the 'sexual revolution' of the preceding years faded, it became all too clear that sexism and repressive gender relations were still deeply entrenched in modern societies. According to Mitchell, the women's movement needed to supplement its sociological and economic focus on women's oppression with a specific focus upon sexual ideology, examining the symbolic forms through which patriarchy and gender roles are internalized. For, if our unequal sexual world is replicated through oppressive social practices such as the conditions of mothering, job discrimination, and unequal wages, it is also profoundly shaped by an ambivalent emotional structure involving fear, envy, aggression, and hatred in gender relations. For Mitchell, and indeed for contemporary feminist politics, such emotional and sexual ideologies – ideologies which so powerfully shape gender relations in modern culture – urgently demand practical examination. From this vantage point, the women's movement will be better placed to understand polarized sexual roles and to rethink the possibilities for restructuring gender relations.

The enterprise of psychoanalytic feminism is today more intellectually fertile and robust than ever before. In fact, the encounter between feminism and psychoanalysis has proved to be of crucial importance in transformations of gender power, sexual identities and practices, and the restructuring of emotional intimacy in modern societies. Broadly speaking, the major divisions in psychoanalytic feminism are between Anglo-American object relations theory on the one hand, and French Lacanian and post-Lacanian theory on the other. As refracted through the object relations lens, feminist theorists analyse sexuality and gender against the backdrop of interpersonal relationships – with particular emphasis on the pre-Oedipal child/ mother bond. Poststructuralist feminists indebted to Lacanian psychoanalysis, by contrast, deconstruct gender terms through recourse to the structuring power of the symbolic order, of language as such. In theoretical terms, the differences between these approaches to understanding women's oppression are very great indeed. In practical terms, however, the issues addressed show strong points of convergence. For example, both Anglo-American and French theories examine the forces which affect women's desexualization and their lack of agency in modern culture; the relationship between maternal and paternal power in infant development; the connections between sexuality, the body, and its pleasures; and the recontextualization of psychoanalytic concepts in social and political terms. In this chapter, I shall review these emphases in Anglo-American and French psychoanalytic feminism, concluding with an examination of the current possibilities for greater dialogue between these theoretical standpoints.

Phallic Power: Sexuality and Psychoanalytic Theory

For Freud, as discussed in chapter 1, castration is of key importance in structuring the small infant's representation of sex and gender difference. It is the presence or absence of the phallus, under the sign of the castration complex, which organizes psychical paths of masculinity and femininity. Freud's starting point is that libido is 'masculine'; a proposition which leads him to speculate that 'the little girl is a little man'. Secondly, Freud contends that the Oedipus/ castration complex affects boys and girls differently. In the case of the boy, it is the father's possession of the mother's body, coupled with a fantasy about the little girl's lack, which gives meaning to the threat of castration – a narcissistic wound which dissolves the Oedipus complex. Yet, once negotiated, the boy learns that his possession of a penis can be used to express his own desire. In the case of the girl, castration is imagined as having been already inflicted, as she learns that both herself and mother lack a penis. This experience of 'penis-envy' actually produces Oedipal desire in the small girl, causing her to reject her mother as a love object and turn to her father in the hope of winning the missing phallus. According to Freud, then, both the boy and the girl must undergo a violent separation from the mother's body – and to this extent both are 'castrated'. However, the psychical distinction between the sexes, as Freud describes it, is negative in a more profound sense for the girl than for the boy. Female 'castration' involves the repression of the girl's earlier masculine sexuality.

Given Freud's account of female sexuality in terms of penis-envy, what possible attraction might psychoanalytic theory hold for feminists? For surely to define human sexuality as resting upon a male norm, with the feminine cast as supplementary and derivative, is only to raise phallocentrism to a higher power. For some feminists, this is precisely the ideological effect of psychoanalysis. Freudian theory, according to this view, is used to deny women an active agency and individuality. The discourse of psychoanalysis in modern societies functions itself as repression, reinforcing the patriarchal insistence on heterosexuality by 'adapting' or 'reinscribing' women within oppressive sexual norms. As Mary Daly argues from this standpoint, the word 'therapist' should be read as 'the/rapist'.[2] In this account, then, Freud is the targeted enemy, the patriarchal father of normalizing discourse.

Instead of taking such an anti-psychoanalytic line, however, the great bulk of contemporary feminist theory has acknowledged, and made use of, the (partial) truth of Freud's account of sexuality – however ideologically suspect it may be in certain respects. Here feminists, of divergent theoretical backgrounds, claim the accuracy of Freud's linkage of masculinity with individuation, agency, and desire on the one hand, and of femininity with passivity, lack, and the object of desire on the other. In general, feminists recognize that cultural processes of individuation pose key problems for a feminist transformation of gender power. For Freud's theory of sexual difference, it is argued, shows the profound desexualization to which women must submit in order to take up gender roles of femininity in modern culture. Whether we speak of the desexualized images of motherhood which circulate through the mass media, or even of the Madonna-inspired 'sexy' woman of the 1990s, the essential point remains the same: an object-like status, which at best only allows women a certain pleasure in being desired, is taken as the central attribute of the feminine.

This much of Freud, then, is generally accepted: modern culture enforces a brutal desexualization of female subjectivity – a desexualization which can make women submissive, passive, envious, and often ill. But it is here that we also find the beginnings of a feminist engagement with, and critique of, Freud. Psychoanalytic feminists say that Freud is descriptive, not prescriptive, about gender and sexuality. Feminist theorists stress that the psychic forces which underpin patriarchy are not inevitable; they can be altered and transformed. From this angle, the view that castration is the sign of femininity itself depends on a series of suppressions and displacements of the social and political forces that structure gender difference.

Contemporary psychoanalytic feminists have gone a long way in tracing out how asymmetrical relations of power impact upon sexuality. Through an in-depth political critique of the primacy of the phallus in personal individuation, feminists have powerfully shown that anatomy is not destiny. Perhaps the most significant emphasis here concerns the *political* links between male power and the status of the phallus in psychoanalytic theory. Broadly speaking, attention has focused on the work of culture as regards the father and his phallus, as the necessary third term which disrupts and divides the child/mother relationship. A number of differing factors are linked to the reproduction of gender asymmetries in this respect. Lacanian feminists highlight the links between language and the phallus as the signifier of difference par excellence – a signifier which, since it cannot be captured or contained, is deconstructed as a 'fraud'. Post-Lacanian feminists focus attention on the imaginary domain of the child/mother dyad, tracing the subterranean influence of patriarchal logic upon the emergence of the child's desire. Alternatively, other developments in feminist thought have concentrated less on the role of the father, focusing instead on the impact of mothering in the reproduction of gender asymmetries. This approach, which has led to a number of fruitful feminist interventions and strategies, is generally associated with object relations theory in psychoanalysis – and it is to this that we shall now turn.

Reversing Freud: Object Relations Feminism

The object relations approach in feminist theory accords prime importance to the early mother/child bond; or, to what psychoanalysis terms the pre-Oedipal period. Its starting point is that the pre-Oedipal stage is fundamental to the infant's psychic structure and emerging sense of self. Unlike Freud's theory, in which sexual difference and gender identity are only constituted with the passing of the Oedipus complex, object relations theory posits a core sense of gender identity. Challenging Freud's account of Oedipally organized gender difference, the object relations school of psychoanalysis underscores the infant's primary, erotic connection with the body of the pre-Oedipal mother – a connection which is conceptualized as the central organizing axis for all human social relationships. The role of the father, accordingly, shifts into the background in this theory. It is the pre-Oedipal mother, taken as the first object of desire, which structures and cements the child's basic sense of selfhood and gender. Love and desire are born through an erotic union with mother; a primary love that exerts a profound influence throughout life.

This re-evaluation of the role of the pre-Oedipal mother in infant development, however, cannot be given a wholly positive gloss. For if the child begins life under the sign of maternal devotion, lived as an erotic union with the body of another, this connection also leads to feelings of intense helplessness and fear. The paradox of desire is that the infant loves the mother, but hates her as well. Such hatred fuels a range of terrifying anxieties over the power, seduction, and engulfment of the pre-Oedipal mother. Accordingly, the infant experiences intense ambivalence concerning the pre-Oedipal mother – an ambivalence that swings between states of idealized love and denigrating hate. And it is precisely from this focus upon pre-Oedipal ambivalence that feminists drawing on object relations theory attempt to trace dominant social constructions of women in modern culture.

The view that our earliest experiences of an omnipotent mother lead to a general fear and loathing of anything female is given powerful expression in the work of the American cultural theorist, Dorothy Dinnerstein. In *The Mermaid and the Minotaur* (1976), Dinnerstein examines the psychic effects of societal nuturing arrangements. Her claim is that, given exclusive female mothering in late-capitalist societies, children of both sexes encounter a social context that violently deforms gender and, especially, female subjectivity. Female mothering, Dinnerstein says, leads us inevitably to fear women. Both sexes are said to fear the power that mother wields over them as infants, a fear which leads children to betray the 'engulfing mother' by turning to the father in search of emotional security. The paternal authority offered by father offers an escape route from the primary ambivalence – involving infantile helplessness, rage, and hate – felt towards the mother. As Dinnerstein puts this: 'It is as we leave infancy that the possibility of transferring dependent, submissive feeling to the second parent – whose different gender carries the promise of a new deal, a clean sweep – entices us into the trap of male dominion.'³ In other words, patriarchy is the outcome of a denial of emotional ambivalence: unconscious pain is denied with respect to maternal authority, coupled with an idealization of paternal authority and power. Yet the psychic costs of this denial are severe. Men and women remain haunted by the memory of maternal dominance. For, although infantile helplessness may have been repudiated, the return of the repressed continually threatens to outstrip masculinist culture. Significantly this situation, says Dinnerstein, is worse for women. Associated with the power of mothering, women are displaced to self-mutilation within the contemporary gender system.

In a subsequent work *The Rocking of the Cradle* (1978), Dinnerstein expands on her account of the psychical dynamics of the child/mother relationship, situating her analysis within a Kleinian framework. Dinnerstein contends that socially predominant ideologies of gender and sexuality are marked by a failure to work through persecutory and depressive anxieties about women, and especially women's identification as mothers. Instead of developing a realistic sense of mother as an independent agent, personal and cultural fantasies proliferate of women as all-powerful and thus as objects of fear. In this context, Dinnerstein locates some of the most pathological features of contemporary culture: man's need to control and humiliate women, woman's collaboration in denigrating her own sex, the domination of nature, sexual violence, the cultural denial of human fragility and death, and so on. The way forward to a transformation of gender, says Dinnerstein, is through shared parenting. 'So long as the first parent is a woman,' writes Dinnerstein, 'women will inevitably be pressed into the dual role of indispensable quasi-human supporter and deadly quasi-human enemy of the self.'

Dinnerstein's work offered one of the first psychoanalytic challenges to mainstream feminist accounts of gender relations. Society, for Dinnerstein, is not something external, which then 'goes to work' on people by imprinting gender power. It is, rather, a force which penetrates to the deepest roots of personal and sexual experience, engendering anti-female feelings in the very act of constituting the self. As such, her work raises important issues about the connections between sexuality, power, and culture. Significant as it is, though, Dinnerstein's critique of gender is severely limited by several major flaws. She assumes, for example, that the avoidance of psychic pain in early life connects with the devaluation of women in a universal, mechanistic way. What this overlooks, however, is that motherhood itself is situated in a social, political, and economic context – a *patriarchal* context which deforms the social organization of parenting. In other words, what Dinnerstein's model cannot adequately accommodate is the impact of ideology – those forms through which social power structures the feelings, thoughts, and representations of everyday social life. This is a serious omission, and it is one which causes Dinnerstein to ignore the point that men, as well as women, are also idealized, envied, feared, and hated. Moreover, Dinnerstein's account of the contemporary gender system runs into a kind of theoretical brick wall since it cannot comprehend resistances, changes, or transformations in gender power. Women and men are simply deemed dependant on patriarchy as a way of side-stepping their neurotic, paranoid reactions to motherhood, child-rearing and nature.

A theory of gender that does discriminate between the lived experience of males and females can be found in the approach taken by the American psychoanalytic feminist Nancy Chodorow. Chodorow, like Dinnerstein, is interested in the political ramifications of exclusive female mothering. She employs psychoanalytic theory for analysing the reproduction of gender asymmetries in modern societies and for tracing paths to social change. Yet, unlike Dinnerstein, Chodorow argues that a mother's love is profoundly different for sons and daughters – a difference that leads to socially structured psychological processes of gender power.

In her pioneering book *The Reproduction of Mothering* (1978), Chodorow argues that mothers experience their daughters as doubles of themselves, through a narcissistic projection of sameness. Chodorow calls this pre-Oedipal bond between mother and daughter a *narcissistic object-attachment*; which means that the mother relates to her daughter as simply an extension of her own life, and not as an independent person. As Chodorow puts this:

> A mother is likely to experience a sense of oneness and continuity with her infant. However, this sense is stronger, and lasts longer, vis-a-vis daughters. Primary identification and symbiosis with daughters tend to be stronger and cathexis of daughters is more likely to remain and emphasize narcissistic elements, that is, to be based on experiencing a daughter as an extension or double of a mother herself, with cathexis of the daughter as a sexual other usually remaining a weaker, less significant theme.[4]

From this pre-Oedipal merging of self and (m)Other, daughters develop a strong capacity for empathy, sensitivity, and intimacy with other people. Yet, because daughters are perceived as the self-same as mother, differentiation is rendered problematic. The female child, in brief, finds it painfully difficult to disengage from the mother's love. Locked within maternal narcissism, the daughter is, in effect, psychically prevented from establishing a sense of independence and individuality. From this perspective, Chodorow reinterprets 'penis-envy', not as biologically pre-given, but as a sign of the daughter's desire for autonomy. The daughter turns to her father, through an awareness of the social privilege that the phallus symbolizes, in the hope of achieving a sense of independence from the mother. Yet, because fathers are emotionally distant and absent (for reasons which we will soon examine), daughters are unable to break with the power and authority of the pre-Oedipal mother.

Accordingly, the sensitivity and concern which is taken as the hallmark of feminine identity – so Chodorow contends – is a direct outcrop of this early pre-Oedipal mother/daughter bond. Daughters grow up with a deep emotional sense of continuity with their mother, a continuity which provides the basis for a strong relational connection in women's adult life. However, this relational component of feminine identity is achieved only at a severe personal cost. Since mothers do not perceive daughters as separate Others, girls remain without any real affirmation of their own sense of self and agency. This results in a confusion of ego boundaries, coupled with a wider estrangement from personal needs, aspirations, and desires. Feelings of inadequate separateness, lack of self-control, and a fear of merging with others thus arise as prime emotional problems for women. Related to this is women's identification with a socially devalued gender category. For Chodorow, women's 'core gender identity' (weak ego boundaries, immersion in narcissism, etc.) comes to mirror their culturally devalued social position. One common way out of these difficulties for women, says Chodorow, is through a defensively constructed set of personal boundaries: denying what is needed within, focusing on what is needed by others – particularly the needs of men.

In similar fashion, Chodorow argues that a distinctly masculine form of personality structure, or core gender identity, exists in modern societies. Reversing Freud through the object relations lens, Chodorow argues that masculine identity is forged against the backdrop of a primary identification with mother, that is, a primary femaleness. This primary love for the mother, says Chodorow, makes the achievement of maleness much more difficult than was originally presumed by Freud. For what boys must at all costs repudiate, if they are to establish successfully a masculine sense of selfhood, is the love and emotional intimacy shared with the mother. Boys must deny their primary bond to female eroticism, repressing their own femininity permanently into the unconscious. The originating cue for this repression, somewhat paradoxically, comes from the mother herself. For it is clear to Chodorow that boys are assisted in the developmental task of making their maleness through the mother's perception of gender difference. From the start of life, Chodorow says, mothers propel their sons towards differentiation and autonomy, prizing assertiveness in interpersonal relations. Chodorow calls this pre-Oedipal mother/son bond an *anaclitic object-attachment*; which means that mothers relate to their sons as different and other from themselves. Mothers thus lead their sons to disengage emotionally from care and intimacy. This prepares boys for an instrumental, abstract attitude towards the world – an attitude which will be expected of them in the extra-familial spheres of work, and public and political life.

The gendered self for Chodorow is therefore constructed relationally. Like Dinnerstein, Chodorow argues that sons and daughters seek to escape from the engulfing pre-Oedipal mother by turning to paternal authority. Yet, unlike Dinnerstein, Chodorow claims that the feelings of powerlessness which lead to an emotional break with mother are handled differently by the sexes. Sons are better placed to establish boundaries, separation, and autonomy because they are recognized by the mother as sexually Other. Daughters, by contrast, develop their emotional life around relationships, nurturance, and care since they are caught in a narcissistic identification with the mother. Significantly, one consequence of this re-evaluation of the role of the pre-Oedipal mother is that the function of the father in psychic differentiation diminishes. Although fathers come to be idealized as representatives of the outside world, they have only a shadowy emotional existence for sons and daughters, even after the passing of the Oedipus complex. In this account, then, paternal authority is viewed as a uniform, repressive 'last-ditch escape from maternal omnipotence'.[5]

What this account of gender relations suggests, then, is that exclusive female mothering produces an ideology of male domination. The absence of any primary attachment to males in pre-Oedipal childhood leads to an idealization of men and a devaluation of women. The only way out of this self-reproducing gender system,

Chodorow argues, is through shared parenting. The inclusion of men in early parenting activities should lead to a breakup of established gender polarity. Both parents would be available to establish a caring, nurturing connection with their children. In this context, children of both sexes would be able to forge emotional intimacy and autonomy through a primary relatedness to mother and father. As Chodorow theorizes this gender transformation:

> Masculinity would not become tied to denial of dependence and devaluation of women. Feminine personality would be less preoccupied with individuation, and children would not develop fears of maternal omnipotence and expectations of women's unique self-sacrificing qualities. This would reduce men's needs to guard their masculinity and their control of social and cultural spheres which treat and define women as secondary and powerless, and would help women to develop the autonomy which too much embeddedness in relationships has often taken from them. (p. 218)

Let me sum up the main threads of Chodorow's theory. Exclusive female mothering is posited as central to the reproduction of gender asymmetries in modern societies. It produces social relations split between connected, empathic female identities on the one hand, and isolated, instrumental male identities on the other. Masculine identity is built on a denial of primary maternal identification resulting in a fragile sense of self, defensively structured by an abstract attitude to the world. Feminine identity is grounded in a strong sense of gender, but is limited in capacity for autonomy and individuality. The only viable route out of contemporary gender aysmmetries, says Chodorow, is through shared parenting.

Chodorow's work presents a powerful and compelling account of those psychosocial forces that distort gender relations. Her theoretical model has exercised enormous influence in feminism, sociology, cultural theory, and psychoanalytic studies.[6] Her claim that there is a basic and stable gender identity for males and females in modern societies has proved attractive to many wishing to understand the persistence of patriarchal domination. In this respect, Chodorow's claims about female psychology are illuminating. Of key importance here is Chodorow's assertion that women want to have children in order to recapture the primary bond of the mother/daughter relationship. The reasoning here is clear. Women's lives are emotionally drained and empty because men are cut off from sexual intimacy and communication. From this angle, the desire to have a child is actually

rooted in the distortions of the current gender system. Conversely
the abstract traits of male selfhood described by Chodorow provide
a direct purchase on the anxieties that many men experience in
relation to intimacy, care, and love. Masculinity, says Chodorow,
necessarily involves the adoption of intolerance, insensitivity, and
emotional coerciveness. From this angle, male sexual dominance
often involving the use of violence towards women, has its roots in
the damaged, fragile, and precarious nature of masculine identity.

Nevertheless, Chodorow's theory has its limitations. To begin
with, there is something too neat and comfortable about Chodorow's
claim that exclusive female mothering produces asymmetric gender
roles. Chodorow presents us with a model of woman as mother, as
primary caretaker, with maternal desire being fixed into narcissistic
or anaclitic modes of identification. Yet is the institution of mothering
really so strongly delimited to these psychic categories? What of
mothers who encourage 'feminine' modes of expression in their sons?
What of mothers who foster 'masculine' aims of autonomy, independence, and achievement in their daughters? What of the increasing
phenomenon of single-parent, mother-led families? The difficulty
here is that Chodorow ignores the vast complexities of family life in
modern societies, and privileges instead a traditionalist style of
mothering which is rapidly in decline today. As Lynne Segal notes: 'I
have found everywhere evidence of the amazing diversity buried
within the ideology of the familial: fathers who were present and
caring, "working" mothers who were strong and powerful within the
home, daughters who bonded tightly with fathers or older brothers,
mothers who could not love their sons, mothers who never accepted
their daughters, mothers who identified with their sons, and so on.'
The reason that such emotional diversity in the parent/child bond
remains missing from Chodorow's work stems from her overconcen-
tration on maternal desire – that is, on how the mother relates to her
child. This focus, when used in isolation from psychoanalysis, has
the effect of viewing the emerging infant as a mere cipher in the
construction of selfhood and gender. Yet it seems more likely, and
certainly more in line with psychoanalytic theory, that identity-
construction itself arises through the internal world of the infant –
the representations, drives, and passions of the emerging gendered
self.

Following directly from this, Chodorow's use of object relations
theory seems to me to involve several misunderstandings of psychoanalysis. Her concept of 'core gender identity', for example, returns
us to a *pre*-Freudian view of subjectivity; one which altogether

brackets the psychoanalytic discovery of the pre-Oedipal bisexual self and instead affirms the consoling unity of personal identity. Consequently, instead of exploring the problematic construction of sexual difference and gender, Chodorow can only describe how culturally dominant sex-roles become interwoven with core masculine and feminine identities. Her whole model, in other words, is a functionalist version of how sexual identities are generated to mirror gender power in patriarchal modern class-society. Thus, as Jacqueline Rose comments, Chodorow's psychoanalytic feminism fails to get beyond a basic sociological notion of 'gender imprinting'.[8] Related to this is the criticism that, in diverting attention from the split and conflict-ridden 'subject' of psychoanalytic discourse, Chodorow collapses the dynamic interplay between psychic and social phenomena. Lost are the vital psychoanalytic concepts of unconscious desire, anxiety, trauma, condensation, and displacement – all of which suggest that gender roles are, at best, only arbitrary and provisional categories. Significantly, this erases the complex, contradictory unconscious realm of sexuality, a realm which is so central to an individual subject's relation to society. Instead, sexual difference is replaced by an unproblematic version of sanitized sex-roles.

Finally, there are substantive problems with the emancipatory claims of this theory. Chodorow argues that, under shared parenting, men would develop the kind of relational qualities that women possess, while women would be free to develop a better sense of social autonomy. Yet if one considers the terms of Chodorow's analysis – that gender-identity is powerfully shaped in negative and polarizing forms – it is not at all clear how women and men might liberate themselves from the destructive gender identities that currently preoccupy them. Is Chodorow, then, simply too optimistic about shared parenting? From a feminist angle, the answer must be yes. Chodorow offers no convincing psychoanalytic reasons as to why shared parenting would eradicate male domination or transform gender power. Neither does she consider that her account of gender transformation fits neatly with dominant cultural fantasies which idealize fathers as figures of separation and agency, while devaluing mothers as models for gender autonomy. The problem, then, is not that increased male participation in child-rearing fails to bring greater intimacy into the parent/child relationship – clearly, it often does. Rather, the difficulty is that there is no reason to suppose that shared parenting, of itself, will alter the power relations between men and women. Chodorow's theory, in other words, fails to consider the structural, symbolic forms of gender hierarchy that so powerfully shape sexuality in modern societies. Instead, her account (at both the descriptive and prescriptive levels) reduces the social to familial ideology – thus screening from view the wider social, cultural, and political forces constitutive of patriarchy.

Feminist Issues in Contemporary Object Relations Theory

Object relations theory of the Chodorow and Dinnerstein kind is thus unable to grapple with the structural determinants which underpin asymmetric gender relations. In both writers' analyses, it is the consequences of exclusive female mothering that is examined, not the symbolic forms which set the institution of mothering within the patriarchal structure of the current gender system. Recent approaches in object relations feminism, however, do focus on the symbolic forms of gender-constitution, and, unlike Chodorow, have not concentrated exclusively on maternal behaviour. Indeed, attention has turned to the psychic world of the developing infant, as related to the structural positioning of mother, father, and the ideological complexities of contemporary gender relations. Though there are many theorists that might have been examined, I have chosen in what follows to concentrate briefly on the conceptual departures of Jessica Benjamin, Madelon Sprengnether, and Jane Flax.

A critical theory of gender, argues Jessica Benjamin in *The Bonds of Love* (1988), should focus on women's desexualization and lack of agency within the wider social context of power relations between men and women. Like Chodorow, Benjamin sees the contemporary gender system as locating the mother at the pole of regressive biological absorption on the one hand, and the father at the pole of progressive agency and authentic subjectivity on the other. Yet, unlike Chodorow, Benjamin refuses to view the psychic world of the developing child as simply mirroring gender asymmetry. On the contrary, Benjamin contends that it is necessary to tackle head-on 'the problem of desire': that is, the identifications and cross-identifications through which the infant establishes basic differences between itself and other people. To do this, Benjamin develops the concept of 'identificatory love', which is a pre-Oedipal phase of rapprochement in which the child seeks to establish a sense of attachment *and* separation with its parental figures. Emotional continuity is central here. With the dawning of love through identification, the small child is able to separate out a sense of self while remaining emotionally connected to others.

However, if one examines the roles of the sexes in modern culture – so Benjamin contends – it becomes clear that pre-Oedipal identificatory love is continually denied and displaced. Children of both sexes cannot maintain their identificatory love for the mother since she is devalued and rendered regressive by current sexual ideology. This leads Benjamin to adopt a similar position to Chodorow. The core of her argument is that, while boys can identify with the father and his phallus to separate from the mother and establish autonomous individuality, the same path to psychic individuation is denied to girls. An alternate, empathic relationship with the exciting father, says Benjamin, is usually refused, the result being women's 'lack' of desire and its return as masochism in idealizations of male power. For Benjamin, what this means is that the tension between dependence and independence, which underpins healthy emotional relationships, breaks down within culture at large. Moreover, sexual relations between men and women grow diseased and deformed into master/slave patterns.

What of the possibilities for change? Benjamin differs sharply from both Chodorow and Dinnerstein in her evaluation of gender transformation. Paternal identification, Benjamin says, can certainly play a progressive role in the achievement of autonomous female subjectivity. Yet, according to Benjamin, any identification with the father is likely to prove counterproductive as long as the cultural devaluation of women remains in place. In this context, an alteration of parenting arrangements – as proposed by Chodorow and Dinnerstein – is itself an insufficient basis to transform gender structures. Non-repressive gender relations, Benjamin argues, depends rather on replacing the cultural split of progressive, autonomous father against regressive mother with new sexual identifications – identifications that permit a less rigid set of sexual roles. This would involve the repudiation of defensive modes of separation – that is, the father's phallus would no longer be used as the dominant medium to beat back an engulfing mother. Instead, children might construct more fluid sexual identifications – expressing both masculine and feminine aspects of identity – in relation to a socially and sexually autonomous mother, and a more empathic, caring father. Two figures of love and idealization – mother and father – are thus located as necessary for the creation of non-patriarchal patterns of socialization.

Pursuing these themes, Madelon Sprengnether in *The Spectral Mother* (1990) contends that psychoanalysis has itself devalued female subjectivity. The phallocentrism of psychoanalysis, according to Sprengnether, is evident in Freud's own ambivalence towards the mother – an ambivalence that at once makes the mother the centrepoint of emotional experience and yet reduces her to a mere 'object' of desire. This romanticization of maternity, Sprengnether says, is reinforced throughout post-Freudian psychoanalysis, from postulations of 'good-enough mothering' in object relations theory to the rich maternal splendour of the Lacanian imaginary order. For Sprengnether, as for Benjamin, assumptions which negate the complexity of women's subjectivity must be rejected and overturned. In this connection, the question for psychoanalytic feminism becomes how to reconceive of the mother in a manner that does not result in the exclusion of the feminine from society and culture. The answer Sprengnether offers is that the 'body of the mother' – in light of the multiple trajectories of her desire – represents an alternative paradigm for the constitution of an elementary form of selfhood. Taking aim at the patriarchal, theoretical gestures of Oedipus and the holy phallus, Sprengnether contends that the mother's body is fluid and plural, a foundation for the emergence of difference and estrangement, the site of an originary, non-violent separation between self and other. The maternal body is thus opposed to the fixed boundaries of Oedipal significations, and functions as a creative source in the replay of non-identity. Ultimately, Sprengnether contends, the maternal body is a locus of otherness and familiarity, difference and identity. Since all human beings enter the world through the body of a woman, maternal subjectivity is a presence that is always coloured by absence. As Sprengnether puts this: 'Rather than fleeing, condemning, or idealizing the body of the (m)other, we need to recognize her in ourselves.'[9]

This raises the vexed question, much debated in feminist theory, as to whether the lifting of repression can be directly connected to the achievement of gender justice. This is an issue which has been taken up in recent times by the American psychoanalytic feminist Jane Flax who argues that the object relational goals of interpersonal communication and dialogue are of central importance to gender transformation.[10] Flax criticizes the tendency in feminist politics to generalize gender roles – as in the commonplace view that women are in touch with their feelings, whereas men repudiate their capacity for intimacy. According to Flax, it is important to recognize that there are different modes of gender-constitution, and that each mode is harnessed to power interests in different ways. In the plural sexual domains of postmodern culture, says Flax, gender is continually dislocated and dispersed. Difficulties with sexuality, love, and intimacy are as common to women as they are to men. In this context,

Flax underscores the object relational focus on emotional communication as essential to interpersonal equality and democracy. Recovering emotional communication with the self and with others is crucial to revaluing the domain of gender. The development of autonomy and respect between the sexes, informed by emotional links of self and other stretching back to the pre-Oedipal stage, is the basis for an open-ended restructuring of gender. What is being stressed here is the capacity of both sexes to re-eroticize interpersonal relations. It is not a question of which of the sexes is better placed to undertake the emotional work of gender struggle. Rather, the human capacity for emotional connection must be made to turn back upon itself, opening sexuality and gender to a more reflexive involvement with the social structures of modern culture.

At this point, we can summarize the key issues raised in object relations feminism in the following terms:

1   Psychical organization is constituted in relationship with the pre-Oedipal mother; a relation which forms internalized object relational patterns which are essential to selfhood and gender identity.

2   Contemporary sexual divisions, especially exclusive female mothering, is pivotal to analysing the reproduction of male-dominant gender relations.

3   The familial structure of modern societies produces male identities with isolated, instrumental relations to the world, and female identities with empathic, caring connections to others and to the social world.

4   Sexual divisions, as currently constituted, fuse to reproduce asymmetrical gender relations of power; relations which are directly bound up with technical frameworks involving economic, social, and political institutions.

5   Gender transformation presumes a recovery of the feminine and female sexuality, rooted in reflexively negotiated relations of care, respect, and emotional communication between the sexes.

Lacanian Feminism

In recent years within psychoanalytic feminism, attention has turned to Lacanian theory in order to advance political debate on subjectivity and sexuality. Feminists who defend and/or recontextualize Lacanian psychoanalysis stress the role of symbolic forms in the structuring of desire – even that primary bond between child and mother, a bond so dear to object relations theorists. For, in contrast to object relations feminism, Lacanians argue that there can be no experience of sexuality and gender which is not generated through the symbolic order of modern culture. To hold otherwise – Lacanians contend – is to read back into the pre-Oedipal stage sexual distinctions which do not arise until after the symbolic law of the Oedipus complex impacts upon the child. In Lacanian feminism, subjectivity and sexuality are by definition tied to language and culture. The symbolic, language, the Law of the Father, the phallus as transcendental signifier: these are, in Lacanian feminism, the mechanisms through which asymmetrical power relations between men and women are reproduced.

In order to understand Lacanian claims about our current gender system, it is necessary to situate Lacan's doctrine in relation to older psychoanalytic debates on female sexuality. Very broadly speaking, these debates revolve around the following, opposing claims: those that rely on traditional Freudian theory, and assert that sexuality is constituted through the effects of 'castration'; and those that derive their theoretical base from post-Freudian clinical work, focusing on the pre-Oedipal development of sexuality and gender.

Let us recall some pertinent features of the traditional Freudian view of sexual difference, previously discussed in chapter 1. Bisexuality, says Freud, is at the bedrock of psychic organization for both sexes. The very persistence of unconscious, infantile sexuality in human development (that is, variability in sexual aim and the contingency of object-choice) means that identity and gender are precarious constructs. Freud's point here is that the unconscious dimensions of sexuality continually undercut any consistent form of identity. Sexual identity, rather, involves repression, and as such is partial and fragmentary in character. But how is sexual identity constituted? For Freud, sexual subjectivity is organized phallically. The psychical distinction between the sexes takes place in a social context which gives it its meaning. That context is patriarchy – the paternal institution of sexual prohibition in the Oedipus complex. This complex initiates sexual division, a division in relation to language, power, social processes, and institutions. Moreover this division, as we have seen, places man on the inside of power, and excludes woman.

By contrast, many psychoanalytic theorists have expressed dissatisfaction with Freud's sexual monism, and have endeavoured to introduce greater complementarity into the psychoanalytic understanding of sexual development. In this connection, the view that femininity arises from a failed sense of masculinity has been firmly rejected by many post-Freudian theorists. Instead, a core sense of gender identity is presupposed for both sexes from the beginning of life. Much more weight is accorded to the infant's developing awareness and experience of gender, which in turn becomes the primary determinant of sexual difference. (As we have seen, the work of Dinnerstein, Chodorow, and others in the object relations school presuppose such a pre-Oedipal gendered subject.) Accordingly, there is a shift in focus here away from the father and Oedipus towards the mother and pre-Oedipal relations.

Casting a careful eye over the complexities of these positions, Lacan's innovation is to develop a language-centred re-reading of Freud's Oedipus complex – the crucial moment of psychic individuation – while incorporating elements of post-Freudian revisionism. What Lacan does, in effect, is to redescribe the primary mother/infant bond as the realm of imaginary desire, while simultaneously shifting gears to the structuring of Oedipal desire, described at the level of the symbolic order. The key term in Lacan's work which explains this division between imaginary unity and symbolic differentiation is the phallus. For Lacan, as for Freud, the phallus is the marker of sexual difference par excellence. The phallus smashes the incestuous unity of the mother/infant relation, and thereby constitutes the identity of a subject. The fundamental difference between Freud and Lacan, however, is that the latter claims to disconnect the phallus from any linkage with the biological penis. The phallus, says Lacan, is illusory, fictitious and imaginary. It exists less in the sense of biology than in a kind of fantasy realm which merges desire with power, omnipotence, and wholeness.

But what role, exactly, does the phallus play in psychic individuation? According to Lacan, the desire of the child – of either sex – is to *be* the exclusive desire of the mother, grounded in an erotic mode of imaginary plenitude. The child, however, soon learns that the mother herself is lacking. The child becomes aware that the mother's desire is invested elsewhere: in the father and his phallus. Significantly, the child's discovery that the mother is lacking occurs at the same time that it is discovering itself in language and culture, as a separate subject. This situation arises, says Lacan, with the entry of a third person (the father) or term (language). It is the symbolic function of the father, as possesser of the phallus, to prohibit Oedipal desire – a prohibition which at one stroke constitutes the repressed unconscious. Lacan himself argues that *both* sexes enter the symbolic order of language as castrated. The moment of separation from imaginary plenitude is experienced as loss, the loss of connection with the imaginary, archaic mother. The pain of this loss *is* castration. The child imagines the phallus as the source of the mother's desire, and from this perspective both males and females come to be lacking – a condition from which children are projected into language and symbolization.

However, though lack cuts across gender, Lacan says that to enter the symbolic is to enter the realm of the masculine. That is, while both male and female children are castrated (the pain that neither can be everything for the mother), the phallus in modern culture comes to be identified with the penis and with male power. Gender identity is thus formed through a privileging of the visible, of having or not having the phallus. Males are able to assume phallic privilege since the image of the penis comes to stand for sexual difference. As Lacan puts this: 'It can be said that the [phallic] signifier is chosen because it is the most tangible element in the role of sexual copulation . . . it is the image of the vital flow as it is transmitted in generation.'[11] What is involved here is the constitution of masculinity as phallic and femininity as non-phallic. Masculinity is constructed around the sign of the phallus, a sign which confers power in most contexts of modern societies. By contrast, femininity is constructed through exclusion from the symbolic realm of power. Femininity is on the outside of language, culture, reason, and power. 'There is no woman,' says Lacan, 'but excluded from the value of words.'[12] Lacan's interpretation of sexuality and gender thus underwrites current stereotypes – male sexuality as active and striving, female sexuality as essentially passive. Of course, it should be noted that this account is consistent with the reality of gender hierarchy in patriarchy. For women have been excluded, brutally and violently, from masculinist culture and discourse. Yet Lacan's description of how one is constructed as a masculine or a feminine subject seeks also to destabilize dominant images of sexuality. Beyond his bleak Oedipal reinforcement of the rule of the phallus, Lacan's self-appointed task is to unmask the 'fraud' of sexual identity. Desire lurks beneath the very signifiers which inform sexuality and gender. According to Lacan, though sexuality is articulated around the phallus, human subjects remain fundamentally split at the core. Gender fixity is thus always open to displacement. Woman as the excluded Other is certainly consistent with the gender structure of modern societies; but it is this absence of the feminine which also threatens to outstrip the very foundations of sexual division.

The implications of the preceding discussion are clear. For Lacan, the phallocentric organization of sexual subjectivity cannot be divorced from the discontinuous nature of unconscious desire. It is within the terms of sexual difference, the symbolic, and the Law of castration that subject positions of masculinity and femininity are lived. Yet such gender organization is in turn always outstripped by the conflictual, fragmentary realm of the unconscious. Sexual subjectivity and loss are inextricably linked for Lacan, and the phallus just *is* that transcendental signifier which represses or covers over the missing object of desire at the level of gender division. Exactly why this loss of imaginary plenitude, and the subsequent impinging of symbolic reality, must be organized in such a one-sided masculine fashion is not something that unduly concerns the phallocentric Lacan – and this is a point which has been taken up by many feminist critics of Lacanian theory. Nevertheless, Lacan's language-centred account of the function of the phallus is important since it demonstrates that sexual difference is not a mere reflex of anatomy. It is, rather, constituted and reproduced through the fantasy effects of the symbolic order.

Lacan's theory was taken up enthusiastically by the feminist critic Juliet Mitchell in her *Psychoanalysis and Feminism* (1974) – a widely read book in which the author employs Freudian and Lacanian psychoanalysis as a means of fusing a discussion of gender power with an Althusserian-Marxist account of modern societies. In her view, Lacan's analysis of the phallic organization of sexuality and language deconstructs gender hierarchy in a way that feminists cannot afford to ignore. It provides an account of sexual difference, not according to some pre-given essence, but according to the phallocentric structure of modern culture. 'If psychoanalysis is phallocentric,' Mitchell writes, 'it is because the human social order that it perceives refracted through the individual human subject is patrocentric. To date, the father stands in the position of the third term that must break the asocial dyadic unit of mother and child.'[13] Thus accepting the Lacanian appeal to the androcentric nature of the symbolic order, Mitchell argues that definitions of masculinity and femininity are constituted through the symbolic – with man as a self-determining, autonomous agent, and woman as the lacking Other, the cause of sexual desire. The political implications of these culturally operative fantasies – so Mitchell argues – are that man imagines himself as a unified entity, and projects his sense of lack and otherness onto woman, which in turn makes the feminine at once unknowable and yet the guarantor of fantasy. Such gender definitions, though illusory, are highly conducive to late capitalism: to the distorting, idealization of family life, the split between the private and public realms, and so on.

As I have argued elsewhere, however, employing the Lacanian concept of the symbolic order to deconstruct gender inequality is misguided.[14] Mitchell's work, as noted, examines how the inscription of gender power in language can be traced to socio-symbolic reproduction. The patriarchal symbolic, for Mitchell, constructs distorted and polarized sexualities, which in turn leads to the reproduction of gender asymmetry. However, apart from preaching the obvious (that is, that gender power is reproduced), Mitchell's analysis mistakenly assumes that the cultural structuration of gender is a stable affair. But what of conflictual sexual ideologies in late modernity? What of the flexibility and fluidity of modern sexuality, in which gender difference is traversed by new heterosexual, gay, and lesbian sexual identities? It is, of course, true that all this takes place within the parameters of a male-dominant socio-symbolic order. Yet these different modes of sexuality highlight the gross limitations of a socio-symbolic reductionist approach to issues of gender power. Such difficulties have their roots in broader theoretical impasses. In Mitchell's reading of Lacan, the symbolic is all-enveloping, constituting polarized gender identities in a singular and oppressive fashion. Yet, in this privileging of the Lacanian symbolic, Mitchell disregards the turbulent and precarious terrain of unconscious sexuality and passion. She ignores the ways in which unconscious, imaginary sexualities often disrupt repressive gender categories, and fails to trace out the interweaving of the imaginary with symbolic forms. Instead, the issue of gender construction is inserted into a conceptual straitjacket.

Not all Lacanian feminists take the symbolic order as a description of the constitution and fixity of gender identity. Jacqueline Rose, who worked with Mitchell in developing a feminist reading of Lacan, contends that psychoanalysis explores the failure of sexual identity as much as its consolidation. As Rose puts this: 'If psychoanalysis can give an account of how women experience the path to femininity, it also insists, through the concept of the unconscious, that femininity is neither simply achieved nor is it ever complete.'[15] What might it mean to say that feminine identity, in some sense, fails? Since woman is consituted through the symbolic order on the side of lack, says Rose, femininity constantly escapes language and cultural categorization. Put simply, women do not slip into feminine roles easily or painlessly. The 'feminine' in modern culture is associated with denial and repression. But it is also associated with resistance, in both the personal and institutional spheres. For example, the refusal to adopt feminine subject positions of passivity is exemplified by hysterics – a resistance to received social meanings in patriarchy. Thus, as lack, as absence, as what is repressed within the male-dominated symbolic, the feminine position is always outside (and possibly beyond) the regulation of the phallic economy. Here Rose takes her cue from Lacan's late work on female sexuality. In his Seminar 'Encore' in 1972–3, Lacan articulates the concept of *jouissance*, a mysterious state of sexual joy, an erotic satisfaction which dissolves the boundaries of self and Other. According to Lacan, women hold a special relationship to *jouissance*, a condition which is not contaminated by patriarchal discourse. In Rose's Lacanian gloss: 'woman is implicated, of necessity, in phallic sexuality, but at the same time it is "elsewhere that she upholds the question of her own *jouissance*" . . . Lacan designates this jouissance supplementary so as to avoid any notion of complement, of woman as a complement to man's phallic nature (which is precisely the fantasy). But it is also a recognition of the "something more", the "more than *jouissance*" . . . Woman is, therefore, placed *beyond* (beyond the phallus).'[16] In brief, women's *jouissance* threatens the disruption of desire to the phallic organization of language and culture, even though little can be said directly of this libidinal condition which remains excluded from symbolic representation.

The work of Rose represents an evocative blending of Lacanian theory and feminist politics, a politics that casts feminine identity as a problem of desire itself. It is not, however, without its difficulties. To begin with, what might a transfiguration in *jouissance* actually look like, outside individuals posturing a certain libidinal pleasure or enjoyment? And what of a critical interrogation of the feminine? Does this simply consist of a potential disruption to the socio-symbolic order, or might it involve a transformation of gender power itself? The problem here, in other words, is that if *jouissance* cannot articulate itself at the level of the symbolic, it is difficult to understand how significant changes in gender relations may come about. Yet it is precisely this issue of the specificity of female sexual subjectivity that will be taken up by post-Lacanian feminists, a feminism which leads to quite a different style of thought about sexuality and culture.

Feminism Beyond Lacan

In recent years, there have been numerous significant attempts to articulate an alternative vision of female sexual subjectivity in French feminism. This approach to revaluing femininity is generally referred to as post-Lacanian feminism, and it has a number of different theoretical manifestations. This branch of feminist psychoanalysis is 'Lacanian' because it adopts a broadly structural interpretation of masculine and feminine gender categories, viewing woman as the excluded Other of masculine discourse and culture. But it is also 'anti-Lacanian' since it opposes the view that woman can only be defined as the mirror opposite of the masculine subject, and thus can never escape the domination of a rigidly genderized discourse. Instead, post-Lacanian feminists evoke a postive image of femininity, an image that underscores the multiple and plural nature of women's sexuality.

One of the most influential sources for this kind of feminism is the work of the psychoanalyst Julia Kristeva. Kristeva's work blends together Lacanian psychoanalysis, structural linguistics, and European philosophy to produce a suggestive account of the relations between unconscious desire, feminine sexuality, and modern social processes. In *Revolution in Poetic Language* (1984), Kristeva contrasts the Lacanian symbolic, the social and sexual system of the Law of the Father, with those multiple libidinal forces which she terms the 'semiotic'. The semiotic is a realm of prolinguistic experience – including bodily drives, feelings, and rhythms experienced by the child in its pre-Oedipal relationship to the mother. For Kristeva, these pre-Oedipal pleasures undergo repression through entry to the social and cultural processes of the symbolic order. That is, the unorganized flux of semiotic experience is channelled into the relatively stable domain of symbolization and language. However, Kristeva contends that the repression of the semiotic is by no means complete; semiotic forms remain present in the unconscious and cannot be shut off from culture. According to Kristeva, our semiotic longing for the pre-Oedipal mother is part and parcel of selfhood, making itself felt through material pressures such as tonal rhythms, slips, and silences in everyday talk. These semiotic pressures, she insists, are subversive of the symbolic Law of the Father since they are rooted in a pre-patriarchal connection with the mother's body. Hence, the disruptive and subversive potential of the semiotic is closely interwoven with femininity. Yet it would be a mistake simply to link the experiences of empirical women to the semiotic, for it is a pre-Oedipal realm of experience that comes into being *prior* to sexual difference. As such, if the semiotic is 'feminine', it is a femininity that is always potentially available to women and men in their efforts to transform gender power.

Kristeva further expands her account of the complex interplay of semiotic and symbolic orders through recourse to the concept of the 'abject'; a kind of pre-object which provides an imaginary lining to human experience and, therefore, allows the infant to separate itself from the pre-Oedipal mother. In her psychoanalytic account, Kristeva argues that the pre-Oedipal mother becomes abject – an object of horror, distaste, and fear. Like Dinnerstein and Chodorow, Kristeva argues that the infant fears the omnipotent powers of the pre-Oedipal mother, and thus expels or abjects her in order to create a separate psychic space. Related to this is the intervention of the 'father of personal pre-history', or pre-Oedipal father, which the infant identifies with in order to break with the omnipotent mother. This imaginary, pre-Oedipal father is understood in Lacanian terms as the mother's desire for the phallus. Yet the crucial point about these psychic processes for Kristeva is that they indicate an internal independence between maternal and paternal power in infant development. Desire of the archaic mother is not fully repressed, according to Kristeva, with entry to symbolization and culture – as Lacan tends to suggest. On the contrary, there is a continual shuttling between the semiotic and symbolic, maternal fragmentation and paternal structuration.

In arriving at these psychoanalytic conclusions, Kristeva attempts to specify moments in which semiotic processes are let loose from the rigidity of the male-dominated symbolic order. She finds a return of the semiotic relation to the pre-Oedipal mother in the writing of certain avant-garde authors, such as Mallarmé, Lautréamont, Artaud, and Joyce. Though these examples are all of male authors, Kristeva finds that this kind of writing embodies central elements derived from the pre-Oedipal semiotic, a 'feminine' articulation of pleasures which defies patriarchal language and culture. In her more recent work, Kristeva attempts to give the idea of semiotic subversion further empirical content through the study of motherhood. In pregnancy, Kristeva says, woman can recover a repressed relation to the semiotic maternal through the profound psychic experience of giving birth to her newborn child. Pregnancy involves a kind of pleasurable, creative linking with an Other. In 'Women's Time', for instance, she argues that pregnancy reproduces 'the radical ordeal of the splitting of the subject: redoubling of the body, separation, and coexistence of the self and of an other, of nature and consciousness, of physiology and speech.'[17] This mode of relating, Kristeva says, involves a potential reconstruction of human social relationships, one in which a new relation to the semiotic body, its pleasures, and its dismantling of fixed oppositions (self/Other, man/woman) can overturn existing masculine culture.

Kristeva's theory of the feminine semiotic, as a mode of experience available to women and men in the restructuring of gender power, has been fiercely contested, both inside and outside feminist quarters. For example, it has been claimed that, in collapsing the feminine with unconscious experience, Kristeva argues for a political pluralism without feminist content.[18] In this critique, women's real experiences of both oppression and active gender struggle are displaced in favour of an abstract, male model of semiotic (literary) practice. From the other side of the coin, Kristeva has also been charged with essentialism and sexual separatism – with reducing semiotic subversion to the biological conditions of motherhood, and thereby erasing the capacity of men (and also of women who choose not to be mothers) to partake in radical gender struggle.[19] Neither of these criticisms is, in my view, accurate. It is important to see that Kristeva is not claiming the semiotic realm as the exclusive province of either women or men – even if there may be an essentialist slippage in her account of motherhood. Rather, Kristeva teaches us to see that, as split, desiring subjects, we all have a pre-Oedipal, feminine connection with the mother, a connection which is potentially subversive of patriarchal logic and thought. There is indeed a real problem, though, in Kristeva's account of the political implications of semiotic subversion. Kristeva assumes that semiotic displacements in language and culture are, in some sense, equivalent to overturning and transforming social and political relations. However, it seems to me that this is a hazardous connection at best. How, exactly, might semiotic silences and displacements be used to overcome repressive gender relations? How, for example, might they bring to an end gender tensions, sexual violence, or pornography? Kristeva's theory in this respect is unconvincing. The possible links between the semiotic and critical self-reflection are sidestepped in her analysis, thus leaving little possibility for a meaningful psychic reorganization of the self.

There may, however, be strong psychoanalytic grounds for supposing that the feminine is itself a space that cannot be adequately theorized. According to the French philosopher Luce Irigaray, the feminine cannot be properly symbolized under patriarchy. Irigaray, taking her cue from Lacan, proposes the feminine as somehow outside language and the symbolic order. Her argument is that the *pre-Oedpial mother/daughter relationship* remains on the 'outside' of symbolic boundaries – an outside that leaves women in a state of 'déréliction', undifferentiated from maternal space. As she puts this, 'there is no possibility whatsoever, within the current logic of sociocultural operations, for a daughter to situate herself with respect to her mother: because, strictly speaking, they make neither one nor two, neither has a name, meaning, sex of her own, neither can be "identified" with respect to the other'.[20]

By contrast, to Lacan, however, Irigaray contends that the idea of woman as outside and Other always threatens subversion, thus transforming the dominant male order of things. The feminine, says Irigaray, contains subversive dimensions to patriarchal language and culture. Here Irigaray's position has certain affinities with Kristeva's notion of the semiotic. However, Irigaray goes further than Kristeva on the nature of female sexuality, proposing a direct link between women, feminine sexuality, and the body. In line with other women of the 'écriture feminine' movement, such as Hélène Cixous, Irigaray grounds the feminine in women's experience of sexuality and the body, an experience which is plural, dispersed, and multiple. Woman, says Irigaray, must recover a true relationship to her feminine sexuality, effecting a range of displacements to patriarchy through writing as a cultural practice.

I would suggest, however, that the question of gender transformation cannot be solved through direct appeal to the body and its pleasures. For to invoke such a strategy is to risk the dangers of biological essentialism – that is, the assumption that there is an unchanging, transhistorical female sexuality which is subversive in all social contexts. While Irigaray is clearly concerned to trace the impact of distorting socio-symbolic forces upon the pre-Oedipal mother/daughter relationship, her appeal to a 'female unconscious' seems to assume that sexuality is magically pre-given. Juliet Mitchell sums up the difficulty with this position: 'You cannot choose the imaginary, the semiotic, the carnival as an alternative to the symbolic, as an alternative to the law. It is set up by the law precisely as its own lurid space, its own area of imaginary alternative, but not as a symbolic alternative. So that politically speaking, it is only the symbolic, a new symbolism, a new law, that can challenge the dominant law.'[21]

Psychoanalytic Feminism and Sexual Emancipation

What do current versions of psychoanalytic feminism suggest about gendered asymmetric relations of power? Most significantly, psychoanalytic feminism highlights the profound yet subtle links between unconscious desire and gender identity – thus raising subjectivity and sexuality as a problem for political debate. Focusing on the unconscious construction of sexual difference, psychoanalytic feminists (from diverse theoretical backgrounds) stress that socio-political change is a difficult and painful endeavour, and that there can be no easy paths to gender transformation. From this angle, then, psychoanalytic feminism is concerned with tracing the reproduction of gender hierarchy and women's subordination; or, as Mitchell puts this, psychoanalysis 'describes' rather than 'prescribes'. As it stands, however, it seems to me that such a descriptive approach to women's oppression cannot really address those issues that are most theoretically and politically difficult today. I have in mind here the horrific rise of sexual violence in the 1980s and 1990s (ranging from sexual harassment to rape and body mutilation), underpinned by the cultural implosion of totalitarian and apocalyptic sexual fantasy. In such a political climate, the language of 'gender internalization' is no longer adequate (if, indeed, it ever was) to understand the social reproduction of sexual identifications and identities. The imaginary and symbolic forms constitutive of gender power need to be addressed in a different fashion, one that focuses on the imbalances and discontinuities of sexual identification as much as on the reproduction of gender significations. We need to know more about the psychic processes of sexual identification, and of how existing identifications interact, conflict, and reinforce one another in the current gender system. We need to know more about the potentialities of such variations for subjectivity, sexuality, and gender differentiation. And we need to know more about the enabling aspects of modern sexuality, enquiring at what point fantasy structures outstrip themselves and marshal human subjects into active forms of gender struggle and commitment.

In my view, if we are successfully to confront such issues, it will be necessary to develop a more open dialogue between competing theoretical approaches in psychoanalytic feminism. A more flexible conceptual approach to sexuality and gender, in particular, will need to tackle head-on the question of linking interpersonal analysis with a consideration of the broader symbolic forms that constitute and reproduce our unequal sexual world. In this respect, the consequences of the restructuring of family life is a good example of the need to overcome theoretical polarization. For the transformation of parenting – as the post-structural Lacanian critique highlights – cannot of itself change the symbolic force of the phallus in determining the meanings of sexual difference. However, and this is where the claims of Lacanian feminists are vulnerable, this does not mean that current transformations in familial ideology are not altering the domain of personal life – from which more wide-ranging social changes might spring. Clearly, we need to know more than we currently do about how the reorganization of the family in late modernity intersects with the reproduction of sexual difference. Is it producing more or less gender-divided identities? This is an area, I argue, that demands sustained theoretical and empirical consideration, not vague polemic.

Finally, what of the possibilities for sexual emancipation? Again, psychoanalytic feminism shows that this is not just some utopian dream. Rather, our liberation from gender oppression is already in process, discernable in the active struggles of women and men to reconstruct the links between personal life and the sociopolitical world. Sexuality and identity is being continually reforged in modern societies. The women's movement, men's groups, gay and lesbian forums: these are critical engagements with the ideological apparatus of patriarchy and the limits of sexual dualism. No one knows how far, or with what consequences, the psychic restructuring of gender may be practically effected. What can be said, however, is that psychoanalytic feminism has a crucial and ongoing role in helping to illuminate and guide the emotional processes by which polarized gender can be transformed.

Table 5.1 Psychoanalytic feminism

Theory	Sexuality and gender asymmetry	Key terms
Object relations feminism (Dinnerstein, Chodorow)	Exclusive female mothering constitutes gender power; transformed through shared parenting	Core gender identity Pre-Oedipal sexuality
Contemporary object relations feminism (Benjamin, Sprengnether, Flax)	Gender asymmetry structured within interpersonal relations	Mother as subject Intersubjectivity
Lacanian feminism (Mitchell, Rose)	Sexuality and gender constituted through socio-symbolic order	Patriarchal symbolic Sexual division
Post-Lacanian feminism (Kristeva, Irigaray)	Pre-Oedipal sexuality distorted by patriarchal symbolic; subversion through feminine imaginary	Semiotic Déréliction Female imaginary

6

The Dislocating World of Postmodernism

Identity in Troubled Times

We have seen that the concept of the human subject undergoes a significant transformation as a consequence of developments in psychoanalytic theory during the twentieth century. How we view the identity of the modern subject, as discussed throughout this book, depends significantly on the type of psychoanalytic approach and descriptive account that is used. In Freudian terms, selfhood can be thought of as a direct outcrop of the unconscious itself; a creative core of representations which continuously condenses and displaces its own roots within the cultural fabric of society. In object relational theories this Freudian subject-centred analysis is overturned in favour of a more interpersonal approach. Object relational theorists, with their differing descriptive accounts, argue that it is more useful to think of self and self-identity as constituted within a network of intersubjective relations; relations that either facilitate or disrupt the psychic underpinnings of self-organization. Kleinians share this intersubjective focus, but critically underscore the internal fantasy processes which link paranoid destructiveness and reparative despair to self-development. In Lacanian psychoanalysis, this potential for self-integration is deconstructed as an imaginary concealment of the absence and lack which haunts subjectivity. Rather than bolstering the narcissistic illusions of the ego, Lacanians trace the subject as repressively inscribed within a symbolic network of unstable signifiers.

It can be argued, however, that all such attempts to theorize the 'subject' are themselves only imaginary fictions. To divide inner reality into so many agencies or functions is simply to engage in an act of conceptual house-tidying, a kind of repressive closure of the complexities and ambiguities of human existence itself. From this angle, the term 'subject' is just a shorthand way of designating at the level of theory the complex, contradictory elements of psychical life. Yet there really is no 'individual subject', as the sum total of psychical traces, elements, and parts. All there is, rather, are the fluid and multiple trajectories of libidinal enjoyment. The indeterminacy of desire, *jouissance*, the death drive, signifiers, bodily zones, intensities: there is only the pure multiplicity of unconscious pleasure unfolding endlessly.

With this vision of desire as decentred and desubjectivized we have entered the era of postmodernism – characterized by its suspicion of grand narratives and totalizing concepts, its deconstruction of all interpretative significance as ideological closure, its debunking of the 'self-identical subject', its euphoric celebration of the particular, the fragmented, the indeterminate, and the multidimensional. 'Postmodernity,' Zygmunt Bauman writes, 'is modernity coming of age: modernity looking at itself at a distance rather than from the inside, making a full inventory of its gains and losses, psychoanalysing itself, discovering the intentions it never before spelled out, finding them mutually cancelling and incongruous. Postmodernity is modernity coming to terms with its own impossibility; a self-monitoring modernity, one that consciously discards what it was once unconsciously doing.'[1] Postmodernism, in this sense, exists as a *radicalized tendency* within the very structure and matrix of modernity. It is, as Jean-François Lyotard comments, a kind of 'working through . . . operated by modernity on itself'.[2] Significantly, this postmodern self-monitoring operates most powerfully at the level of theory itself, in and through a critique of the theoretical realm as traversed by random intensities and forces of libidinal desire. Postmodernism, as Samuel Weber argues, proclaims that the 'self-dissimulating distortions' uncovered by Freudian psychoanalysis saturate the entire field of theoretical understanding; and to this, we might add, one place which cannot escape such scrutiny is psychoanalytic discourse.[3]

The postmodern theories to be encountered in this final chapter develop powerful, and often disturbing, readings of psychoanalysis; deploying and refashioning psychoanalytic concepts, perhaps somewhat paradoxically, to launch sustained critiques on the theoretical operations of psychoanalysis. Through a discontinuous presentation of theory, the standpoints considered trace the interrelation between self and society in the global network of our late modern age.

Deleuze and Guattari on Capitalism and Schizophrenia

In their celebrated work *Anti-Oedipus* (1977), Gilles Deleuze and Félix Guattari elaborate a vision of schizophrenic desire as the basis for a postmodern account of social and political organization. *Anti-Oedipus*, a book which scandalized French psychoanalysis and generated heated disputes among intellectuals at the time, develops a postmodern psychoanalysis from two main perspectives. First, through using psychoanalytic theory against itself, tracing how the repressive inscription of desire within language is reinforced by the practice of psychoanalysis. Second, through the dismantling of grand theory in favour of a multiple, desubjectivized account of desire; an account that constantly threatens to undermine its own internal coherence. Deleuze and Guattari proclaim that schizophrenia is the most promising guide to understanding the nature of desire in modern culture. They propose a celebration of the fluid and multiple intensities of schizophrenic desire, intensities which they oppose to the repressive functioning of social institutions and the Law. To this end, they develop the notion of a 'subjectless machine', a kind of schizophrenic overflowing of desire that produces and reproduces itself in aimless circulation. Against the Oedipalizing logic of capitalist discourse, where desire is channelled into prescribed pathways under the sign of the commodity, Deleuze and Guattari posit the impersonalized flows of schizoid desire, a productive network of libidinal articulations which potentially might short-circuit the symbolic order of capitalist production.

Deleuze and Guattari configure the social world as a complex of libidinal and symbolic forms; forms that continuously displace one another. Against this backdrop, they present a speculative account of the historical development of capitalist production. In its early stages, capitalism is said to have severed the economic realm from symbolic forms such as kinship systems, customs, religious beliefs, and so on. Capitalist production, at this historical point, depends crucially upon a more or less stable collectivity, with pre-given social roles and identities. The emergence of monopoly capitalism, however, radically transforms the social world: it sweeps away *all* traditional types of social relations, as the economic bites deeply into the symbolic realm itself. The creation of an international capitalist system, it might be said, breaks down the symbolic framework of the local community and of tradition. Deleuze and Guattari refer to this process as the 'deterritorialization' of social codes. What this means, in brief, is that capitalism ruthlessly dismantles bourgeois cultural forms and moral codes, replacing these with the exchangeability and anonymity of the commodity form. In this connection, Deleuze and Guattari argue that the logic of capitalist economic relations is deeply interwoven with the discontinuities of schizophrenic desire. Like the indifference of the commodity itself, schizophrenia knows no symbolic limit, no constraint of reality, no high-minded guilt born of the superego. Instead, schizoid desire produces itself in fragments of pleasure, slicing capitalist temporality into the fluidity of the moment. 'The order of desire,' write Deleuze and Guattari, 'is the order of *production*; all production is at once desiring production and social production.'[4]

Capitalism, however, not only deterritorializes outmoded social forms, but constantly 'reterritorializes' them in startling new ways. Against capitalism's dismantling of pre-existing social boundaries, Deleuze and Guattari point to a proto-fascist, paranoiac tendency, a tendency at the heart of modernity, to restructure schizoid flows into unified forms and meanings. What is being emphasized here is the oppressive nature of late capitalist society, its recoding of desire into the repressive, structural affairs of international banking, stock markets, insurance companies, and so on. Schizophrenic and paranoiac desire: both forms of production are to be found at different levels of the social system. Global capitalism effects a profound deterritorialization of social forms into schizoid flows on the one hand, while simultaneously recoding these flows into the symbolic circuit of culture on the other. From Perrier water to Playboy magazine: schizophrenic flux-signs of desire are endlessly recoded to support the economic logic of capitalist life.

Like several of the psychoanalytic theorists we have looked at in earlier chapters, Deleuze and Guatarri see the familial structure of Western culture as the key institutional mode of repressing desire in capitalism. Central to their interpretation of the Oedipus complex is the notion of a 'subjectless machine'. Desire prior to Oedipus, Deleuze and Guattari contend, is multidimensional, discontinuous, and shifting. Desire just *is* the production of 'machine parts', spilling out across libidinal surfaces, and pluralized in its operations through contact with other human 'machines'. As Deleuze and Guattari reconceptualize the pre-Oedipal moment: 'The breast is a machine that produces milk, and the mouth a machine coupled to it' (p. 1). At this point, then, desire is schizoid and subjectless, an impersonal force of production. But not so after the effects of Oedipalization. The impersonal force of schizoid desire, according to Deleuze and Guattari, is repressively codified through Oedipus. That is, the Oedipus complex works to *personalize desire*, referring all unconscious productions to the incestuous sexual realm of the family network. Oedipus, then, is a prime instance of the capitalist recoding of desire. Deleuze and Guattari argue that psychoanalysis in modern societies functions as a repressive force which projects desire into the person-alized, neuroticized structures of 'daddy-mummy-me'.

However, Deleuze and Guattari are by no means suggesting that this paranoic process of capitalist reterritorialization is complete. For them, the schizoid nature of desire constantly escapes the well-ordered structure of capitalist production, at which point there is a dismantling of received social meanings. The schizoid pullulations of desire, argue Deleuze and Guattari, are transgressive, polymorphous, and fragmenting. In its anarchic, heterogeneous lines of libidinal intensity, schizophrenic desire offers paradoxically to outstrip the centralized, unified organization of capitalist Law in which it is encoded. 'Schizophrenia,' write Deleuze and Guattari, 'is desiring production at the limit of social production' (p. 35). Like the avant-garde of Surrealism, Deleuze and Guattari are fascinated by the notion of transgression, the breaking of limits, the undoing of rules. Smashing through the boundaries of ordinary life, schizoid desire is pure production: desire turning in upon itself to further the produc-tion of desire.

This valorization of the absolute positivity of desire, it should be noted, is in direct contrast to the Lacanian model of the unconscious. Whereas Lacan posits unconscious desire as a product of lack, that lost object which the subject strives constantly to fill, the cravings of the schizo-subject are conceived instead as pure affirmation. Lacan's referral of desire to lack, absence, and failure – so Deleuze and Guattari contend – is itself the projection of Oedipus into contempor-ary theory, institutions, and affairs. Psychoanalysis, both traditional and Lacanian, constructs desire as loss for the purpose of adapting human subjects to the social order.[5] From this angle, psychoanalysis deciphers and reinscribes Oedipal compulsions for identification which are essential to the ego-centred, neurotic structures of subject-hood of late capitalism. In this manner, the signs of power constitute us as subjects through and through. In contrast, Deleuze and Guattari emphasize the multiple paths of desire, their schizoid proliferations, openings, zigzags, and flows. To designate this, they propose a 'schizoanalysis' which interprets unconscious desire hydraulically as a desiring machine; as flows of libidinal energy which at once anchor and destabilize the social process. As they put this:

> To discover beneath the familial reduction the nature of the social investments of the unconscious. To discover under the individual fantasy the nature of group fantasies. Or, what amounts to the same thing, to push the simulacrum to the point where it ceases to be an

> image of an image, so as to discover the abstract figures, the schizzes-
> flows that it harbours and conceals ... To overturn the theatre of
> representation into the order of desiring production: this is the whole
> task of schizoanalysis. (p. 271)

For Deleuze and Guattari, schizophrenia is revolutionary since it
defies identification, categorization, and differentiation. According to
this view, unconscious desire represents nothing, neither representation nor the sign. It simply *is* – indeterminate, impersonal production.
Hence, the factory metaphor of 'desiring machines'.

A number of social and political implications arise from the
foregoing analysis. To begin with, the work of Deleuze and Guattari
seeks to undermine traditional conceptions of political and revolutionary action. Politics, embedded in desiring and social production,
is not something that can be rationally refashioned, since the socio-
political world is caught up in the territorialization of norms. So too,
blueprints for social and political transformation will be unsuccessful
because such activity and planning will necessarily involve a paranoiac encoding of desire. But in what important sense, then, is social
change possible? It would seem that the only means for overcoming
cultural oppression, for Deleuze and Guattari, lies in the schizophrenic process itself. Their case suggests that the best thing is to
push the schizophrenic process as far as it will go, to the point where
the social system is broken apart by the libidinal forces it seeks to
suppress. In the words of Deleuze and Guattari's commentator Brian
Massumi: 'Schizophrenia as a positive process is inventive connection, expansion rather than withdrawal.'[6] To turn the process of
schizophrenia against the logic of capitalist production might just
allow us to construct alternative social relations – relations that
permit a spontaneity and intensity of desire free from cultural
constraint.

Anti-Oedipus offered a timely critique of psychoanalysis and
Lacanianism at the time of its publication in France. Most commentators would now agree, however, that 'schizoanalysis' itself is fatally
flawed. There are at least three core objections which can be made to
the work of Deleuze and Guattari in this respect. In the first place,
there is no reason to assume, even granted that subjectivity may be
usefully decentred and deconstructed, that desire is naturally rebel-
lious and subversive. To treat the unconscious as *ipso facto* politically
transgressive is to invoke a libertarian theory of the subject, one
which tends uncritically to celebrate the flows of desire in opposition
to the symbolic order of representation. But this simple prioritization

of schizoid processes over the socio-symbolic network fails to consider the social and political forms in which desire is embedded; it fails to examine the ideological context in which persons attempt a psychical reorganization of the self. The fact that desire is routinely displaced and projected onto others as well as properly owned and nurtured, that fantasy-objects yield pleasure and enjoyment but also disturb and terrify, is completely lacking in this perspective. It contains no adequate account of psychic interiority, nor can it theorize the intersubjective domain of self-other relations. What this approach theorizes, rather than the subject and unconscious enjoyment, is the mind-shattering flux of schizoid desire. Significantly, however, no account of the psychical determinants of this condition is offered. Deleuze and Guattari assume that desire is in some sense true to itself, that its primal positivity is damaged only when it becomes enmeshed in the socio-symbolic of modern societies. But this individualist emphasis eliminates both the concept of the unconscious (there is no originary unconscious in this perspective, since it is seen as a decentred effect of entry into the symbolic), and of the human subject as agent. Self-autonomy, interiority, the unconscious: these essential elements of identity are disowned. As a consequence, the individual is seen as no more than various organs, intensities, and flows, rather than a complex, contradictory identity with a differentiated mode of psychic organization.

This issue might not be quite as significant if it were not for the emancipatory claims made by Deleuze and Guattari for schizophrenia; which leads us to the second major objection to their work. According to Deleuze and Guattari, the troubles of modernity are to be erased through the expressive disorder of schizoid desire. To grasp the limitations of this view we need to look no further than to psychoanalytic portraits of schizophrenia. What these findings reveal is a world, not of euphoric celebration, but of disintegration, fragmentation, terror, and emotional devastation. In schizophrenia, Freud wrote, the individual rejects reality and turns desire back upon itself with a vengeance.[7] This destroys the self to its very core. Consequently, psychotic delirium is experienced as pure fragementation – bits of persons and objects are randomly experienced without the structuring force of a meaningful, symbolic order. As Kovel puts this: 'The centre of schizophrenia is annihilation: the person becoming schizophrenic remains materially present and conscious, but ceases to be.'[8] This annihilation of self, perhaps not surprisingly, leads to the psychical destruction of others – that is, of intersubjectivity. Having repudiated social reality, the schizophrenic is left with nothing to invest in but a substitutive fantasy world. But this fragmented world is not really any kind of 'world' at all: previous terrors and anxieties are now poured into delusions and hallucinations, which rebound upon the subject with unbearable force, producing terrifying vulnerability.

Against this backdrop, is it reasonable to assume that liberation might be uncovered in 'the glaring, sober truth that resides in delirium'? That is, how should we rate Deleuze and Guattari's celebration of schizophrenia? Not very highly, and it is important to outline why. Whatever the 'intensity' of schizoid desire, Deleuze and Guattari completely fail to consider the pain and emptiness of the psychotic experience. As such, their romanticized account of schizophrenia cannot provide any moral criterion. For example, how might an individual disconnected from subjectivity and intersubjectivity attempt to achieve critical self-reflection? If it is through the disordered flow of schizoid desire itself, is there nothing to be said about the rights of other persons? Clearly, if schizoid desire is accorded absolute entitlement for itself, we are dealing with a deep-lying potential for violence to the self, to others, and to society. Of course it might be argued, as some of Deleuze and Guattari's commentators have done, that to value the schizophrenic *process* in itself is not to sing the praises of *clinical* schizophrenia.[9] In this reading, it is the schizophrenic process – that breakdown of symbolic forms into random flows, images, and part-objects – which is seen as potentially transformative of our repressive conditions of life. This case, however, still recklessly ignores the relations between psychical structure and social life. Any emancipatory theory of alternative social arrangements must provide for a means of constituting the individual within socially valued forms; a structuration of the individual which, psychoanalytically speaking, involves the overcoming of infantile omnipotence and the acceptance of decentred subjectivity. Deleuze and Guattari offer no such means. Their vision, even when read as a valuation of schizophrenia as process, projects the individual out of the social-historical world and into a carnivalesque hyperspace.

Thirdly, serious difficulties arise from Deleuze and Guattari's work for the interpretation of contemporary culture. Their social analysis and critique hinges on the point that the expressiveness and positivity of desire is ruined through insertion into the cultural order of representation. But it might be as well to question what type of cultural order Deleuze and Guattari have in mind here. For it seems that in defending the cravings of the schizoid-subject against the repressions of modernity, Deleuze and Guattari slide into an indiscriminate rejection of institutionality as such. All political and social systems become, in effect, 'terroristic' – regardless of their modalities of power and law. But surely the claim that some orders of representation are not more repressive than others is highly problematic. What, for example, of the vital political differences between liberal democracy and fascism? What of the impact of symbolic forms and ideologies, such as religious fundamentalism, nationalism, and political militancy? Surely these socio-symbolic forms affect the possibilities for self-realization and autonomy in crucially distinct ways. Deleuze and Guattari's work, in this respect, is unconvincing. By flattening out the complex, contradictory reproduction of modern societies into a mechanistic account of the 'terror of norms', Deleuze and Guattari are left without any secure footing to elucidate the revolutionary political agency which they wish to see realized. Instead, Deleuze and Guattari are left with little more than a romantic, idealized fantasy of the 'schizoid hero'.

Lyotard on Libidinal Intensities

In the work of Deleuze and Guattari, a primary emphasis is placed on the disorder of desire. Schizoid desire signals the recovery of repressed differences, the multiplication of libido in a new era of postmodernity. Similar theoretical directions can also be found in the early work of Jean-François Lyotard, who explicitly poses the question of political society as the problem of desire in *Economie Libidinale* (1974). But whereas Deleuze and Guattari interpret the political in terms of schizoid desire against repressive desire, 'revolutionary' desire against 'fascist' desire, Lyotard turns instead to the mutual imbrication of the social and libidinal, law and desire. Ideology for Lyotard is not simply a matter of the repressive closure of desire. On the contrary, the ideological can be described as itself libidinal, inscribed always on the 'inside' of desire. What is needed, therefore, is not the projection of some utopian realm 'beyond' our socio-political condition, but a reconfiguration of the libidinal intensities and singularities of social life itself.

There is an intrinsic link, Lyotard says, between the order of discourse and desire. The social order, though dependent on a repression of desire, is traversed by the libidinal sphere, structured in and through unconscious representation, fantasy, and drive energy. A discursive repression of desire is thus always potentially open to transformation by the operations of desire itself; just as repressive political regimes, no matter how ideologically secure they may appear, are liable to be overthrown by citizens desiring alternative forms of life. Lyotard expresses this by noting that the return of the repressed 'violates the order of speech'. Yet Lyotard altogether rejects the libertarian view that such violation is inherently good, and discursive repression bad. All social and political systems, he argues, negotiate networks of discourse and desire. Instead of prioritizing desire over signification, as in Deleuze and Guattari's *Anti-Oedipus*, Lyotard, by contrast, draws attention to differing modalities of desire and the structure of their production. Highlighting ambivalences in Freud's account of the unconscious, Lyotard discerns two aspects of desire: desire-as-wish (fantasy) and desire-as-force (libido). Desire-as-wish, the figural component of the unconscious, is the representation of a lost object. Here the human subject fantasizes images of the self, of others, and of the world as a compensation for various lacks or exclusions. In this regime, desire operates under the sign of lack, absence, and negativity. By contrast, desire-as-force, the energetic component of the unconscious, is pure energy, libido, and primary process. In this regime, desire functions through the act of its own production, endlessly reproducing itself in some transcendental process of repetition.

Lyotard wishes to claim desire-as-force as inherently positive and affirmative. He advocates, in Nietzschean fashion, a celebration of unconscious intensity and power. On the basis of this vision, Lyotard speaks of the primacy of libidinal intensities. He describes the functioning of a 'libidinal band'; a flux or scramble of energy cathexes; intensities lodged across the surfaces of the body. How might we imagine this 'libidinal band'? Libidinal intensities are not focused upon 'objects of desire' (such as Oedipal figures), for this is the province of desire-as-wish. They consist, rather, of the flux of desire itself, energy in a state of continuous nonlinear movement. Lyotard refers to a rotation of the libidinal band that constantly disrupts all intersections of self and other, of internal and external, of the differentiation of 'this' from 'not-this'. The whole notion is somewhat like the 'action painting' of Jackson Pollock, in which lines of figures interweave without end. However, libidinal intensities cannot be really understood in this way either. There is no point, Lyotard warns, of trying to capture the best image of the libidinal band, nor of seeking to observe it, since we are dealing with a force that is *prior* to representation and conceptual thought. Indeed, conceptual thought is itself only possible through a cooling of libidinal energy, through a binding of the intensities of desire. As such, it is really impossible to talk of this unconscious realm without deforming it in the act of doing so.

In the case of what Lyotard calls the 'libidinal band', then, we are dealing less with a domain of direct description than with a kind of fiction – a fiction which at once precedes and exceeds representation, significiation, and meaning. Yet if it is the case that libidinal intensities constitute and account for the realm of representation, it is certainly not Lyotard's purpose simply to oppose the libidinal to the social sphere. Lyotard, to his credit, rejects as politically naive proclamations about the 'truth of desire'. As he puts this, there is no 'place where desire would be clearly legible, where its proper economy would not be scrambled'.[10] The opposition of desire and signification, then, cannot make sense of the process of social transformation. A new vision is required to understand the structure of libidinal and social formations. For Lyotard, this involves the dissolution of representation and of theory as a *medium* of the libidinal band itself. 'The representative chamber,' he writes, 'is an energetic system' (p. 11). Western knowledge, enlightenment domination, science, and technology: such discourses and practices – so Lyotard contends – are themselves libidinal. But in what manner, more concretely, might this contribute to social and political critique? Lyotard's specification of the libidinal nature of social practices, discourses, and concepts is rooted in an attempt to de-legitimize the totalizing, objective pretensions of contemporary affairs and institutions. By showing that desire constitutes the social through and through, Lyotard wishes to highlight that 'knowledge' is itself only one mode of libidinal intensity among others. From this angle, Lyotard's critique appeals to the singularities and intensities of desire against the repressive claims of enlightenment reason.

To attempt to salvage the singularities of libido may not be that easy, however. If desire is a split, contradictory realm – divided between desire-as-wish and desire-as-force – so too the intensities of the libidinal band are deeply structured by the discontinuities of unconscious force itself. Such are the effects of the dualism of Eros and the death drive, a dualism which Lyotard invokes to conceptualize the limits of symbolization. This is not just, as most interpretations of Freud hold, because the death drive displaces the narcissistic unity established by Eros. It is because, as Lyotard rightly emphasizes, the disruptive, unbound force of the death drive is part and parcel of the various manifestations of Eros. Holding this in mind, it can be said that the deathly force of the libidinal band leads to a complete annihilation of the symbolic network itself; or, as Lyotard puts it, the primary chaos of the death drive reveals 'the limit of representation and of theory'. From a psychoanalytic perspective, Lyotard is referring to symbolic, not biological, death. The disruptive energy of the death drive produces the moment of discontinuity, of rupture, at which point there is a short-circuit in the socio-symbolic order. Here human subjects can briefly glimpse social reality in its full libidinal plenitude – heterogeneous, fluid, and multiple.

At this point, we get to the heart of Lyotard's political analysis in Economie Libidinale. It is to trace the libidinal intensities lodged in cultural representations and social meanings. 'What would be interesting,' writes Lyotard, 'would be to stay where we are, but at the same time silently to grab all opportunities to function as good conductors of intensities' (p. 311). According to this view, it is simply mistaken to believe that desire does not flow freely enough in contemporary society – as Deleuze and Guattari contend. For the fact of the matter, according to Lyotard, is that desire circulates endlessly around objects, surfaces, and bodies. In this connection, late capitalism for Lyotard is an immense desiring system. He describes postmodern capitalist society as a culture swamped with flashy commodities and signs, in which all social forms are colonized by the economic logic of exchange. Yet the implications of this for radical politics are not necessarily bad news. For, according to Lyotard, the exchangeability and anonymity glimpsed in contemporary social processes parallels the aimless flux of the libidinal band itself. 'If desire is not to be opposed to capitalism,' as Geoffrey Bennington says of Lyotard's position, 'it can be recognized in capitalism.'[11] Lyotard thus advocates embracing the fragmentation of desire as a way of intensifying the lived experiences of postmodern culture. The challenging and exhilarating task of postmodernism is to recognize that desire is always already realized, to extract pleasure from the fragments and surfaces in which identities are constituted.

However, all of this, from the standpoint of critical psychoanalytic theory, is deeply problematic. The difficulties with Lyotard's conception of libidinal intensities relate, above all, to certain assumptions about human subjectivity and agency. Lyotard's celebration of the energetic component of the unconscious is achieved at the cost of displacing the vital role of representation in psychical life. Lyotard contends, as we have seen, that representation is only a local effect of energy forms and intensities. Yet this altogether erases the fundamental stress upon representation in Freud's interpretation of the self. According to Freud, as discussed in chapter 1, representation and desire are inextricably intertwined. Selfhood for Freud is anchored in a psychical structure that creates representations, drives, and desires. This interweaving is a permanent feature of psychical life, and lies at the basis of how men and women image themselves and each other in institutional social life. By severing the representational space of the self from unconscious desire, seeing the former as a reductive outcrop of the latter, Lyotard is able to imagine that the libidinal economy moulds all cultural productions to their roots. Yet how far is it really possible to disentangle the libidinal forms of social life from the representational structures in which they are embedded? How can we disconnect the way we feel about personal and social life from the images we have of ourselves and other people? The problem here is surely clear. The energy basis at the root of social organization cannot be shifted along cultural representations as easily as Lyotard thinks. This is because representation and desire, signification and affect, are deeply tied together. And it is from this angle that some forms of cultural representation predominate over others in modern societies.

These ambiguities connect to deeper theoretical and political problems. Lyotard argues for a multiplication of libidinal formations, for the intensification of pleasure within this multiplicity, in opposition to the dominant forms of rationality in modern societies. Yet Lyotard's political dilemma is that the concept of libidinal intensities is cast so wide that it is rendered effectively fruitless for critical social analysis. As Peter Dews has argued, Lyotard's position is bereft of any moral or political orientation.[12] The problem of arguing for the 'dissimulation of intensities', in short, is that it can be ideologically marshalled by conservative political forces as well as by the Left. Indeed, the intensity of affect derived from the institutionalization of a brutal, authoritarian political regime – witness contemporary South Africa or Bosnia in ex-Yugoslavia – can be great as the libidinal intensity derived from the liberal affirmation of difference and singularity. As such, Lyotard's position really fails to pose any kind of threat to the dominant structural powers of contemporary society.

The Experience of Postmodernity

Notwithstanding the foregoing criticisms, the work of Deleuze and Guattari, and of Lyotard, offer provocative images of what it feels like to live in the modern world. Everyday experience, according to these images, is characterized by psychic fragmentation and dislocation. Modern culture, simply, is an immense desiring structure, fracturing social space through its schizoid tendencies toward deterritorialization while also managing to create unity through a depersonalized incorporation of libidinal intensities. Significantly these fragmenting trends create new forms of personal identity otherness, fantasy, and symbolism.

Modernity has been understood as the historical trajectory of modernization. The key processes of modernization – such as industrialism, bureaucratic organization, technology, and science – can be said to have unleashed profound cultural transformations. The rise of nation-states, corporate capitalism, the industrialization of war new communication technologies: these are the central institutional features of the modern world. For many theorists, this crisis-ridden system of global interconnectedness in which we now live is experienced by people ambivalently – as exciting adventure and terrifying risk, perpetual disintegration and renewal. Modernity is seen as an institutional setting which simultaneously empowers and constrains people, engendering their deepest hopes and fears. The modern task as discussed in chapter 3, is the creative engagement with changing forms of life, the reflexive involvement with a disorientating socio-cultural and economic world context. This is not an easy endeavour For, just as a growing sense of turmoil and flux infuses modern institutions and affairs, so too self-identity is recast through experiences of disorientation and discontinuity. In this context, mature and creative psychic-organization depends upon an open, revisable sense of self-identity – a willingness to embrace emotional support and change in the affairs of day-to-day life. In Winnicott's terms, the transitional realm of intersubjectivity is the essential condition for the development of such creative self-organization. In Giddens's picture of modernity, people handle dangers and fears through reflexive monitorings of trust.

For postmodern theorists, however, changes in social, cultural, and political conditions are so far-reaching that it is deemed inappropriate to talk of self-identity at all. Changes in the proliferation of generalized communication; the dispersal of economic production and consumption; global, multinational capitalism; the multiplication of new political movements and identities; the fracturing of knowledge and information: postmodern society is a *radicalized* modernity, a world of cataclysmic change, dynamism, and intensity. By a perverse kind of internal logic, postmodernity breaks up social reality into chunks of experience without reference, structure, or unity. Of particular relevance in this context is the proliferation of images, messages, signs, and codes disseminated through the phantasmagoria of the mass media. For postmodern theorists, this proliferation of images in postmodern social space entails a radical breakdown in our sense of subjective reality. Postmodernity multiplies, dislocates, and disperses the psychological forms of everyday reality. It destroys modern structures of time, space, history, and truth, and replaces them with a celebration and pluralization of brute immediacy. Indeed it has been suggested by some that it is now impossible to achieve any kind of critical distance for the illumination of social experience at all. Faced with the multiplication of social reality, the trusted distinctions between meaning and non-meaning, truth and fantasy, surface and depth can no longer be sustained.

Fredric Jameson has proposed, in what is now regarded as a classic essay on postmodernism, a more direct relationship between contemporary identity and culture on the one hand, and socio-economic processes on the other.[13] Jameson interprets the fluidity and multiplicity of postmodern cultural experience as a symptom of 'multinational capital'. The globalizing tendencies of late capitalism, he argues, breaks up the fabric of cultural social space and the personal sphere, creating 'a new and historically original penetration and colonization of Nature and the Unconscious'. This global process of complete social commodification involves the dissolution of selfhood and psychical structure, with 'postmodern hyperspace' proclaimed by Jameson as 'transcending the capacities of the individual human body to locate itself, to organize its immediate surroundings perceptually and cognitively to map its position in a mappable external world' (pp. 83–4). Social space becomes profoundly imaginary, fantastical, overheating the very social imagination to which it is bounded. The whole thing is something akin to the Lacanian child in its pre-mirror, imaginary phase – in which no divisions exist between self and world. Thus, for Jameson, the postmodern human subject is caught within a global, computational network of random signifiers and cultural representations which seduce and tantalize, but ultimately fail to make sense.

Jameson proposes a list of the dominant characteristics of postmodern culture. These include 'The Waning of Affect', 'Euphoria and Self-Annihilation', 'Loss of the Radical Past', 'The Breakdown of the Signifying Chain', and 'The Abolition of Critical Distance'. All of these refer to the fragmentation of subjecthood, dispersed across the global, multinational capitalist system. In postmodern culture, according to Jameson, 'there is no longer a self present to do the feeling'. Social identity, rather, is forged in and through fragments of language, media messages, and television images. Yet the press-button society of postmodernism leaves us cold, and without bearings. As cultural production becomes increasingly depthless and meaningless, so also does the self. Jameson, in a series of discussions about contemporary painting, contrasts the alienated subject of modernism with the fragmented subject of postmodernism. He points to Munch's painting *The Scream* as a cultural emblem of modernist solitude and isolation, of the 'age of anxiety', contrasting this with the postmodern depthlessness of Warhol's painting *Marilyn*, in which the repetition of the image of Marilyn Monroe is used to demonstrate the breakdown of trusted distinctions between people and their images. In this connection, postmodernism can be said to raise commodification to the second power, using the world of late capitalism to generate new forms of cultural representation.

For Jameson, as for Deleuze and Guattari and Lyotard, there are profound links between postmodern social experience and schizophrenia. Following Lacan, Jameson contends that biographies of self-identity are written against the backdrop of a unification of past, present, and future. Experiencing language and representation as temporally linked to social life is the psychological basis upon which a sense of psychological well-being rests. Contemporary postmodern social conditions, however, profoundly derail the relationship between self and language, desire and discourse. The dislocations and terrors of postmodern experience leads to a breakdown of the signifying chain itself. The present becomes dispersed, the past and future isolated. Desire randomly connects to bits of persons, experiences, and objects, as subjects live amongst a 'rubble of distinct and unrelated signifiers' (p. 72). In this context, the dissolution of self accompanies a transmutation of feelings. As Jameson notes: 'This is not to say that the cultural products of the postmodern era are utterly devoid of feeling, but rather that such feelings – which it may be better and more accurate to call "intensities" – are now free-floating and impersonal, and tend to be dominated by a peculiar kind of euphoria.'

Discussions about schizophrenia as a psychic metaphor for the postmodern tend to operate on different theoretical and cultural levels. In the 'schizoanalysis' proposed by Deleuze and Guattari, the schizoid pullulations of desire are given a positive gloss. Deleuze and Guattari celebrate the positivity of the flux of desire as a potential displacement to the repressive structures of late capitalism. In the work of Lyotard, a different tack is taken. The intensities of schizophrenic desire are not resistant to socialization, but already define and situate language, society, and cultural politics. The emancipatory prospects for postmodernity thus depend upon a progressive reappropriation of the singularities of libidinal intensity. For Jameson, schizophrenic desire also best captures the nature of the postmodern condition. Yet, according to Jameson, this fragmentation of self is not something to be celebrated, since to do so would play directly into the hands of the dominant cultural logic of capitalist reproduction. All these accounts of postmodern psychical experience can be found in current psychoanalytic studies and cultural and social theory. The broader issue raised by 'schizophrenic fragmentation' as an emblem of the postmodern, however, is whether the term can usefully serve at this level of cultural generality. Certainly it is possible to deploy 'schizophrenic fragmentation', like Jameson, as a benchmark for the assessment of postmodernism. Yet even this approach to understanding contemporary selfhood and society contains serious problems and contradictions.

One objection to the kind of cultural analysis just discussed is that it cannot really account for its own claims. If postmodern subjectivity really is fragmented, decentred, discontinuous, and schizoid in character, then how might it be possible for some cultural critics to map the psychical determinants of the contemporary world? That is, how is it possible to overcome the deforming, schizoid imaginary structures of the contemporary world in the act of interpreting them? It has been argued that such an objection really misses the point of postmodernism. It has been suggested that the work of Deleuze and Guattari, and of Lyotard, avoids this objection by disrupting the linear presentation of theory in favour of the displacements of desire itself. According to this view, the underlining of the flux of desire as the baseline of the contemporary environment is mirrored in the discontinuous, fragmentary form of postmodern discourse. In the postmodern world we know that all theory is necessarily partial and provisional; and that, therefore, any account of the postmodern condition will be bound up with the conditions of desire. There are still serious difficulties, however, with this conception of postmodern theory and practice. For one thing, to employ deconstructive strategies in critical theory, no matter how fragmentary and multidimensional, is not the same as embracing the central characteristics of psychosis or schizophrenia. For the fact of the matter is that the postmodern cultural practice under consideration uses metaphors, symbols, and interpretative strategies – the very psychical processes closed down and foreclosed in schizophrenia. This suggests that postmodern cultural forms might not be as brittle and fragmented as imagined. Has the capacity for critical self-reflection and analysis been impoverished by postmodernity? Can postmodern identity only be equated with fragments of language or discourse? The complex, contradictory ways in which people search for individual and collective identity, I argue, requires greater analytical depth than the foregoing postmodern theories provide.

Another objection to the postmodern celebration of schizophrenic renewal is the charge of naturalistic essentialism. As I argued earlier, it is clear that psychoanalysis does not view psychosis as any form of emancipation. On the contrary, schizophrenia is conceived as a kind of psychical murder, an annihilation of self and of symbolic connectedness to the world. In this context, the postmodern search for schizophrenic cultural forms that would allow us to be *ourselves*, free from the constraints and limitations of the social-historical world, is simply ill-defined. It is an approach framed upon a naive naturalism (desire as somehow, almost magically, always true to itself), and to that extent it offers little space for any critical examination of the changing relations between self and society. As Jacqueline Rose puts it, there is a 'sanitization' of schizophrenia in postmodern theory, a kind of cleaning up operation, in which this psychic model becomes 'strangely divested of some of the most difficult aspects of the psychic itself.'[14] To that extent, too, the social domain is also sanitized, as devoid of the realities of political change, social transformation, and ideological conflict. More specifically, there is a failure to attend to the political content of self-organization, as well as the social conditions structuring desire. It is important to see, therefore, that schizophrenia, and related psychotic categories, are not alternatives to the social order of modern societies. They are rather painfully desperate psychical forms experienced within the organizing social, political, and ideological conditions of the modern world.

Related to this is the feminist objection that the schizophrenic metaphorization of the postmodern serves to silence issues of sexual difference and gender power. There is some agreement among feminists that the internal fragmentation of contemporary selfhood is itself the product of an insipid intensification of patriarchal power. Certainly, it might be thought that this is a difficult claim to sustain in the light of recent gender transformations and the advances of the women's movement. However, many feminists argue that postmodern social, cultural, and political conditions are now affecting sexuality in a dramatic way, generating violence and hatred at the heart of sexual fantasy. Significantly, much of the writing on postmodernism examined in this chapter displaces questions of sexual difference onto the general categories of fragmentation and disintegration. This however, is a very curious displacement. For schizophrenic fragmentation is itself a disavowel of sexual difference. In schizophrenia, the psychotic denies the fact of castration, rejecting the *gendered structures of social life* in the process. Yet the relation between sexual difference, fragmentation, and new forms of gender power are not raised in the theories examined.

Postmodernism as Repression: Excavating the Imagination

Postmodern thinking about self and society emphasizes the dislocation and fragmentation of contemporary experience. Postmodernity, as we have seen, arises at that point in which the interchangeability and indifference of economic commodification penetrates deeply into the communicational networks of modern culture itself. In the contemporary social-theoretical writings of the psychoanalyst Cornelius Castoriadis, however, this expansion of the term 'commodification' conjoins the economic realm to everyday social experience only at the cost of displacing the creativity of the social-historial process. For Castoriadis, postmodernity is itself a cultural symptom of a society that has come to forget its own creative self-institution. Against this cultural tendency, Castoriadis is concerned with examining the psychoanalytic, social, and political mechanisms by which human creation emerges in subjectivity and in history. To do this, Castoriadis develops in *The Imaginary Institution of Society* (1987) the concept of the *radical imaginary*, by which he means a purely originary architecture of representations, drives, and desires through which self and society are constituted and reproduced. The radical imaginary, as it affects personal and social life, is an open-ended stream of significations and passions; it is thus a productive core which permits human subjects to create and reproduce society anew.

The term 'imaginary', says Castoriadis, has been reductively understood in traditional thought. For the imaginary has been cast as no more than a reflection or copy of the external world. The Lacanian conception of the 'imaginary order' is a prime example. In the Lacanian imaginary, the small child receives a reflection from the mirror, a reflection which functions as a distorted image for the drafting of the self. By contrast to Lacan, Castoriadis argues that the 'imaginary does not come from the image in the mirror or from the gaze of the other. Instead, the "mirror" itself and its possibility, and the other as mirror, are the works of the imaginary.'[15] Human imagination, Castoriadis proposes, is creation *ex nihilo*. The dimension of the imaginary is pure creation, the making and remaking of images and forms as an explicit self-production. This does not mean, absurdly, that human beings are unconstrained in their individual and collective activity. On the contrary, Castoriadis links the self-creating nature of cultural production to the *instituted imaginary representations* which belong to society and to history. The productive core of the social field, whether at the level of individual fantasy or at the level of Western global expansion, arises through this structuration of imaginary representations.

To speak of 'imaginary representations' as being at the core of the social world is certainly at odds with the bulk of contemporary theory; and it is usually from this angle that Castoriadis is criticized in poststructural psychoanalysis and postmodern circles. Such critics argue that the whole concept of representation, the idea that some transcendental signified automatically assigns a set of stable meanings to individuals, has seriously come to grief since the model supplied by Saussurean or post-Saussurean linguistics. This kind of criticism, however, actually targets an empirical model of representation, which posits a one-dimensional, functional connection between personal thoughts and external reality. Yet the imaginary dimension of representation for Castoriadis is entirely different in scope. It does not denote an organic bond between image and thing, idea and object. Rather, through a brilliant reinterpretation of Freudian psychoanalysis, Castoriadis speaks of a 'representational flux' which lies at the heart of the radical imaginary and its ever-erupting significations. The unconscious, says Castoriadis, exists *as* representational flux; representations that are continually overdetermined and interwoven with the cultural fabric of society. Following Freud, Castoriadis argues that, from the beginning of life, all representations are geared towards the pleasure principle. What is important in the representational or phantasmatic dimension of the unconscious is pleasure, satisfaction, and enjoyment. The hallucination of the breast by the infant is a key Freudian instance of representation as a source of unconscious pleasure.

To the radical imaginary of the individual subject corresponds what Castoriadis calls the 'social imaginary' of culture and social institutions. The social imaginary, to be sure, is not simply the sum of individual fantasies in society. The social imagination draws upon the effective investments of individual subjects, certainly. But, through the institutionalization of social practices, the social imaginary always exceeds the domain of the radical imagination. Here, as it were, there is a structuring of the radical imagination in and through symbolism, language, tradition, and custom. Castoriadis explains the social imaginary as follows:

> This element, which endows the functionality of each institutional system with its specific orientation, which overdetermines the choice and connections of symbolic networks, which creates for each historical period its singular way of living, seeing and making its own existence, its world and its relation to it, this originary structuring, this central signifier-signified, source of what is each time given as indisputable and indisputed sense, support of the articulations and distinctions of what matters and what does not, origin of the augmented being of the individual or collective objects of practical, affective and intellectual investment – this element is nothing other than the imaginary of the society or period concerned.

Self and society, in brief, are constituted within the activity of the creative imagination. The imaginary dimension of personal and social life always outstrips the world of external reality. Consider capitalism, for example. Capitalism organizes personal activity, social structures, and institutions in order to affirm itself as accumulation and commodification. The imaginary element of capitalist relations, however, cannot be localized as such. Certainly, objects such as cars and televisions are 'seen' in daily life. But the actual commodity 'car', or the commodity 'television', are invisible objects. The realm of commodification exists through fantasizing, through the social imaginary.

Social life is necessarily structured by the activity of the imagination, which is manifested in what Castoriadis terms a 'world of significations'. Any such world of signification is the generation of radically different imaginary patterns, patterns driven and overdetermined by the image-creating realm of the unconscious. What is at stake here is the essentially productive core of society. 'The imagination,' says Castoriadis, 'gives rise to the newly thinkable.'[16] The philosophical systems of Kant and Hegel, the scientific discoveries of Newton, Einstein, or Darwin, the institutionalization of Gods and Spirits: such world-constitution *is* the creative imaginary dimension of society.

Institutionalized society exists in and through these imaginary conditions. Yet cultural forms can harden in such a way that the productive core of the social imaginary diminishes. Here it is as if social life becomes uncoupled from the creative imagination and its source of inspiration. From this perspective, society becomes profoundly alienated, fetishising reality through a dull repetition of the self-same. Such a 'retreat into conformism' is how Castoriadis describes postmodern social conditions. Ideological regression, intellectual poverty, the waning of social and political conflict, the destructive expansion of technoscience: these and other features of our postmodern age represent a flattening of the creative imagination, what Castoriadis describes as our 'second-order imaginary'.

Castoriadis's work as a whole represents an original psychoanalytic contribution to the analysis of what one might call the imaginary tribulations of modern culture. Castoriadis makes an urgent plea for the recovery of the human imagination in the widest sense. Charting the enormous dangers of destructive social practices in the postmodern age, Castoriadis seeks to disclose new possibilities for the contemporary imagination. As Castoriadis says of the postmodern political situation: 'For the resurgence of the project of autonomy, new political objectives and new human attitudes are required, of which, for the time being, there are but few signs. Meanwhile, it would be absurd to try to decide if we are living through a long parenthesis, or if we are witnessing the beginning of the end of Western history as a history essentially linked with the project of autonomy and codetermined by it.'[17]

Table 6.1 The dislocating world of postmodernism

Theoretical model	Conception of self and society	Key terms
Deleuze and Guattari	Modernity as repressive fusion of desiring and social production; transgression through schizophrenia	Schizoanalysis Deterritorialization Reterritorialization
Lyotard	Libidinal intensities lodged in social institutions and affairs; multiplication of intensities affirmed through postmodernity	Libidinal band Desire-as-force
Jameson	Schizoid fragmentation as postmodern cultural experience	Breakdown of signifying Chain Postmodern hyperspace
Castoriadis	Intersection of radical and social imaginary; postmodernism as general conformism	Radical imaginary Social imaginary Second-order imaginary

Conclusion: Psychoanalysis as Critical Theory

In the course of this book I have examined the central theoretical trajectories in contemporary psychoanalysis. Freudian theory, ego psychology, object relations, Kleinianism, self-psychology, Lacanian and post-Lacanian theory, feminist and postmodern psychoanalysis: all of these approaches, notwithstanding divergences in their basic assumptions, provide valuable insights into the difficulties of living in the modern world. In discussing these standpoints, I have also set out a number of critical remarks concerning their readings of selfhood, unconscious desire, and contemporary culture. In these concluding pages, I want briefly to develop some thoughts about the nature of psychoanalysis as a critical theory.

I began this book by arguing that psychoanalytic theory is an inherently critical, political discourse. I mean by this that psychoanalysis is a critical reflection on the central modes of feeling, valuing, and caring in modern societies. Very often, the political credentials of psychoanalysis are evaluated in terms of rigidly individualist categories, notably as concerns psychoanalytic practice. In such accounts, politics is related to psychoanalysis only in terms of therapy, which is then assessed as either conformist or radical in nature. I have tried to show throughout this book, however, that the political is part and parcel of psychoanalytic discourse at a much deeper level. I have suggested that what is at issue in psychoanalysis is the interlacing of repressed desire and power-relations, of unconscious passion and cultural reproduction. Of course, the variety of psychoanalytic approaches considered in this book offer complex, contradictory positions on this focus of concern. However, in all of these approaches, political and social connections of many kinds are treated as central to the very condition of human subjectivity. From Sigmund Freud to Jean Laplanche, psychoanalytic theory has been intricately interwoven with political values and ideological assumptions. Indeed psychoanalysis places a question mark against the ideology of subjectivity itself – bringing the question of the subject back to political issues of desire, gender, language, history, and society.

The political significance of psychoanalysis, therefore, lies precisely in tracing the imprint of the social, cultural network upon unconscious passion. As Herbert Marcuse puts this: 'psychoanalytic categories do not have to be "related" to social and political conditions – they are themselves social and political categories'.[1] It is characteristic of psychoanalytic discourse, as I have tried to show, to deconstruct the complex interplay between unconscious desire and social life.

What I have suggested, in brief, is that a strategy of *theoretical linkage or cross-referencing* is the most fruitful and productive way to engage with psychoanalytic doctrine. What is required is an openness to differences within psychoanalytic theory, differences which I believe might serve as the medium for rigorous critical reflection. This is not to say, however, that we should attempt a synthesis or integration of psychoanalytic approaches. Any such ideal of conceptual unity in contemporary psychoanalysis is, in my opinion, misplaced. For the theoretical divergences here are simply too great. As we have seen, there is little common ground on the role of pre-Oedipal development, the wider cultural effects of Oedipus, the dynamics of splitting, and the like. What I am suggesting, rather, is that the articulation of differences in psychoanalytic theory will allow us at least to make a start in comprehending the heterogeneity of unconscious desire in its relation to the self, to others, and contemporary culture. Only through the articulation of differences shall we be able to set psychoanalysis within the wider social context, and to theorize the kinds of political effects which theories produce.

Theodor Adorno, one of the most astute commentators on the radical potentials of psychoanalysis, well knew the dangers of conceptual isolation or closure. For Adorno, it is quite mistaken to imagine that we might affirm a moment of psychic experience which is not at the same time a condensed imprint of the subject's struggles in the social and political domain. From this viewpoint, the idea that there are impartial or non-political modes of psychoanalytic criticism is simply a theoretical fantasy, a fantasy aimed at erasing contradiction, antagonism, and differentiation. Commenting on the historical tendency to separate psychoanalysis from the social and political world, Adorno writes: 'The more strictly the psychological realm is conceived as an autonomous, self-enclosed play of forces, the more completely the subject is drained of his subjectivity. The objectless subject that is thrown back upon himself freezes into an object. It cannot break out of its immanence and amounts to no more than equations of libidinal energy. The soul that is broken down into its own laws is a soul no longer.'[2] The general point to be derived from this is as follows. Theories which are incapable of thinking through the social, historical constitituion of psychic experience will be, on the whole, unable to confront the reality of contradiction and conflict – dimensions of experience implicitly distilled in their readings of selfhood and desire. Crises of identity and desire, in other words, will remain entirely within an imaginary orbit of illusion, in which social conflict and the contradictions of modernity are wished away.

By contrast, I have argued throughout this book that it is vital to recover the central organizing role of power relations and patterns of cultural domination in the constitution of identity and repressed desire. If psychoanalysis is to remain effective as a critical theory, it must necessarily step back from the tendency to see the self solely in terms of the 'psychic', and instead confront head-on the issue of the construction of the unconscious in the field of the social and political. Only if this is achieved will psychoanalysis be able to confront issues of new political importance in social and cultural enquiry – such as the resurgence of racism and nationalism, changing cultural definitions of masculinity and femininity, problems of human agency, and the like.

A critical psychoanalytic theory, in order to be reflective and encounter otherness, must display an openness about conceptual approaches and methods of study. No single theory will have the whole truth. No single theory will be able to confront the contemporary, multidimensional identities of the postmodern world. For these reasons, I have suggested that it is necessary to recognize the interlocking concerns of psychoanalytical theories, and to recognize that these doctrines are bound up with political ideologies in ways which always outstrip their modes of thinking. The variety of theories in contemporary psychoanalysis, I have suggested, are therefore better understood as *images* of what it feels like to live in the multidimensional world of modernity. The Freudian stress on ambivalence, the object relational discourse on connection and relatedness, the Kleinian underwriting of splitting, the Lacanian emphasis on otherness, the postmodern account of fragmentation and dispersal: these are ideological forms engendered in and through the late modern age. Yet consideration of these images does not occur in a realm closed off from the social world. Critical thinking about different psychoanalytic theories is connected in an essential way to transformations in self-identity and social relations. 'As the understanding of Freudianism is changed,' Paul Ricoeur comments, 'so is the understanding of oneself.'[3] Critically reflecting on psychoanalytical doctrines, and putting them into practical engagement with each other, might indeed help alternative subjectivities and social futures to be realized.

Notes

Introduction

1 For a discussion of the institutional politics of psychoanalysis see S. Turkle, *Psychoanalytic Politics: Freud's French Revolution* (London: Barnet, 1979) and S. Frosh, *The Politics of Psychoanalysis* (London: Macmillan, 1987). For discussions of the scientific validity of psychoanalysis see J. Habermas, *Knowledge and Human Interests* (London: Heinemann, 1972) and A. Grunbaum, *The Foundations of Psychoanalysis* (Berkeley: University of California Press).

Chapter 1

1 Dennis Wrong, 'The over-socialized conception of man in modern sociology', *American Sociological Review*, 26 (1961), pp. 183–93.

2 Sigmund Freud, An Outline of Psycho-Analysis, in *The Standard Edition of the Complete Psychological Works of Sigmund Freud*, tr. J. Stachey (London: Hogarth Press, 1935–74), XXIII, p. 154.

3 Philip Rieff, *Freud: The Mind of the Moralist* (Chicago: University of Chicago Press, 1979).

4 Freud, *Inhibitions, Symptoms and Anxiety*, SE, XX, p. 170.

5 Freud, *The Ego and the Id*, SE, XIX, p.

6 Freud, 'Some psychical consequences of the anatomical distinction between the sexes', *SE*, XIX, p. 252.

7 Slavoj Žižek, *The Sublime Object of Ideology* (London: Verso, 1989), p. 49.

8 Cornelius Castoriadis, *The Imaginary Institution of Society* (Cambridge: Polity, 1987), p. 104.

9 See Heinz Hartmann, *Essays on Ego Psychology* (New York: International Universities Press, 1964).

10 Russell Jacoby, *Social Amnesia* (Boston: Beacon Press, 1975).

11 Harry Guntrip, *Schizoid Phenomena, Object Relations and the Self*, (London: Hogarth Press, 1968), p. 422.

12 D. W. Winnicott, 'Ego distortion in terms of true and false self', in *The*

Maturational Process and the Facilitating Environment (London: Hogarth Press, 1965), p. 147.

13 Jean-François Lyotard, *The Postmodern Condition: A Report on Knowledge* (Manchester: Manchester University Press, 1986).

14 See Jacques Lacan, 'The mirror stage as formative of the function of the I', *Ecrits: A Selection* (London: Tavistock, 1977), ch 1.

15 Gilles Deleuze and Félix Guattari, *Anti-Oedipus: Capitalism and Schizophrenia* (New York: Viking, 1977).

16 See Jean Baudrillard, *L'échange symbolique et la mort* (Paris: Gallimard, 1976). For a useful overview of Baudrillard's writings in English see Mark Poster (ed.), *Jean Baudrillard: Selected Writings* (Cambridge: Polity Press, 1988).

Chapter 2

1 Sigmund Freud, 'Civilized sexual morality and modern nervous illness', in *The Standard Edition of the Complete Psychological Works of Sigmund Freud*, IX, p. 203.

2 Freud, *Totem and Taboo*, SE, XIII, p. 74.

3 Freud, 'Analysis terminable and interminable', SE, XXIII, p. 243.

4 Paul Ricoeur, *Freud and Philosophy: An Essay on Interpretation* (New Haven: Yale, 1970), p. 307.

5 Freud, *Civilization and Its Discontents*, SE, XXI, p. 122.

6 Freud, *Civilization*, p. 145.

7 Erich Fromm, 'The method and function of an analytic social psychology: Notes on psychoanalysis and historical materialism', in A. Arato and E. Gebhardt, *The Essential Frankfurt School Reader* (New York: Continuum, 1985), p. 483.

8 This summary of the essential needs of mankind in Fromm's theory is detailed in ch. 3 of *The Sane Society* (London: Routledge, 1991), pp. 30–66.

9 John D. Cash, 'Chasing the decentred subject: Ideology since Freud', MS, Australasian Political Studies Association, 1990, p. 19.

10 Herbert Marcuse, *Eros and Civilization* (London: Ark, 1956), p. 258.

11 Marcuse, *Eros*, p. 143.

12 For further discussion of this point see my *Social Theory and Psychoanalysis in Transition: Self and Society from Freud to Kristeva* (Oxford: Blackwell, 1992), pp. 94–102.

13 Joel Kovel, 'Narcissism and the family', reprinted in his *The Radical Spirit: Essays on Psychoanalysis and Society* (London: Free Association, 1988), p. 199.

14 Christopher Lasch, *The Culture of Narcissism* (London: Abacus, 1979), p. 82.

15 Christopher Lasch, *The Minimal Self: Psychic Survival in Troubled Times* (New York: Norton, 1984), pp. 195–6.

Chapter 3

1 Erik H. Erikson, *Childhood and Society* (Harmondsworth: Penguin, 1965), pp. 239–41.
2 Erik H. Erikson, *Identity, Youth and Crisis* (New York: Norton, 1968), pp. 22–3.
3 Erik H. Erikson, *Gandhi's Truth* (New York: Norton, 1969), p. 433.
4 Nathan Leites, *The New Ego* (New York: Aronson, 1973). See also Mark Poster, *Critical Theory of the Family* (London: Pluto, 1978).
5 D. W. Winnicott, 'Primary maternal preoccupation', in *Through Paediatrics to Psycho-analysis* (London: Hogarth Press, 1958), p. 304.
6 D. W. Winnicott, *Playing and Reality* (Harmondsworth: Penguin, 1974), p. 83.
7 See Nancy. J. Chodorow and Susan Contratto, 'The fantasy of the perfect mother', *Feminism and Psychoanalytic Theory* (Cambridge: Polity, 1989).
8 Anthony Giddens, *Modernity and Self-Identity: Self and Society in the Late Modern Age* (Cambridge: Polity, 1991), p. 39.
9 Giddens, *Self-Identity*, pp. 182–3.
10 Giddens, *Self-Identity*, p. 185.
11 Hannah Segal, *Introduction to the Work of Melanie Klein* (London: Hogarth Press, 1986), p. 26.
12 See Hannah Segal, 'Silence is the real crime', *Int. Rev. Psycho-Anal*, 14 (1987), pp. 3–12.
13 Michael Rustin, *The Good Society and the Inner World: Psychoanalysis, Politics and Culture* (London: Verso, 1991), p. 20.
14 Cornelius Castoriadis, *The Imaginary Institution of Society* (Cambridge: Polity Press, 1987), p. 285.
15 Stephen Frosh, *Identity Crisis: Modernity, Psychoanalysis and the Self* (London: Macmillan, 1991), p. 51.
16 Heinz Kohut, *The Restoration of the Self* (New York: International Universities Press, 1977), p. 86.
17 Jay R. Greenberg and Stephen A. Mitchell, *Object Relations in Psychoanalytic Theory* (Cambridge, Mass: Harvard University Press, 1983), p. 363.

Chapter 4

1 Jacques Lacan, *Ecrits: A Selection* (London: Tavistock Press, 1977), p. 2.
2 Jean Laplanche and Serge Leclaire, 'The unconscious', *Yale French Studies*, 48 (1972), p. 154.
3 Jacques Lacan, 'Fonction et champ de la parole et du langage en psychanalyse', *Ecrits* (Paris: Seuil, 1966), p. 319.
4 Cornelius Castoriadis, 'The state of the subject today', *Thesis Eleven*, 24 (1989), p. 7.

5 See Paul Ricoeur, *Freud and Philosophy: An Essay on Interpretation* (New Haven: Yale, 1970), pp. 395–406; Jean-François Lyotard, 'The dream-work does not think', in A. Benjamin (ed.), *The Lyotard Reader* (Oxford: Blackwell, 1990); Cornelius Castoriadis, 'Psychoanalysis: project and elucidation', in his *Crossroads in the Labyrinth*; and Jean Laplanche and Serge Leclaire, 'The Unconscious', *Yale French Studies*, 48 (1972).

6 Malcolm Bowie, *Lacan* (London: Fontana, 1991), p. 199.

7 Jacques Lacan, *Ecrits: A Selection* (London: Tavistock Press, 1977), p. 152.

8 Louis Althusser, *Lenin and Philosophy and Other Essays* (London: New Left Books, 1971), p. 161.

9 Paul Hirst, 'Althusser and the theory of ideology', *Economy and Society*, vol. 5, no. 4 (1976), p. 406.

10 Christian Metz, *Psychoanalysis and Cinema* (London: Macmillan, 1982), p. 45.

11 Slavoj Žižek, *The Sublime Object of Ideology* (London: Verso, 1988), p. 45.

12 Slavoj Žižek, *Looking Awry: An Introduction to Jacques Lacan through Popular Culture* (Cambridge, Mass: MIT Press, 1991), p. 128.

13 Jean Laplanche, *New Foundations for Psychoanalysis* (Oxford: Blackwell, 1987), p. 128. All subsequent references to this work will be given parenthetically in the text.

14 See Rose in J. Fletcher and M. Stanton, (eds) *Jean Laplanche: Seduction, Translation, Drives* (London: ICA, 1992), p. 61.

Chapter 5

1 Juliet Mitchell *Psychoanalysis and Feminism* (London: Penguin, 1974), XV.

2 Mary Daly and Jane Caputi, *Websters' First New Intergalactic Wickedary of the English Language* (Boston: Beacon, 1987), p. 230.

3 Dorothy Dinnerstein, *The Mermaid and The Minotaur* (New York: Harper and Row, 1976), p. 186.

4 Nancy J. Chodorow, *The Reproduction of Mothering*, (Berkeley: University of California Press, 1978).

5 Nancy J. Chodorow, *Feminism and Psychoanalytic Theory* (Cambridge: Polity, 1989), p. 71.

6 For example, see Issac D. Balbus, *Marxism and Domination* (Princeton: Princeton University Press, 1982), ch. 9; and R. W. Connell, *Gender and Power* (Cambridge: Polity, 1987), ch. 9.

7 Lynne Segal, *Is The Future Female?: Troubled Thoughts on Contemporary Feminism* (London: Virago, 1987), p. 140.

8 Jacqueline Rose, *Sexuality in the Field of Vision* (London: Verso, 1986), p. 60, no. 28.

9 Madelon Sprengnether, *The Spectral Mother: Freud, Feminism, and Psychoanalysis* (Ithaca: Cornell University Press, 1990), p. 246.

10 Jane Flax, *Thinking Fragments: Psychoanalysis, Feminism, and Post-modernism in the Contemporary West* (Berkeley: University of California Press, 1991).

11 Jacques Lacan *Ecrits: A Selection* (London: Tavistock Press, 1977), p. 287.

12 Jacques Lacan, *Encore: Le Seminaire XX* (Paris: Seuil, 1975).

13 Juliet Mitchell, *Women: The Longest Revolution* (London: Virago, 1984), p. 274.

14 Anthony Elliott, *Social Theory and Psychoanalysis in Transition: Self and Society from Freud to Kristeva* (Oxford: Blackwell, 1992), ch. 6.

15 Rose, *Sexuality* p. 7.

16 Ibid., pp. 75–6.

17 Julia Kristeva, 'Women's time', in T. Moi (ed.), *The Kristeva Reader* (Oxford: Blackwell, 1986), p. 206.

18 Andrea Nye, 'Woman clothed with the sun: Julia Kristeva and the escape from/to language', *Signs*, 12 (summer 1987), pp. 664–86.

19 Drucilla Cornell and Adam Thurschwell, 'Feminism, negativity, intersubjectivity', in S. Benhabib and D. Cornell (eds), *Feminism as Critique* (Cambridge: Polity, 1987), pp. 149–51.

20 Luce Irigaray, *This Sex Which Is Not One* (Ithaca: Cornell University Press, 1985), p. 143.

21 Mitchell, *Women*, p. 291.

Chapter 6

1 Zygmunt Bauman, *Modernity and Ambivalence* (Cambridge: Polity, 1990), p. 272.

2 Jean-François Lyotard, 'Defining the postmodern', in Lisa Appignanesi (ed.), *Postmodernism: ICA Documents* (London: Free Association Books, 1989), p. 10.

3 Samuel Weber, *The Legend of Freud* (Minneapolis: University of Minnesota Press, 1982).

4 Gilles Deleuze and Félix Guattari, *Anti-Oedipus: Capitalism and Schizophrenia* (New York: Viking, 1977), p. 296. All subsequent references to this work will be given parenthetically in the text.

5 In an interview, Guattari comments: 'Lacanianism isn't just a re-reading of Freud; it's something far more despotic, both as a theory and an institution, and far more rigid in its semiotic subjection of those who accept it.' Félix Guattari, *Molecular Revolution: Psychiatry and Politics* (London: Penguin, 1984), p. 49.

6 Brian Massumi, *A User's Guide to Capitalism and Schizophrenia: Deviations from Deleuze and Guattari* (Cambridge, Mass: MIT Press, 1992), p. 1.

7 'In schizophrenia', Freud writes, 'after the process of repression the

libido that has been withdrawn does not seek a new object, but retreats into the ego; that is to say, that here the object-cathexes are given up and primitive objectless condition of narcissism is re-established.' 'The unconscious', in *The Standard Edition of the Complete Psychological Works of Sigmund Freud*, XIV, pp. 196–7. For a lucid discussion of the thought-processes of psychotic states see Stephen Frosh, *Identity Crisis* (London: Macmillan, 1991), ch. 6.

8 Joel Kovel, 'Schizophrenic being and technocratic society', in D. Levin (ed.) *Pathologies of the Modern Self* (New York: New York University Press, 1987), p. 336.

9 Massumi, *A User's Guide*; and also Ronald Bogue, *Deleuze and Guattari* (London: Routledge, 1989).

10 Jean-François Lyotard, *Economie Libidinale* (Paris, 1974), p. 133. All subsequent references to this work will be given parenthetically in the text.

11 Geoffrey Bennington, *Lyotard: Writing the Event* (Manchester: Manchester University Press, 1988), p. 39.

12 Peter Dews, *Logics of Disintegration* (London: Verso, 1987), p. 138.

13 Fredric Jameson, 'Postmodernism, or the cultural logic of late capitalism', *New Left Review*, 146 (1984), pp. 53–93. All subsequent references to this work will be given parenthetically in the text.

14 Jacqueline Rose, ' "The man who mistook his wife for a hat" or "A wife is like an umbrella": Fantasies of the modern and postmodern', ICA Documents, 6, p. 31.

15 Cornelius Castoriadis, *The Imaginary Institution of Society* (Cambridge: Polity, 1987), p. 3.

16 Cornelius Castoriadis, 'Logic, imagination, reflection', *American Imago*, vol. 49, no. 1, spring 1992, p. 30.

17 Cornelius Castoriadis, 'The retreat from autonomy: Postmodernism as generalized conformism', *Thesis Eleven*, 31 (1992), p. 23.

Conclusion

1 Herbert Marcuse, *Five Lectures: Psychoanalysis, Politics and Utopia* (London: Allentane, 1973), p. 44.

2 Theodor Adorno, 'Sociology and psychology', *New Left Review*, 46 (1967), p. 81.

3 Paul Ricoeur, *Freud and Philosophy: An Essay on Interpretation* (New Haven: Yale, 1970), p. 420.

Further Reading

For those wishing to explore further any or all of the various traditions in psychoanalytic theory the following books are recommended. The central works discussed throughout this book, plus other important texts, are listed as suggested reading in a set order.

Freudian Psychoanalysis

Sigmund Freud, *The Standard Edition of the Complete Psychological Works of Sigmund Freud*, tr. J. Stachey, (London: Hogarth Press, 1935–74)

Philip Rieff, *Freud: The Mind of the Moralist* (Chicago: University of Chicago Press, 1979)

Paul Ricoeur, *Freud and Philosophy: An Essay on Interpretation* (New Haven: Yale, 1970)

Peter Gay, *Freud: A Life for Our Time* (London: Dent, 1988)

J. Laplanche and J. B. Pontalis, *The Language of Psycho-Analysis* (London: Hogarth, 1980)

American Ego Psychology

Anna Freud, *The Ego and the Mechanisms of Defence* (London: Hogarth, 1941

Heinz Hartmann, *Essays on Ego Psychology* (New York: International Universities Press, 1964)

—— *Ego Psychology and the Problem of Adaptation* (London: Hogarth Press, 1959)

Erik H. Erikson, *Childhood and Society* (London: Penguin, 1965)

—— *Identity, Youth and Crisis* (New York: Norton, 1968)

—— *Gandhi's Truth* (New York: Norton, 1969)

Object Relations Theory

W. R. D. Fairbairn, *Psychoanalytic Studies of the Personality* (London: Routledge and Kegan Paul, 1952)

Harry Guntrip, *Schizoid Phenomena, Object Relations and the Self* (London: Hogarth, 1968)

Michael Balint, *Primary Love and Psycho-Analytic Technique* (New York: Liveright, 1965)

Jay R. Greenberg and Stephen A. Mitchell, *Object Relations in Psychoanalytic Theory* (Cambridge, Mass: Harvard, 1983)

Stephen A. Mitchell, *Relational Concepts in Psychoanalysis* (Cambridge, Mass: Harvard, 1988)

D. W. Winnicott, *The Maturational Process and the Facilitating Environment* (London: Hogarth, 1965)

—— *Playing and Reality* (Harmondsworth: Penguin, 1974)

Charles Spezzano, *Affect in Psychoanalysis: A critical synthesis* (Hillsdale: The Analytic Press, 1993)

Kleinian Theory

Melanie Klein, *Love, Guilt and Reparation and Other Works 1921–1945* (London: Virago, 1988)

—— *Envy and Gratitude and Other Works 1946–1963* (London: Virago, 1988)

Hanna Segal, *Introduction to the Work of Melanie Klein* (London: Hogarth, 1986)

Juliet Mitchell (ed), *The Selected Melanie Klein* (London: Penguin, 1986)

W. R. Bion, *Second Thoughts* (London: Heinemann, 1978)

—— *Seven Servants* (London: Maresfield, 1984)

Otto Kernberg, *Borderline Conditions and Pathological Narcissism* (New York: Jason Aronson, 1975)

Donald Meltzer, *The Kleinian Development* (Perthshire: Clunie, 1978)

Richard Wollheim, *The Thread of Life* (Cambridge: Cambridge University Press, 1986)

Michael Rustin, *The Good Society and the Inner World: Psychoanalysis, Politics and Culture* (London: Verso, 1991)

Self-Psychology

Heinz Kohut, *The Analysis of the Self* (New York: International Universities Press, 1971)

—— *The Restoration of the Self* (New York: International Universities Press, 1977)
—— *Self Psychology and the Humanities* (New York: Norton, 1985).
R. Stolorow, B. Brandchaft, and G. Atwood, *Psychoanalytic Treatment: An Intersubjective Approach* (Hillsdale, New Jersey: The Analytic Press, 1987)

Lacanian and Post-Lacanian Psychoanalysis

Jacques Lacan, *Ecrits: A Selection* (London: Tavistock Press, 1977)
—— *The Four Fundamental Concepts of Psychoanalysis* (London: Penguin, 1979)
—— *The Seminar of Jacques Lacan, Vol. 1: Freud's Papers on Technique 1953–54* (Cambridge: Cambridge University Press, 1988)
—— *The Seminar of Jacques Lacan, Vol 2: The Ego in Freud's Theory and in the Technique of Psychoanalysis 1954–55* (Cambridge: Cambridge University Press, 1988)
—— *The Ethics of Psychoanalysis 1959–60: The Seminar of Jacques Lacan* (London: Routledge, 1992)
B. Benvenuto and R. Kennedy, *The Works of Jacques Lacan* (London: Free Association, 1986)
Malcolm Bowie, *Lacan* (London: Fontana, 1991)
Ellie-Ragland Sullivan, *Jacques Lacan and the Philosophy of Psychoanalysis* (Chicago: University of Illinois Press, 1986)
Ellie-Ragland Sullivan and Mark Bracher (eds), *Lacan and the Subject of Language* (New York: Routledge, 1991)
David Macey, *Lacan in Contexts* (London: Verso, 1988)
Louis Althusser, Ideology and ideological state apparatuses' and 'Freud and Lacan', in *Essays on Ideology* (London: Verso, 1984)
Christian Metz, *Psychoanalysis and Cinema* (London: Macmillan, 1982)
Teresa De Lauretis and Stephen Heath (eds), *The Cinematic Apparatus* (London: Macmillan, 1985)
Slavoj Žižek, *The Sublime Object of Ideology* (London: Verso, 1988)
—— *Looking Awry: An Introduction to Jacques Lacan through Popular Culture* (Cambridge, Mass: MIT Press, 1991)
—— *Enjoy Your Symptom* (London: Routledge, 1993)
Jean Laplanche, *New Foundations for Psychoanalysis* (Oxford: Blackwell, 1987)
J. Fletcher and M. Stanton (eds), *Jean Laplanche: Seduction, Translation, Drives* (London: ICA, 1992)

Psychoanalytic Feminism

Dorothy Dinnerstein, *The Mermaid and The Minotaur* (New York: Harper and Row, 1976)

Nancy J. Chodorow, *The Reproduction of Mothering* (Berkeley: University of California Press, 1978)

—— *Feminism and Psychoanalytic Theory* (Cambridge: Polity, 1989)

Jessica Benjamin, *The Bonds of Love* (New York: Pantheon, 1990)

Madelon Sprengnether, *The Spectral Mother: Freud, Feminism, and Psychoanalysis* (Ithaca: Cornell University Press, 1990)

Jane Flax, *Thinking Fragments: Psychoanalysis, Feminism, and Postmodernism in the Contemporary West* (Berkeley: University of California Press, 1991)

—— *Disputed Subjects: Essays on Psychoanalysis, Politics and Philosophy* (New York: Routledge, 1993)

Juliet Mitchell, *Psychoanalysis and Feminism* (London: Penguin, 1974)

—— *Women: The Longest Revolution* (London: Virago, 1984)

Jacqueline Rose, *Sexuality in the Field of Vision* (London: Verso, 1986)

Julia Kristeva, *Revolution in Poetic Language* (New York: Columbia University Press, 1984)

—— *Tales of Love* (New York: Columbia University Press, 1987)

—— *In The Beginning was Love: Psychoanalysis and Faith* (New York: Columbia University Press, 1988)

J. Fletcher and A. Benjamin, *Abjection, Melancholia and Love: the Work of Julia Kristeva* (London: Routledge, 1990)

Luce Irigaray, *This Sex Which Is Not One* (Ithaca: Cornell University Press, 1985)

M. Whitford, *Luce Irigaray: Philsophy in the Feminine* (London: Routledge, 1991)

Teresa Brennan (ed.) *Between Psychoanalysis and Feminism* (London: Routledge, 1989)

H. Cixous and C. Clement, *The Newly Born Woman* (Minneapolis: University of Minnesota Press, 1986)

Drucilla Cornell, *Beyond Accommodation* (New York: Routledge, 1992)

Critical Theory and Psychoanalysis

Herbert Marcuse, *Eros and Civilization* (London: Ark, 1956)

—— *Five Lectures: Psychoanalysis, Politics and Utopia* (London: Allen Lane, 1973)

Theodor Adorno, 'Sociology and psychology', *New Left Review*, 46 (1967)

David Held, *Introduction to Critical Theory* (London: Hutchinson, 1980)

Martin Jay, *The Dialectical Imagination* (Boston: Little Brown and Company, 1973)

Jürgen Habermas, *Knowledge and Human Interests* (London: Heinemann, 1972)
—— *Communication and the Evolution of Society* (London: Heinemann, 1979)

Postmodern Psychoanalysis

Gilles Deleuze and Félix Guattari, *Anti-Oedipus: Capitalism and Schizophrenia* (New York: Viking, 1977)
—— *A Thousand Plateaus: Capitalism and Schizophrenia* (Minneapolis: University of Minnesota Press, 1987)
Félix Guattari, *Molecular Revolution: Psychiatry and Politics* (London: Penguin, 1984)
Brian Massumi, *A User's Guide to Capitalism and Schizophrenia: Deviations from Deleuze and Guattari* (Cambridge, Mass: MIT Press, 1992)
Jean-François Lyotard, *Economie Libidinale* (Paris, 1974)
—— *The Differend: Phrases in Dispute* (Minneapolis: University of Minnesota Press, 1988)
A. Benjamin (ed.), *The Lyotard Reader* (Oxford: Blackwell, 1990)
Geoffrey Bennington, *Lyotard: Writing the Event* (Manchester: Manchester University Press, 1988)
Frederic Jameson, 'Postmodernism, or the cultural logic of late capitalism', *New Left Review*, 146, pp. 53–93
Jacqueline Rose, 'Fantasies of the modern and postmodern', ICA Documents, 6, pp. 30–4
Cornelius Castoriadis, 'The retreat from autonomy: Postmodernism as generalized conformism', *Thesis Eleven*, 31 (1992), pp. 14–23

Psychoanalysis and Contemporary Theory

Anthony Elliott, *Social Theory and Psychoanalysis in Transition: Self and Society from Freud to Kristeva* (Oxford: Blackwell, 1992)
Peter Dews, *Logics of Disintegration* (London: Verso, 1987)
Stephen Frosh, *Identity Crisis* (London: Macmillan, 1991)
Anthony Elliott and Stephen Frosh (eds), *Psychoanalysis in Contexts* (London: Routledge, 1994)
Cornelius Castoriadis, *The Imaginary Institution of Society* (Cambridge: Polity Press, 1987)
—— *Crossroads in the Labyrinth* (Cambridge, Mass: MIT Press, 1984)
Mikkel Borch-Jacobsen, *The Freudian Subject* (Stanford: Stanford University Press, 1982)
Jacques Derrida, *The Post Card* (Chicago: University of Chicago, 1987)

Index of Names